AF312301

Transforming India's External Security Using its Ancient Strategic Culture

Transforming India's External Security Using its Ancient Strategic Culture

Gp Capt Rajesh R Chaudhary

Introduction by
Air Marshal **Anil Chopra** PVSM AVSM VM VSM (Retd)

KNOWLEDGE WORLD
KW Publishers Pvt Ltd
New Delhi

in association with

Centre for Air Power Studies
New Delhi

Copyright © 2021 Centre for Air Power Studies, New Delhi

The Centre for Air Power Studies is an independent, non-profit, academic research institution established in 2002 under a registered Trust to undertake and promote policy-related research, study and discussion on the trends and developments in defence and military issues, especially air power and the aerospace arena, for civil and military purposes. Its publications seek to expand and deepen the understanding of defence, military power, air power and aerospace issues without necessarily reflecting the views of any institution or individuals except those of the authors.

Centre for Air Power Studies
P-284, Arjan Path
Subroto Park
New Delhi 110010

Tele: (91-11) 25699131

E-mail: capsnetdroff@gmail.com
website: www.capsindia.org

All rights reserved. No part of this book may be reproduced or transmitted in any form or by any means, electronic or mechanical, including photocopying, recording or by any information storage and retrieval system, without permission in writing.

ISBN 978-93-91490-51-5 Hardback
ISBN 978-93-91490-54-6 ebook

Published in India by Kalpana Shukla

KNOWLEDGE WORLD

KW Publishers Pvt Ltd
4676/21, First Floor, Ansari Road
Daryaganj, New Delhi 110002
Phone: +91 11 43528107
Marketing: kw@kwpub.in
Editorial: production@kwpub.in
Website: www.kwpub.in

Printed and bound in India

CENTRE FOR AIR POWER STUDIES

VISION

To be an independent centre of excellence on national security contributing informed and considered research and analyses on relevant issues.

MISSION

To encourage independent and informed research and analyses on issues of relevance to national security and to create a pool of domain experts to provide considered inputs to decision-makers. Also, to foster informed public debate and opinion on relevant issues and to engage with other think-tanks and stakeholders within India and abroad to provide an Indian perspective.

Dedication

This book is dedicated to my parents, my wife and my children who supported me and stood by me during the Covid pandemic and encouraged me to complete my project.

Contents

Acknowledgements

I am obliged to the Indian Air Force for providing me the opportunity to indulge myself in the field of academic pursuit and research. I am thankful to Centre for Air Power Studies (CAPS) for providing me with a conducive environment to pursue my research. I am grateful and indebted to the present Director General CAPS, Air Mshl Anil Chopra PVSM VSM VM VSM (Retd) for guiding me and standing by me for my project. He has been a constant source of support and advice for my work. I am grateful to the previous Director General, CAPS, Air Mshl KK Nohwar PVSM VM (Retd) for supporting and guiding me during the initial period of my research work. I extend my sincere thanks to Air Vice Mshl Manmohan Bahadur VM (Retd), former Additional Director General CAPS, for mentoring me in pursuing my research. He has introduced me to research writing and methodologies. I express my sincere gratitude to the present Additional Director General, CAPS Air Vice Mshl Anil Golani for patiently going through my drafts and guiding me in making my work more comprehensive. He has greatly helped me in my research by assisting me in getting valuable inputs from experts. I am thankful to the library staff comprising Smt Sushma Zutshi, Ms Surabhi Sareen and Shri Rohit for constantly supporting me with all the research materials for my work, in spite of Covid restrictions. I also express my sincere thanks to the support staff at CAPS who do a wonderful work in providing all the assistance and support required to pursue research. I express my gratitude and thanks to Ms Kalpana Shukla and her entire publishing team at KW Publishers especially Mr Sushanta Gayen for their assistance and support in bringing out this book.

Preface

The book began as a research project on civil military relations. The topic for civil military relations was chosen because of my experience of working for four years in Air Headquarter as Director dealing with Air to Air Refuelling and my dealings with the Ministry of Defence. As would happen with any researcher of civil military relations, I referred to the theoretical works on the subject by theorists like Samuel Huntington's *Soldier and the State*, works of Peter Feaver, Morris Janowitz, Rebecca L. Schiff and others. The subject in the Indian context has been dealt by various authors like Apurba Kundu, Ayesha Ray, Steven I. Wilkinson, Anit Mukherjee, and many others. As I found during the course of my initial research; the foundational argument of the study of civil military relations rests on two pillars or objectives; the first and the most important one is how to control and prevent the military from becoming a threat to civil society and the second being how to have an effective military while achieving the first objective. This is the theoretical foundation on which most research work on civil military relations is based. These theoretical constructs are largely based on the study of Western societies (predominantly American) and their experiences. They have also been supplemented by studies on African societies and developing or underdeveloped countries.

What I learnt from my initial research forced me to think in an alternate direction. Here was a situation where a country like India which has a civilisation more than 6500-7000 (considering the Indus Valley Civilisation) years old, was being evaluated on a theoretical construct which was based on some other value and belief systems far removed from it. It was naïve to assume that a continuous civilisation as old as India would not have distinct cultural values and strategic culture imprinted on it. The institutional structure of the Indian military may be a legacy of the British, but the ethos of soldiering dates back to the Vedic and the Epic ages. Therefore, if I had to study the civil military relations of India and suggest a way forward, I had no option but to study the Strategic Culture of India since ancient times. It was here that my path diverged from what has been followed by other researchers on the subject till now.

The second and the third chapters deal with India's past before the British colonisation. While the second chapter is about the military strength of Indian empires and the evolution of military culture, the third chapter attempts to understand India's approach to war, right from the ancient period. Claims have been made that Indians are pacifist and theorists have gone to the extent to say that India did not have a strategic culture. Nothing can be far from truth. The second and especially the third chapters make you understand that India elevated its war fighting to the realm of ethics. War is brutal and causes untold suffering, the military ethos of India tied up war with ethics to minimise its brutality. It ensured that war between armies did not have an undue adverse effect on the civilian population. I have drawn relevant lessons from the second and third chapters and utilised them subsequently.

The fourth chapter explores the evolution of India's higher defence organisation and its civil military relations and the various changes that it has undergone. I have also explored the civil military relations that existed during the British rule and how it evolved to hand over a legacy to India. In the next chapter I have analysed the present security architecture of India which deals with external security. I have attempted to understand the deficiencies that exist in this structure even though the present government has undertaken major steps like consolidating the NSCS, and creating the CDS and DMA to strengthen external security.

Present and future security threats would require a comprehensive approach to deal with it. The time has come to think about comprehensive national power to deal with present and future security challenges. It is the approach that India has tried to follow while dealing with the Chinese belligerence in Ladakh. The concept of comprehensive national approach is what I have used while trying to understand the deficiencies in the present external security structure. This brings out shortcomings and deficiencies which do not appear to be so if analysed with a prism of the past. But if there needs to be a revamp in the security architecture it would need to become future-proof.

I have briefly analysed the USA and China's military reforms and the conclusion is that India needs to follow its own path. It is important and necessary to learn and adopt technology but institutions would need to be built based on own ethos and culture rather than adopting other's solutions, especially for a country like India. I have tried to amalgamate the deficiencies of the present external security architecture with the lessons learnt from the past. The aim is to recommend a structure which uses India's inherent strengths as learnt from its strategic culture and takes care of its weaknesses of the past as well as present deficiencies.

The structural solution that I have proposed is built on cohesion between the civil and the military. Rightly so because external security today is not the exclusive domain of either the civil or the military. Security since ancient times in India has been one of the fundamental responsibilities of the state, the other being welfare. Therefore, military should not be the only responder for external security threats. It can be the pivot around which the external security architecture is built, but there can be no running away from a comprehensive approach to external security. Similarly, build-up of national power or military capability should be a national responsibility. The present ministerial structure leads to functioning in silos by various components which directly affect external security.

The structure and the changes that I have recommended is by no means the only solution, there can be many. The proposed structure leads to integration between not only the various arms of the military but also integrates the military with the civil structure. It also addresses the complexity in the civil military equation by providing a structure for their integration. The proposed structure may appear unwieldy but it is so because, it requires a major deviation in the way we have thought and operated till now. It is a structure which has not been adopted anywhere else in the world, but then India since ancient times is a nation which evolved its own unique ideas and concepts, which have been followed by others.

Jai Hind.

Introduction

It is the responsibility of the State to ensure security and welfare for its citizens. This has also been the raison d'être of states in India since ancient times. Economic prosperity is fundamental to achieving welfare. However, for a nation to be able to pursue economic prosperity, it needs to ensure security. Economic growth and security are complimentary. A nation is secure if it is capable of protecting not only its territorial integrity but also its national interests even in the face of armed conflict. Hard military power is the pivot of national security.

In a democratic setup the civil structure and the military are interlinked. The political structure is responsible for governing the country. The military is an instrument of the government for security and furthering of national interests. The Higher Defence Organisation or the civil military interface which controls the military is responsible for its effectiveness to a great extent. Therefore, it is imperative that this setup acts as an enabler for the military to achieve a state of preparedness wherein it can provide effective options to the government, for not only ensuring territorial security but also for protection and furtherance of national interests.

After independence the governance and military structures that India adopted were the legacy of the British Empire. It was prudent to continue with them initially, but subsequently there could have been a relook at them and they could have been restructured as per India's ethos and requirements. Why was this important? It was because India is an ancient and continuous civilisation with a legacy of more than 5000 years. It has a military culture which spans millennia. It is one of the few ancient civilisations of the world which thrives even today. Many of its ancient concepts are timeless and are as relevant today as they were in the past. Being a country with such a civilisation India should have modelled its institutions based on the lessons of its past.

India's military culture has been vividly described in the epics and other texts. The art of war was well developed in India. The Mauryan Empire had a massive standing army. The extent of the empire covered almost the entire Indian subcontinent except for the southernmost areas of peninsular India. In spite of having one of the strongest militaries of the period, it never ventured for military conquest beyond the subcontinent. This feature of not attempting military conquest beyond the subcontinent was displayed by all the great empires of India. This does not indicate passive approach to statecraft; rather wars were continuously fought between the various kingdoms to establish supremacy. But unlike Europe which colonised and exploited various countries, India never exhibited such exploitative military conquests. The Gupta Empire displayed similar strategic behaviour. Throughout history the attempts by the various empires were to ensure domination over the Indian subcontinent.

Ancient India produced various treatises on statecraft. Kautilya's *Arthashastra* is well known and highly researched today. The Shanti Parva and Anushasana Parva of the *Mahabharata* extensively deal with statecraft and duties of the king. Ethics in war was practised in India from the period of the Epics. The Chola Empire had a powerful navy which spread its influence to South East Asia and the Maldives. India in the medieval period also displayed strategic weaknesses. The cultural and strategic conditioning through the ages provides uniqueness to India. Therefore, it is incumbent for India to learn and utilise the lessons of its strategic culture while creating institutions for the present. Over 70 years after independence, India must work towards remodelling its institutions.

The Higher Defence Organisation of India evolved with civilian control over the military, which at times was used even to exercise bureaucratic control. It led to the military being detached from the security decision making structure of the government. The Service headquarters were designated as attached offices of the Ministry of

Defence and effectively they could provide inputs only when asked for. This side-stepping of the military from primary security decision making, in a country where the military as per the Arthshastra was one of the most important constituents of the state, had its downstream effects on security. There were some who created a fear of possible coup, despite the Indian military having remained, since ancient times, committed to the state guided by the ancient Indian principle of Dharma. This created distortions in the civil military relations in India and affected the preparedness of the military.

India since independence has faced multiple security challenges. Pakistan has displayed existential animosity towards India and this is likely to continue. In the 1950s India led by Prime Minister Jawaharlal Nehru's policies tried to build friendly relations with China. However by annexing Tibet and Aksai Chin areas, China became a security threat to India. It has refused to settle the border issues and continues to lay claim to more territories of India. It has utilised every opportunity to harm Indian interests. With increase in its economic and military strength, it has begun to display hegemonistic ambitions and has been repeatedly attempting to nibble away at Indian territory. Chinese influence on India's immediate neighbours is inimical to the security of India. The collusion of China and Pakistan create a major security challenge for India.

The recent Chinese actions in Eastern Ladakh, has made it imperative for India to adopt a comprehensive approach to external security. National approach to external security has been dominated by diplomacy since independence. India needs to incorporate military and economic strategy into it. Indian ministries presently act in silos dictated by their responsibilities as per the AoB and ToB Rules. Creation and sustenance of national power would need a whole of government approach rather than being the responsibility of only the military. There is also a requirement to integrate capability build up and operational planning between the three arms of the military. An integrated approach by the military combined with economic strength and diplomacy is the need of the hour looking at the security challenges that India faces.

India lost the 1962 war, largely due to failure of the higher defence organisation at that time, as a consequence of Krishna Menon's rather authoritarian and arbitrary approach of higher defence management. He literally began functioning as a Chief of Defence Staff (CDS) without the experience of any service. Things are now on the mend. An Integrated Defence Staff (IDS) is in place. A military man as CDS has been appointed. His charter is evolving. He is the single-point adviser to the defence minister. If a service Chief differs with the CDS, he can go directly to the defence minister. Country is also toiling to find ways to improve inter-service integration through new joint structures, a work that is actively in progress.

External security and higher defence management is a complex theme. Gp Capt RR Chaudhary, Senior Fellow at the Centre for Air Power Studies (CAPS) has chosen to write on "Transforming India's External Security using its Ancient Strategic Culture". In this process he has carried out deep research, and some out-of-the-box thinking to produce a commendable document. The central issue remains that India continues to face handicaps of disjunctions, both vertical and horizontal, in civil-military relations and equations. This results in delayed decision making and in turn impacts security preparedness. Chaudhary has looked closely at the Civil-Military Relations (CMR) as expounded by Western thinkers and as it existed in ancient India. He subsequently covers the evolution of Higher Defence Organisation (HDO) and CMR in India. He charts the history of India's military prowess before British rule. He also has a closer look at the ancient strategic culture of India, and draws lessons from it. He then analyses India's present external security architecture and the need for greater further integration through institutional changes. He highlights the need for much more coordination and joint work between ministries of Defence, External affairs and Finance for a holistic approach to national security. The proposal to have an overarching Ministry of External Security may seem farfetched and appear to be trampling on the domains of other ministries, but the finer points of logic for such integration needs attention. For a country that has serious boundary disputes with two nuclear armed neighbours and has fought many wars with them, there is clearly a need for a comprehensive approach to national security. Transforming India's external security structure and strategic culture is the need of the hour.

Air Marshal **Anil Chopra**
PVSM AVSM VM VSM (Retd)

Abbreviations

AAP	Annual Acquisition Plan
AoB Rules	Allocation of Business Rules
AOC	Air Officer Commanding
ANC	Andaman Nicobar Command
ARC	Administrative Reforms Commission
CCP	China Communist Party
CCPA	Cabinet Committee on Political Affairs
CCS	Cabinet Committee on Security
CDS	Chief of Defence Staff
CES	Chief of External Security
CGDA	Controller General of Defence Accounts
CMC	Central Military Commission
CPC	Chinese Communist Party
C-in-C	Commander in Chief
CISC	Chief of Integrated Staff to the Chiefs of Staff Committee
COAS	Chief of Army Staff
COSC	Chiefs of Staff Committee
CMR	Civil-Military Relations
CSD	Canteen Stores Department
C2	Command and Control
DAC	Defence Acquisition Council
DAP	Defence Acquisition Procedure

DCC	Defence Committee of the Cabinet
DDP	Department of Defence Production
DDRD	Department of Defence Research and Development
DESW	Department of Ex Servicemen Welfare
DGDPS	Director General Defence Planning Staff
DGMO	Director General of Military Operations
DIA	Defence Intelligence Agency
DMA	Department of Military Affairs
DMC	Defence Ministers Committee
DoD	Department of Defence
DPC	Defence Planning Committee
DPS	Defence Planning Staff
DPM	Defence Procurement Manual
DPP	Defence Procurement Plan
DRDO	Defence Research and Development Organisation
DSSC	Defence Services Staff College
EAM	External Affairs Minister
ECC	Emergency Committee of the Cabinet
EEZ	Exclusive Economic Zone
FADS	Financial Advisor Defence Services
FOC	Flag Officer Commanding
GAD	General Armaments Department
GLD	General Logistics Department
GoM	Group of Ministers
GPD	General Political Department
GSD	General Staff Department
HADR	Humanitarian Assistance and Disaster Relief
HDO	Higher Defence Organisation
IB	Intelligence Bureau

ICDP	Integrated Capability Development Plan
IDS	Integrated Defence Staff
IDSA	Institute of Defence and Strategic Studies
INDU	Indian National Defence University
JCS	Joint Chiefs of Staff
JPC	Joint Planning Committee
JIC	Joint Intelligence Committee
JS	Joint Secretary
KRC	Kargil Review Committee
LTIPP	Long Term Integrated Perspective Plan
LTPP	Long Term Perspective Plan
MEA	Ministry of External Affairs
MES	Ministry of External Security
MoD	Ministry of Defence
MoF	Ministry of Finance
MR	Military Regions
NDA	National Defence Academy
NCTF	Naresh Chandra Task Force
NSC	National Security Council
NSCS	National Security Council Secretariat
NSAB	National Security Advisory Board
NTRO	National Technical Research Organisation
PLA	People's Liberation Army
PM	Prime Minister
PMO	Prime Minister's Office
PSO	Principal Staff Officer
R&AW	Research and Analysis Wing
RBI	Reserve Bank of India
RIAF	Royal Indian Air Force
RIN	Royal Indian Navy

RM	Raksha Mantri (Defence Minister)
SCAP	Services Capital Acquisition Plan
SCG	Strategic Core Group
SFC	Strategic Forces Command
SPG	Strategic Policy Group
SR	Special Representative
ToB Rules	Transaction of Business Rules
VCDS	Vice Chief of Defence Staff

1. Introduction to Civil-Military Relations in Indian Context

What is the academic discipline of Civil-Military Relations (CMR) and why should we study it? The term CMR consists of two parts: Civil and Military. The capability of a State to be able to enforce its will is largely defined by its military strength and every State aspires to increase the effectiveness of its military as an important enabler of national power. The civil component of CMR in a democratic society comprises the political system and the bureaucracy in the form of various institutions which interact with the military. The capability of the military in terms of its force structure and resources is partly determined by the way it is handled by the civil component. Importance of military effectiveness for national sovereignty and survival is a given. World history is testimony to the fact that civilisations and states which became militarily weak were subjugated by the strong. In case of ancient civilisations like Egypt, Greece, Persia (before Islamic dominance) and many others, the effect of military subjugation was so strong that it altered their culture and belief systems. Thus the importance of a strong military backing a strong civilian set-up for national security cannot be overemphasised. A cordial relationship between the two would typically ensure that the country progresses on a path that makes it an effective 'power'. In context here the term 'study of the military' would only encompass the study of its overall efficacy at the strategic level to fulfil the national intent and will not include the aspects of the military at the operational level. The grand aim of good CMR would be to achieve a structure in which the civilian set up, while controlling the military, enables it to achieve capabilities and effectiveness to comprehensively fulfil all the security objectives of the State. The attempt will be to analyse Civil-Military Relations purely in the Indian context and so, it would be prudent to look into the history of India to help understand the structures of the military and society and their interaction in ancient times.

Importance of History for CMR

For the purpose of this book the term India when used in the historical sense would encompass the entire Indian sub-continent (geographical landmass comprising present India, Pakistan, Bangladesh and Nepal). Great empires rose and disintegrated in this landmass. In this geographical area, political boundaries kept changing but the concept of India always remained the same throughout its civilisational history. Alexander Cunningham, the British archaeologist who served in colonial India, cites Greek historian Strabo on how the country beyond the Indus was described to Alexander of Macedon by those well acquainted with it: "These learned men described the land known as India as a rhomboid an unequal quadrilateral, in shape with the Indus to the west, the mountains to the north and the sea on the East and the South"[1]. By citing Alexander Cunningham, Shyam Saran, a former Foreign Secretary of India, brings out the fact that India, since ancient times, has a political history rooted in a defined geography. The history of India,while being covered in detail subsequently in the book, will be the history of the Indian subcontinent. The mention of India before independence will generally relate to the entire Indian subcontinent unless specified otherwise.

India's history can be traced to the Indus Valley civilisation. India's great civilisation would only have continued to flourish if it was supported by a competent military culture to protect and sustain it. Post the invasion of Alexander in 326 BC, Chandragupta Maurya had founded the Mauryan Empire (321 BC to 185 BC). The Mauryan Empire united most of the Indian sub-continent, at least a century before the Qin united only a part of Han China.[2] The mighty military of the Mauryan Empire prevented the overrun of India by the Greeks under Selecus Nikator. A treatise on statecraft 'Arthshastra' written by Chanakya, who was Chandragupta Maurya's mentor, describes in detail the relationship of the military with the state's administration. It is one of the most important expositions on military and statecraft. It describes the structure of the state's administration, ways to conduct diplomacy, duties of the king, management of the treasury, functions of spies, laws of the state, military and the security of the state by utilising both diplomacy and military in a coordinated approach; thus, the '*Arthshastra*' touches on every aspect of the governance of the state[3]. During the period of the Gupta Empire (250 AD to 550 AD), generally known as the golden age of India, diplomacy and military had become cohesive. The military department was the most important one and was directly supervised by the king. The foreign minister, Mahasandhivigrahika, worked in close cooperation with the military and campaigns launched by the forces were decided with his inputs. Which kingdom was to be annexed and which could remain as a feudatory state was decided by his department[4]. This indicates the presence of a very high degree of cohesion between the military and the foreign policy apparatus of the state. This cooperation between various organs of the state and the military, remained true upto the Mughal Empire, especially for those periods where political unification was achieved. The past militaries and their administration,thus hold valuable lessons in CMR for today. As the aim of CMR is to ensure all round security of the State by enhancing the capability of the military, it would be imperative to learn the relevant lessons from the militaries of the past. The second chapter of the book would deal with militaries and their administration, especially of those empires where political unification happened, and draw germane lessons of CMR for the present.

CMR as We Understand Today

Let us look at the basics of CMR in the present milieu. The military is created by a state to ensure its protection and its very existence. If that be so then what are Civil-Military relations and how do they impact the military, the state and society at large? Civil-Military relations are the relationships of the military with the various organs of the State and vice versa. Civil-Military relations are a subset of the larger construct in which the 'Civil' controls the military. One of the first books of modern times to theorise Civil-Military relations was '*The Soldier and the State*', written by Samuel Huntington. As stated by him, Civil-Military relationship is the relationship of the officer class of the military with the governing organs of the state and the freedom which the officer class has to conduct their military business as is perceived by them.[5] Subsequently, a number of authors have written on the topic. David Pion Berlin[6] in his foreword of the book '*Who Guards the Guardians and How*' states that 'if democracy is to survive and flourish in today's world, it must strike a balance between controlling the armed forces and ensuring their effectiveness'.[7] The primary question is 'Quis custodiet ipos custodet'; i.e. who will guard the guardians and how. Peter D Feaver in his article on Civil-Military Relations, written for the Annual Review of Political Sciences in 1999 presents CMR as a simple paradox: "The very institution created to protect the polity becomes a threat to the polity"[8]. Feaver cites many literature written during the cold war period (Kerwin 1948, Smith 1951, Lasswell 1950, Ekirch 1956, Mills1956, Millis et al 1958, Morris Janowitz 1960) along with Samuel Huntington's *Soldier and the State*. The basic premise is the fear of military intervention in the affairs of the state at one end and the takeover of the state by the military at the other extreme. In his article Feaver states that all initial studies on CMR were largely based on the understanding of the American society and its people. This was the cold war period when USA was trying to balance the requirements of having a large military with its traditional suspicions of the threats to liberty posed by standing armies[9]. American war experience in Vietnam produced another set of studies by political scientists on the subject. Later, these studies branched out to include institutionally oriented examination of post-colonial CMR in some countries. These studies have become a benchmark for any research in the field of CMR and most authors look at CMR through this prism.

CMR has been studied in the Indian context by several authors. Ayesha Ray, *Soldier and the State in India*; R Chandrasekhar, *Rooks and Knights*; Steven I. Wilkinson, *Army and Nation*; Anit Mukherjee, *The Absent Dialogue;* Apurba Kundu, *Civil Military Relations in British and Independent India*, are a few of them. All these authors have extensively referred to the western authors mentioned above for their theoretical understanding in their analysis of the Indian experience of CMR. Raj Shukla in his article written for the Manekshaw Paper of Centre for Land Warfare Studies in 2012 argues that "Conflict between the civil and military components may not always be manifestly visible but it is the underlying theme across the politico-military histories of nations. In that sense, CMR is an exquisite dispute, embody as it does, myriad complexities and nuances of the relations between civilian and military leadership"[10]. Raj Shukla also extensively quotes western authors starting from Samuel Huntington, Morris Janowitz, Peter Feaver and the others. It would appear to any reader of Civil Military Relations that the picture that has been created is one in which there is constant friction between the military and the state and that this friction needs to be controlled.

Before exploring CMR in the Indian context any further, it will be worthwhile analysing Peter Feaver again. As mentioned earlier, Feaver has stated that the origin of most contemporary studies on CMR, were based on analyses of the American society and its people. So if CMR is to be understood in the Indian context it needs to be based on the understanding of Indian society. This argument gains traction all the more because India is an ancient society and a continuous civilisation. It has its own culture, ethos and ethics which have evolved over thousands of centuries. Its rich military traditions date back to the epic age of the Ramayana and Mahabharata and before that to the Vedic period. Therefore, for a correct understanding of CMR in the Indian context it will be necessary to understand the strategic culture of India and its military ethics.

Strategic Culture

The concept of Strategic Culture evolved in the late 20th century. It was first introduced by Jack Snyder in 1977 when he tried to explain the different approach that the Americans and Soviets had to a limited nuclear war. "Strategic culture can be defined as the sum total of ideas,conditioned emotional responses, and patterns of habitual behaviour that members of a national strategic community have acquired through instruction or imitation and share with each other with regard to nuclear strategy".[11] In his path breaking argument he stated that the Soviet response to a nuclear war will be different from the American and it will be conditioned by Soviet strategic culture. Ken Booth defines Strategic Culture as "the concept of strategic culture refers to a nation's traditions, values, attitudes, patterns of behaviour, habits, symbols, achievements and particular ways of adapting to the environment and solving problems with respect to the threat or use of force".[12] His subsequent exposition is more important: "The strategic culture of a nation derives from its history, geography and political culture, and it represents the aggregation of the attitudes and patterns of behaviour of the most influential voices; these may be, depending on the nation, the political elite, the military establishment and/or public opinion". Strategic culture, thus, permeates a nation's thinking consciously or in a subconscious way. India's civilisational history and culture makes it imperative to develop a clear understanding of its own unique strategic culture. On the importance and relevance of strategic culture Ken Booth states "Strategic culture helps shape behaviour on such issues as the use of force in international politics, sensitivity to external dangers, civil-military relations and strategic doctrine. As a result of continuities in these matters, it is legitimate to talk about a particular national 'style' in the theory and practice of strategy".[13]

India would benefit by aligning its policies and institutions with its own strategic culture because that is what this nation sub-consciously is. While analysing India's strategic culture the concept of 'military ethics' as stated by Kaushik Roy "the norms of behaviour of armies and polities during wartime and the collective set of ideas that gave birth to such norms"[14] would also be studied.

India's Strategic Culture – Evolution

To understand India's strategic culture one would have to start with the concept of the king. Indian historian A.S. Altekar[15] quotes the Mahabharata to show that "the state was regarded as a divine institution; a king's right to govern was partly due to his divine creation and partly due to the arrangement of his subjects governed by him to prevent anarchy".[16] He further states that the version narrated in the Dighanikaya[17] also agrees with that of the Mahabharata.[18] Kingship also arose out of military necessity of having a leader during war and the king had to be a capable general whose leadership had to be acknowledged by all. The duties of the King during the Vedic and the Epic periods are enumerated in the Dharamsastras[19] and later on are also described by Kautilya in his 'Arthshastra'. An important development in the evolution of society that happened in India during the early Vedic period was the emergence of the Kshatriya varna or warrior class. They took up the profession of arms, were respected in society as protectors and were the upholders of the highest values of the society.[20] Hermann Kulke and Deitmar Rothermund in their Book '*A History of India*' state that "even in Early Vedic times a distinction was made between the ordinary free members *(vish)* of a tribe and the warriornobility *(kshatriya)*, from among whom the tribal chieftain *(rajan)* was selected. The Brahmins, as priests, were also mentioned as a distinct social group in these early Vedic texts".[21] These varnas or class later evolved into the four castes in India.[22] The Brahmin priest was at the apex of the social hierarchy. The king was generally from the Kshatriya class but his powers were not absolute. He had to rely on the advice of his priest called the purohit. The interdependence of the nobility and the priesthood is stressed time and again in the Vedic literature. The purohit used to accompany the king and his army even to the battlefield[23]. The priest was the interpreter of the Dharmasastras, and the king had to refer to him for guidance. "It was the duty of the

Brahmins to define and interpret *dharma* (the Hindu code of conduct), and the Kshatriyas had to implement the rules and regulations laid down by the Brahmins in accordance with *dharma*"[24]. This arrangement, apart from providing legitimacy to the king, also placed a check on his actions and usually kept him on the path to follow his 'Dharma' as per the scriptures. There are examples of kings who tried to wield absolute power but they were regarded as tyrants and oppressors and they would lose their divine right to rule[25]. The duty of the king to follow his 'Dharma' and be veracious as per the scriptures finds mention in the Arthshastra as well as in Kamandaka's 'Nitisara' (book on statecraft written during the period of the Gupta empire). As per Stephen P Rosen "texts advising Indian rulers on how to govern their people have survived and have provided the basis for descriptive analyses of Indian politics"[26]. The yearning of kings to be righteous runs as a common thread throughout Indian history. There were exceptions but the desire for legitimacy and greatness generally persisted.

The primary duty of the Kshatriya class was to serve the state by participating in war. "They were to defend the realm, to protect the people and the Dharma, not to forget a kindness or a hurt, not to back out when challenged to fight or gamble, and in the words of the Great epic they considered it a sin to die in bed"[27]. The origin of the Kshatriya class ensured that the rest of the society remained unaffected from war. "The necessary education, drill and discipline to cultivate militarism were confined to one community and this prevented the militant attitude from spreading to other communities and kept the whole social structure unaffected by actual wars and war institutions"[28]. S.V. Vishwanath in his book *International Law in Ancient India* quotes the *Sukraniti* and Mahabharata to state "persons living in enemy territory were on no account to be slain or made prisoners of war as long as they were peaceful. The civil population of places under military occupation were not under ordinary circumstances to be interfered with"[29]. War, whatever be the reason it is waged for, results in death, destruction and misery for both the sides. Ancient India had realised this and by the epic period there were elaborate code and ethics of war to minimise suffering. B.K. Majumdar may be right when he states that "the Epic and the Puranic literature holds before us an excellent military code making a near approach to the laws of war as laid down in modern International Law"[30]. These ethics of war continued to be followed even later in history as can be inferred by the remarks of the famous historian and Indologist A L Basham, "the chivalrous rules of war based on very old traditions and codified amongst the martial people of western India in post Mauryan times must have had some effect in mitigating the effects of war both for the combatants and the non-combatants. It is doubtful if any other ancient civilisation set such humane ideals of warfare".[31]

During the Epic period, warfare was divided into two types, dharmyuddha and kutayuddha. Dharmyuddha was carried out following the ethics of war. In kutayuddha, deceit and deception was allowed. The aim was to win at all costs. In the ancient books of India, Dharmyuddha has been kept at a very high pedestal compared to kutayuddha, though in Mahabharata, Shri Krishna advises the Pandavas to take recourse to deceit at times to win a righteous war. The end justified the means. Kautilya in *Arthshastra* gives a practical advice; if you are strong follow dharmyuddha otherwise resort to kutayuddha[32]. Nonetheless Indians strived to follow higher ideals in war even during medieval period of India's history. A.S. Altekar states that "there can however be no doubt that there was a constant effort to follow the higher ideal as far as possible; otherwise the Rajput code of chivalry could not have survived till the medieval times"[33]. This is testimony to the strategic culture and military ethics of India. By the definition of strategic culture as given earlier, the conditioning of India that has happened over millennia, will affect and shape its response and behaviour. The scope of the present chapter limits further exposition on this topic; the third chapter of the book would cover in detail the strategic culture and military ethics of India and its likely effect on CMR in the present milieu. CMR in the Indian context will have to factor the strategic culture of India and cannot be based on studies done on some other people or society.

A study of the strategic culture of India will enable the understanding of relevant lessons which can then be used while analysing the present CMR and Higher Defence Organisation (HDO). The present CMR and HDO are a legacy of the British rule in India; therefore a brief understanding of the British rule and its CMR structure in India would be essential to understand the present system.

History of CMR from British Rule

The fourth chapter of the book would cover the history of CMR during the British rule in India and post-independence. Modern India inherited its defence setup from the British. By the end of the 17th century and early 18th century the British East India Company had established three presidencies in India viz. Bombay, Calcutta and Madras. The first presidency was setup in Bombay and these presidencies had their own armies under its Commander-in-Chief (C-in-C). In 1748 the Commander-in-Chief of Bengal presidency was given command of all the East India Company's forces. In 1784 a Governor-General was appointed to manage the affairs in India by an act of the British Parliament. All the three presidential armies came under his control. In 1787 to enable the Governor-General to exercise control over these Armies, an Army Department was setup under a Military Member of the Governor General's Executive Council[34]. The Military Member worked as the interface between the Commanders-in-Chief and the Governor General. The Military Member was a military officer junior in rank to the Commander-in-Chief. In 1858 by an act of British Parliament the military and naval forces of the East India Company were transferred to the British Empire. In 1909 the post of the Military Member was abolished and replaced with Army Secretary who worked under the direct control of the Commander-in-Chief. The Army Secretary was an army officer of the rank of Major General. In 1921 the designation of the Army Secretary was changed to Defence Secretary and an officer of the Indian Civil Service replaced the army officer on this post. The Military Department was changed to the Ministry of Defence (MoD), by the Ministry of Defence Act of 1946 passed by Clement Atlee's[35] government. The MoD became the coordinating agency between the military and the Viceroy's government.

After independence the MoD started functioning under a Cabinet Minister. However, little changed as far as the functionality was concerned and the Higher Defence Organisation (HDO) of India continued to function as was devised by the British. After independence, on the advice of Lord Ismay, who was the Chief of Staff to the Governor General, a series of committees were set up to manage defence. At the apex was the Committee of the Cabinet, comprising the Prime Minister (who also held the External Affairs portfolio), Home Minister, Defence Minister and Minister for Information and Broadcasting. Next was the Defence Minister's Committee (DMC), with him as the chairman and the three Service Chiefs, Defence Secretary and Financial Advisor of the MoD as member. Then there was the Chiefs of Staff Committee (COSC) comprising the three Service Chiefs. Two sub-committees were created to service the COSC, the Joint Planning Committee (JPC) and the Joint Intelligence Committee (JIC). In 1955 the nomenclature of C-in-C for the service chiefs was changed to Chiefs of Staff. In 1961, the Allocation of Business (AoB) / Transaction of Business (ToB) Rules were promulgated and the three Services became attached offices of the MoD. Their access to the political hierarchy got blocked except through the MoD. Thus, largely, the military structure that independent India started functioning with was whatever it inherited from the British with additional bureaucratic control imposed, without a review of what the country would actually need for the future.

India inherited a military which had been created and modelled by the British for their basic intent of ruling British India. The purpose of the army had been twofold, the first was to effectively deal with any uprising within the country and the second was to defend from external aggression and aid the British Empire in fighting its wars. After Independence both these objectives had changed; however, the Indian leaders largely decided to continue with what they had inherited. Ayesha Ray in her book *The Soldier and the State in India* has observed that the Indian policy makers post-independence were preoccupied with the enormous task of economic reconstruction and democratic consolidation which made them less attentive to military affairs. The British had no interest in creating any new defence structure which could meet the future military requirements of a newly independent nation and the Indian political leadership's disinterest in military affairs led to an isolated military and a dysfunctional defence policy.[36] Stephen P Cohen and Sunil Dasgupta in their book on India's military modernization *Arming without Aiming* have correctly analysed that India's leaders post-independence, preserved the structure of the colonial state and its institutions, including the armed forces, police and the bureaucracy. As per them, for the Indian leaders, maintaining continuity was more important, despite imperfections and contradictions in the way these institutions could serve the new state of India. They further state that, for the armed forces, institutional continuity was allowed but strong political, and subsequently, bureaucratic supervision was incorporated.[37] Indian leaders, before independence, had only seen the army furthering the interests of the British and hence most were strongly critical of the military and considered it an undue financial burden.[38] This impression affected to a large extent the shaping up of the higher defence organisation of the country and the military's role in the decision making structure post-independence. Even India's inability to wrest control of entire Kashmir after Pakistan attacked it, did not force the government to rethink its military management. The MoD, staffed with bureaucrats, became the primary organisation to control the military. The first review of the military happened only after the defeat of 1962 by the Chinese.

The defeat of 1962 should have resulted in major revamping of the security structure of India. It resulted in only individuals holding important portfolios being changed. Defence Minister Krishna Menon was replaced with Y.B. Chavan, Lt Gen J.N. Choudhuri replaced the army chief Gen Thapar. "There were no operational or hierarchical changes which could strengthen the decision making apparatus of the Indian Higher Defence Organisation"[39]. The control of JIC was shifted from the COSC to the Cabinet Secretariat. The debacle of 1962 however led to major expansion, logistical improvements and modernisation of the military. The wars of 1965 and 1971 were fought with the same structure but with much better coordination. It is to the credit of the Prime Ministers of India that during the wars of 1965 and 1971 they interacted directly with the military leadership even though no organisational structure facilitating the same existed. A major review of the defence setup happened with the setting up of the National Security Council (NSC) in 1998 and after the Kargil War of 1999. Along with the NSC a Strategic Policy Group (SPG) and a National Security Advisory Board (NSAB) were also created. The NSC, SPG and NSAB were supposed to provide advice to the Prime Minister for long term policy formulation affecting security of the country. Post Kargil war in 1999, a Kargil Review Committee (KRC) was setup. The recommendations of the KRC were examined by a Group of Ministers (GoM) whose mandate was to review the national security system. They recommended setting up of a Strategic Forces Command (SFC), a joint Andaman Nicobar Command (ANC) a Defence Intelligence Agency (DIA) and an Integrated Defence Staff (IDS). The Service headquarters were recommended to be renamed as integrated headquarters of the MoD. However, functionally things remained the same between the Service Headquarters and the MoD. This changed on December 30, 2019 with the creation of the post of Chief of Defence Staff (CDS) and the Department of Military Affairs (DMA) in the MoD.

Present MoD Set-Up

In India the military is controlled by the MoD. MoD is responsible for the overall defence of the country and for ensuring the implementation of all government policies about defence. The MoD has five departments:

- Department of Defence (DoD);
- Department of Defence Production;
- Department of Defence Research and Development (DR&D);
- Department of Ex-Servicemen Welfare;
- Department of Military Affairs (DMA);

DMA is a new department which has been created along with the establishment of the CDS and it would function directly under him. Department of Defence is headed by the Defence Secretary. It is responsible for the defence of India and the nation's defence policy. It deals with capital acquisition for the defence forces, Canteen Stores Department (CSD), Coast Guard, Reserves for the three services, Cantonment matters and NCC along with other subjects as listed in the AoB Rules, 1961. The Department of Defence Production is headed by a Secretary and deals with matters relating to defence production, Ordnance Factory Board and Defence PSUs. The Department of DR&D is headed by a Secretary and its function is to advise the government on scientific aspects of military equipment and logistics and the formulation of research design and development plans. The department of Ex Servicemen Welfare deals with all resettlement, welfare and pensionary matters of Ex-Servicemen.[40] As per the Allocation of Business Rules, all the three services (Army, Navy and the Air Force) and their headquarters were listed under the Department of Defence prior to the creation of DMA. This changed on 30 December 2019 and now the three services, their headquarters and Integrated Defence Staff (IDS) function under the newly created DMA.

Prior to the creation of DMA, MoD used to be predominantly staffed by the civilian bureaucracy. It was the interface between the military and the political leadership. The MoD,because of being primarily staffed with civilians without expertise in military matters, was ill-equipped to provide strategic directions to the military. Prior to the creation of CDS and DMA, in the MoD structure that India had, there was a mismatch between the political leadership, the bureaucrats as representative of the executive and the military. The situation was best stated by one of the former Naval Chiefs, Admiral DK Joshi, who stated that "*the root cause in the dysfunctional and inefficient business model that we have is that the professional competence, domain expertise, accountability, responsibility and authority, these all reside in separate silos in different locations.*"[41] The Army, Navy and the Air Force,each carried out their separate evaluation of the force structure that they needed, based on the threat perception provided by MoD. Each Service predominantly looked after its own requirements and there was no integrated approach. For all their procurements, major reallocation of forces from one place to another involving permanent moves, major restructuring of their cadres, and other major decisions, they had to take prior sanction from the MoD. However, they were free to manage their training. The MoD did not provide any roadmap to the services for the future simply because it was not established, equipped or staffed to do so. It functioned as the manager of the three services and only audited the proposals of the Services to ensure that they followed the basic laid down rules and procedures without any value addition to it. According to Late Air Commodore Jasjit Singh, India had an "ossified system of defence management" and the "structure of the ministry is a major factor for its inefficiency".[42] Any contact between the political leadership and the military was through the MoD. As brought out earlier this led to a divide between the MoD and the military. The military felt that the MoD was not a facilitator in their functioning. The MoD felt that the military needed to be kept under tight civilian control. There was thus a disconnect between the MoD – which had complete authority over all matters related to defence – and the Armed Forces who are actually responsible to fight for the defence of the nation. Authority rested on one end with the MoD while responsibility was on the other end with the Armed Forces. Anit Mukherjee had summed up the situation in his book *The Absent Dialogue* when he stated that "the pattern of civil-military relations in India compromises the effectiveness of the military".[43] This was the truth of Civil-Military relations in India; it had become Bureaucratic-Military relations.

The creation of the DMA, more than the CDS, has finally integrated the military with the MoD. As per the AoB Rules, 1961 which lists out the responsibilities of the various departments in the ministries; DMA is responsible for, the Armed Forces of the Union and their headquarters, IDS, procurement except capital acquisition, promoting jointness in procurement, training and staffing and jointness in operations. This will result in considerable decision making autonomy for the military, speed up the routine decision making process and go a long way in reducing friction between the Civil and the Military. However, the AoB Rules also specify that the DoD headed by the Defence Secretary is responsible for the "defence of India and every part thereof including defence policy and preparation for defence and all such acts as may be conducive in times of war to its prosecution and after its termination to effective demobilisation".[44] The responsibility of the defence of the nation is that of the Defence Secretary who is a generalist bureaucrat and not that of the CDS who is a professional. The Defence Ministry is headed by the Defence Minister. He is responsible for each of the departments of the ministry and represents the political and executive authority. Thus, the final responsibility for defence is his whether it is with DoD or DMA. The delegation of responsibility for defence of the country and all issues related to war, down from the Defence Minister to the Defence Secretary and not to the CDS signifies the continuation of bureaucratic control over the military. This is not the same as civil control or state control of the military. Apart from delegation of routine affairs of the military to the DMA nothing much appears to have changed. The fifth chapter would analyse the entire external security apparatus of the country and its effectiveness in maximising the security and military capability of the country.

CMR for the Future

Future wars will require capabilities to deal with counterinsurgency, low intensity warfare across the spectrums, very short and high intensity war, cyber war and potential nuclear conflict in addition to conventional conflict. This will require competencies and synergy across the various spectrums of warfare between all agencies having a stake in the defence of the country. Attaining the full potential of military effectiveness is therefore an inescapable necessity. Analyses of the Civil-Military structure leads to two conclusions. First is that there is a requirement of increasing the synergy between the three Services. Since independence the three Services have operated in different silos and capability build-up has happened independently. There is a necessity to increase jointness of effort[45]. CDS has been mandated by the government to do this. Creation of the DMA is by far one of the most important decisions taken by the government affecting the military since independence.

The second, and more important, issue is of integrating the military in the strategic decision making of the country. Before deliberating on this further let us understand the definition of grand strategy. Ashley Tellis has cited Paul Kennedy's useful definition of grand strategy as, "*the capacity of [a] nation's leaders to bring together all of the elements, both military and non-military, for the preservation and enhancement of [a] nation's long-term (that is, in wartime and peacetime) best interests.*"[46] Since independence, India's military has remained isolated from the national decision making. George Tanham in his work 'Indian Strategic Thought, An Interpretive Essay' states that '*India has pursued the policy of tight civilian control over the military to a point where the military have almost no input at all in the formulation of higher defence policy and national strategy*'.[47] He further states citing his conversation with K Subrahmanyam, held in Washington D.C. on April 29, 1992:

> "The Cabinet Committee on Political Affairs (CCPA) rather than the military makes the major strategy and military decisions. The civilian Minister of Defence and his civilian staff receive recommendations from the services, make decisions, and pass on the most important issues to the CCPA for decisions. A section of the Ministry of Finance with an office in the Ministry of Defence has a near veto on all expenditures proposed by the services, and an input to the recommendations to the Ministry of Defence. The Ministry of Defence in essence serves as a higher headquarters that makes all the decisions; the service chiefs have no statutory power to make government decisions. They are limited to operations and operational plans".[48]

Over the years the military has become involved in the defence planning process, however major policy decisions have been steered mainly by the bureaucracy. The bureaucracy functions as a layer between the military and the political leadership and the military has often been consulted directly by the political hierarchy only during times of crises. India is a democracy where governments may change every five years. The bureaucracy in India is generalist as there is no concept of developing domain expertise. Hence, their knowledge on military capabilities and other military matters will be, at best, superficial. Involvement of the military in policy making institutional structures, therefore, becomes vital. A nation cannot have a grand security strategy by excluding the military from its formulation, while at the same time it cannot be left to the military alone. With national security being a function of multiple domains it has become imperative to develop a cohesive structure comprising all elements of national power. India has robust institutions in the IFS, IAS, IPS and other central government services. Officers in these services develop a good understanding of the functioning of the country as they grow in service. The Indian Military is a professional service whose ethos has evolved through centuries. What is required is to develop institutions that could synergise the individual capability of each service. What we have ended up creating are structures which have generated a sense of divide between the civil and the military. In the past the most important strength of a State was the military. It still is, but the present world order has led to an equally important role for diplomacy. Military strength of yesteryears has given way to 'Diplo-Military' strength. In today's world, military strength or economic strength or diplomatic strength in isolation is not sufficient to deal with external security. Hence, the concept of diplo-military needs to be integrated with economic strength. Military, diplomacy, economic strength and intelligence incorporate all the tangible and intangible aspects of a nation that constitutes national power that comes into play while dealing with other nations. A nation which wields this integrated strength will be able to achieve its national objectives. This book in chapter six, proposes the creation of such an institution as a remedy for not only the existing Civil-Military friction but as a solution for providing the right Diplomilitary directions for a comprehensive and effective national security strategy.

This institution would provide strategic direction to the military and to the nation's foreign policy based on a synergistic whole of government approach. It would be capable of synergising all the individual capabilities of separate institutions to create a policy making structure which would provide unified advice to the political hierarchy. Such an institution will also ensure defence savings as it would lead to a synergistic build-up of capability of the armed forces as per the perceived requirements of the nation. Moreover, it would transform the defence manufacturing sector also, as it would be able to project long term and short term defence requirements, leading to better coordination with industry for their fulfilment. This is the real Civil-Military cohesion that India needs. It would lead to a whole of government approach not only for national security but also for technological and industrial development of the country in the field of defence and related sectors. As mentioned earlier before analysing the present CMR and security structure of India, understanding its strategic culture would be necessary. Towards this, the next chapter attempts to briefly understand the military prowess of India before the British rule.

Notes

1. Shyam Saran, *How India sees the World, Kautilya to the 21st Century*, (New Delhi, Juggernaut Books, 2017), p. 10.
2. Ibid.
3. For further reading refer Kautilya, *Arthshastra,* trans. R Shamasastry (Bangalore: Government Press, 1915), available online at https://archive.org/details/ArthashastraOfChanakyaEnglish_201506/page/n17/mode/2up, accessed on December 26, 2019.
4. For more on this refer Dr AS Altekar, "The Administrative Organisation" in *The Vakataka – Gupta Age* ed. RC Majumdar (Banaras: Motilal Banarsidass Publishers and Booksellers, 1954).
5. Samuel P Huntington, *The Soldier and the State*, (London: Harvard University Press, 1957), p. 3.
6. David Pion Berlin is a Latin Americanist widely known for his research and writings on civil-military relations and military political thoughts.
7. David Pion Berlin, "Foreword" of *Who Guards the Guardians and How, Democratic Civil-Military Relations,* (Austin: University of Texas Press, 2006), p. ix.
8. Peter D Feaver, "Civil – Military Relations," *Annual Review of Political Science, 1999.* 2:1, 211-241.

9. Ibid.
10. Raj Shukla "Civil Military Relations in India" *Manekshaw Paper No. 36, 2012*, (CLAWS, KW Publishers, 2012), p. 5.
11. Jack Snyder, *The Soviet Strategic Culture: Implications for Limited Nuclear Operations*, R-2154-AF (Santa Monica, CA: The Rand Corp., Sep 1977), p. 8.
12. Booth K. (1990) *The Concept of Strategic Culture Affirmed.* In: Jacobsen C.G. (eds) Strategic Power: USA/USSR. Palgrave Macmillan, London, p. 121 at https://doi.org/10.1007/978-1-349-20574-5_8, accessed on August 18, 2020.
13. Ibid.
14. Kaushik Roy, *Hinduism and the Ethics of Warfare in South Asia From Antiquity to the Present,* (New York, Cambridge University Press, 2012), p. 9.
15. A.S. Altekar was an archaeologist, historian and numismatist. He was a professor of history at India's famous university, Banaras Hindu University and has authored many books on ancient Indian history. He participated in and led many archeological excavations from 1936 to 1955.
16. AS Altekar, *State and Government in Ancient India,*(Varanasi, Motilal Banarsidas Publishers, 1949), p. 13.
17. Dighanikaya is a Buddhist scripture and the first of five Nikayas which contains long discourses of Gautama Buddha. For more refer Walshe, Maurice O'Connell, *The Long Discourses of the Buddha- A translation of the Dighanikaya*, (Boston, Wisdom Publications, 1995).
18. For more on the origin of the State and King in ancient India also refer Ram Sharan Sharma, *Aspects of Political Ideas and Institutions in Ancient India*, (Varanasi, Motilal Banarsidas Publishers, 1959).
19. The Dharmashastras are ancient Indian religious and legal treatises,which advocate moral laws and principles for devout duty and righteous conduct. The Dharmashastras contain valuable information about the life of ancient Indian society. For details of various modern publications on Dharmashastra refer Ministry of Culture, Government of India website of Indira Gandhi National Centre for the Arts at http://ignca.gov.in/texts-on-dharmashastra-wellspring-of-indian-code-for-life-3/
20. Sarv Daman Singh, *Ancient Indian Warfare with Special Reference to the Vedic Period*, (Leiden: E.J. Brill Publishers, 1965), p. 138.
21. Hermann Kulke and Deitmar Rothermund, *A History of India, 3rd edition*, (London, Routledge, 1998), p. 39.
22. To ensure social harmony society was divided on the basis of the duties that they performed. This was the origin of caste system in India. For more on this refer *War in Ancient India* by VR Ramchandra Dikshitar (Madras: Macmillan and Co. Limited, 1944), p. 4.
23. S. D. Singh, n. 20, p. 141.
24. K. Roy, n. 14, p. 29.
25. For more on this refer AS Altekar, *State and Government in Ancient India,* (Varanasi, Motilal Banarsidas Publishers, 1949), pp. 99-103.

26. Stephen P Rosen, *Society and Military Power in Ancient India*, (New York, Cornell University Press, 1996), p. 66.
27. Bimal Kanti Majumdar, *The Military System in Ancient India"*,(Calcutta, Firma, 1960), p. 28.
28. V.R. Ramachandra Dikshitar, *War in Ancient India*, (Madras, Macmillan and Co. Ltd., 1944), p. 6.
29. S.V. Vishwanatha, *International Law in Ancient India*, (Bombay, Longman Greens and Co., 1925), pp. 134-135.
30. Bimal Kanti Majumdar, *The Military System in Ancient India"*, (Calcutta, Firma, 1960), pp. 40-41.
31. AL Basham, *The Wonder that was India* (New Delhi: Rupa & Co, 1954), p. 127.
32. Kautilya, *Arthshastra, Book X, Chapter3*, trans. R Shamasastry (Bangalore: Government Press, 1915), p. 525.
33. Altekar, n. 16, p. 299.
34. Lt Gen S.K. Sinha (Retd), *USI National Security Lectures – Higher Defence Organisation*, (New Delhi, United Services Institution of India, 1991), p. 11.
35. Clement Atlee was the British Prime Minister in 1946 who oversaw the independence and partition of India.
36. Ayesha Ray, *The Soldier and the State in India* (New Delhi, Sage Publications, 2013), p. 39.
37. Stephen P Cohen and Sunil Dasgupta, *Arming Without Aiming* (Washington D.C: Brookings Institution Press, 2010), p. 4.
38. Ibid, p. 3.
39. Wg Cdr (Dr) R. Venkataraman, *India's Higher Defence - Organisation and Management*, (New Delhi, KW Publishers, 2011), p. 103.
40. Ministry of Defence India, "About Ministry" mod.gov.in/about-ministry accessed on May 10, 2020.
41. C. Uday Bhasker. "Will Modi Reform India's Higher Defence Management". *India Strategic*, (December 2014), at https://www.indiastrategic.in/2014/10/02/will-modi-reform-indias-higher-defence-management/ accessed on February 25, 2020.
42. Jasjit Singh, "Higher Defence Management: Principles and Practice in India," CLAWS Journal, (Summer 2013): pp. 9-10.
43. Anit Mukherjee, *The Absent Dialogue* (New Delhi: Oxford University Press, 2020) p. 5.
44. Cabinet Secretariat of India, "Business Rules / Allocation of Business Rules", (April 29, 2020), p. 44, at https://cabsec.gov.in/businessrules/allocationofbusinessrules/completeaobrules/ accessed on July 29, 2020.
45. For more on Jointness in Indian military refer: Air Mshl V. Patney (Retd), "Jointness in Armed Forces and Institution of Post of Chief of Defence Staff are Mutually Exclusive", *Journal of Defence Studies*, Vol. 2, No. 1, 2008, pp. 31-39, and Vice Admiral P. S. Das (Retd.), "Jointness in India's Military—What it is and What it Must Be", *Journal of Defence Studies*, Vol. 1, No. 1, 2007, pp. 1-12.

46. Ashley J. Tellis, *Nonalignment Redux: The Perils of Old Wine in New Skins*, (Washington D.C: Carnegie Endowment for International Peace, 2012) p. 4, at https://carnegieendowment.org/2012/07/10/nonalignment-redux-perils-of-old-wine-in-new-skins-pub-48675 accessed on February 27, 2020.
47. George Tanham, Indian Strategic Thought, An Interpretive Essay, (California: Rand Corporation, 1992) p. 70, at https://www.rand.org/pubs/reports/R4207.html accessed on January 18, 2020.
48. Ibid., pp. 73-74.

2. Brief History of India's Military Prowess before British Rule: Lessons for the Present

Those who do not learn from the past are condemned to repeat it.

– George Santayana

Introduction

A nation's military is one of the quantifiable measures of its national power. The aim of good civil military relations is to ensure the availability of a military which, apart from providing security from external aggression, can also act as an instrument of national power to further the interests of the state. Social scientists like Colin Grey and Ken Booth in their work on strategic culture have clearly brought out that strategic culture is a factor which should be an important determinant in shaping civil military relations. As brought out in the previous chapter the endeavour of the study is to situate the civil-military relations in India on the understanding of India's strategic culture rather than completely relying on western concepts, which have been arrived at by studying western societies. It does not mean disregarding the vast ideas developed by western studies, but the effort is to understand India from an Indian perspective. Why is this important? It is because India has an ancient history and unlike many cultures, it is one of the few societies which have continuity with its ancient past. This continuity is likely to have led to its conditioning along a strategic pattern. The objective is to find out if this continuity and conditioning exists; and if it does, then how has it affected the strategic thought process, and consequently, the strategic culture of India. The final aim is to draw lessons relevant in the present milieu for national security. The intent is to split the study in two parts. The first part, i.e., this chapter will aim to study the military prowess that existed in India during various phases of its history. India has witnessed three great empires of Mauryas, Guptas and Mughals. It is not that other militarily powerful kingdoms did not exist in India but these empires either directly controlled or had considerable influence over most of the Indian sub-continent. More importantly they were not one generation empires; they created military and civil institutions which enabled their survivability for a considerable period. Consequently, these empires will be studied in greater detail. The next part of the study, undertaken in the next chapter will attempt to explore the continuity and conditioning of India's strategic culture.

History offers many lessons. It helps in understanding the past empowering you to appreciate the present and shape the future. It enables the appreciation of societal progress and its ideas and beliefs. India has a certain continuity of its unique culture, beliefs and traditions. Cultures, traditions and history of a society are deeply influenced by its geography. George Tanham in his RAND sponsored study on the strategic culture of India has rightly asserted that "geography has profoundly affected India's history and culture and therefore its strategic thinking and strategy"[1]. Boundaries of kingdoms within the Indian subcontinent have changed from time to time but Indian history is the history of societies which evolved in the subcontinent bounded by the Himalayas on one side and the sea on the other sides.

Geography of India

Geographically India is an isolated landmass with natural barriers like the Himalayas and the oceans. The northwest is bound by the Hindukush Mountain ranges and its continuation the Karakoram mountains. These ranges and the mighty Himalayan Mountain ranges from the entire northern boundary. In the east, India is separated from Myanmar by the north-south aligned Arakan Yoma hills and its extension Naga and

Patkai hills which themselves are part of the Purvanchal ranges which then merge into the Himalayas. These mountains effectively form a physical barrier between Indian subcontinent and the rest of Asia. The Indian Ocean, Bay of Bengal and the Arabian Sea have ensured isolation in the south with Sri Lanka and Maldives being the only neighbours. This causes the country to had demarcated and defensible borders. North India, which is generally referred to the area north of the Vindhya Ranges, is the most fertile region of the country; it is also known as the Indo-Gangetic plain. North India also has dry plateaus and sandy deserts. The Aravalli ranges are in the west-north overlooking the plains of Agra-Delhi and Vindhya ranges are in the west-central part of the country. In the south the Western Ghats and the Eastern Ghats run parallel to the western and the eastern coast. In between them is the Deccan Plateau. The Western and the Eastern Ghats merge in the Nilgiri hills. Major river systems in the south like the Mahanadi, Krishna, Kaveri and Godavari originate in the west and flow into the Bay of Bengal. In the south most of the political boundaries were formed because of the effect of natural barriers. The watershed between major rivers has traditionally been the boundaries between various kingdoms. Ancient Indian geographers have divided India into five distinct parts:[2]

- Dakshinapatha – the country south of the Narmada/Vindhyas.
- Madhya Desa – the country between the Himalaya and the Narmada but bounded by Prayagraj in the east and Pehowa in the west.
- Uttarapatha – the northwest including the eastern part of Afghanistan.
- Purva Desa – the country east of Varanasi/Prayagraj.
- Pascha Desa – the country west of Ujjain/Devasabha (Dewas) including Sind and Baluchistan.

As can be seen from the geography of the subcontinent, it was largely isolated from the rest of the Asian landmass, though in the north-west region the Himalayas had passes (Khyber, Bolan and Gomal) which were used by Alexander, the Kushans, the Turks and the Moghuls for gaining access to the Indian sub-continent. The subcontinent had good river systems and a fertile land. As far as natural resources were concerned it was a land of plenty. It had tropical climate and because of abundance of natural resources life was relatively easy. This led to the development of a unique culture and an underlying unity in the entire Indian subcontinent in spite of linguistic differences[3]. The areas surrounding the Indian subcontinent were not as richly endowed as the sub-continent itself. Because of natural abundance of resources there was no incentive for Indians to venture out to conquer other territories and bring back wealth. This may be one of the many reasons as to why there has always been an influx of plunderers into India and never from India to other Asian regions. The history of India in this geographical landmass began with the early Indus valley civilisation[4].

Indus valley Civilisation

Archaeological excavations suggest that the Indus Valley Civilisation was situated in the Indian subcontinent largely along the banks of the Indus but also at other places like Lothal, Dholavira, Rakhigarhi, etc. As per contemporary understanding the Indus Valley civilisation refers to a period of almost 5000 years ago. The exact age is controversial with claims ranging from 7000 BC to 2000 BC[5]. Excavations at these places have revealed an advanced civilisation with intricate urban planning and advanced engineering. Baked brick houses, elaborate drainage systems, water supply systems, and clusters of large non- residential buildings have been found at these sites. The excavations indicate advanced architecture with dockyards, granaries, warehouses, brick platforms and protective walls. It was a civilisation with well-developed urban economy. The Indus script has not been deciphered till now. The excavations have yielded very less information about the military culture of the Indus people. Very few weapons have been found. This may be due to still incomplete knowledge of this culture or incomplete excavations. "At its height say around 4000 years ago, the Indus valley civilisation probably had the largest population of the ancient world"[6].

It is highly improbable that a civilisation that existed for close to 5000 years over such a vast area covering the banks of the Indus River and its tributaries and the mythical Saraswati River, had no military. However, sufficient archaeological information and knowledge is not available at present, to enable an analysis of either the security structure or the military of this magnificent civilisation.

Vedic Period

The exact dating of the Vedic period is still ambiguous with various historians having differing claims. The literatures of ancient India like the Vedas, Puranas and the Epics (Ramayana and Mahabharata) are testimony to the existence of militaries and military culture during the Vedic period. As per these literatures the necessity of a king arose from the requirement of having a leader during war and to ensure a lawful society during peace. "The Vedic evidence proves beyond doubt that the office of the king, the supreme commander in battle grew out of warfare".[7] The Taittiriya Samhita a part of the Yajur Veda (one of the four Vedas), speaks of the conflict between the gods and Asuras, where the gods held on to Indra, the strongest as their leader.[8] The Aitareya Brahmana (part of the Rig Veda) mentions the defeat of the gods at the hands of the Asuras. "Through our lack of a king they conquer us, said the gods, 'let us make a king'. They made Soma king and with him as their leader they conquered all quarters".[9] That the king fought and led his army in person is amply demonstrated by the famous battle of the ten kings in the Rigveda, and the warlike deeds of monarchs like Divodasa, Sudas, and Trasadasyu.[10] Fighting for the right cause was 'Dharma'. The king was also responsible for the administration of the kingdom. Thus, welfare and administration of the kingdom merged with the military at the level of the king who was a military leader too.

As per Vedic literature the two important political organisations of the period were Sabha and Samiti. The members of the aristocracy generally made up the Sabha. During early Vedic periods even, women were members of the Sabha but during later periods they ceased to be part of it. The Sabha performed political and administrative functions. Several references show that the Sabha exercised judicial functions also.[11] In contrast, Samiti was a conference of the common people as well as the rich patrons. The king also attended the Samiti. The functions of the Samiti embraced several non-political activities like philosophy and religious activities but its most important political function was the election of the king.[12] The Samiti was considered to be a great asset to the king as it represented the thoughts and beliefs of the society. Its importance in society is stated in the Rig Veda. "A king prays for the destruction of his rivals and claims to have mastered their thoughts (chitta), their way of life (vrata), and their Samiti".[13] The Atharva Veda mentions the army as a regular institution of the state, like the Sabha and Samiti were. There existed harmony between the society and the military.

The military was led and controlled by the aristocracy. During the early Vedic period there came into existence a 'varna' or caste (one of the four castes based on division of functions in society) whose function was mainly waging of war. This was the Kshatriya varna. Hermann Kulke and Deitmar Rothermund in their Book '*A History of India*' state that "even in Early Vedic times a distinction was made between the ordinary free members *(vish)* of a tribe and the warrior nobility *(kshatriya),* from among whom the tribal chieftain *(rajan)* was selected"[14]. Thus, there was conception of a community in ancient India only for war fighting. All teaching, learning, and training for war were done by this community. The king, who usually belonged to the Kshatriya varna, was assisted in his role by the chief priest or Purohit who also used to accompany him during battles. This is amply illustrated in the battle of the ten kings as mentioned in the Rig Veda, where Vasistha advises King Sudasa, whereas Vishvamitra advises his adversarial kings. The king used to appoint a Senani who assisted the king during battle and took care of the army. Next to the Senani was the head of multiple villages called the Gramani, as villages used to be called Grams. "A passage in the Atharva Veda suggests the association of the Gramani with vigour, riches and plenty".[15] The Gramani had his own military contingent which he led during war, under the control of the Senani. Thus, it is found that the military and civil society, even though separated functionally, were enmeshed, resulting in strong coordination between the two.

During the Vedic period there is a clear distinction between the warrior and the common man in society. The formation of the Kshatriya caste resulted in the rest of society being isolated from the travails of war and concentrated on their profession of tilling land or carrying out trade. Sarv Daman Singh in his research thesis 'Ancient Indian Warfare' states that "the growing complexity of life and the division of functions explain the rise of the warriors as a class distinct from the patient tillers of the soil pictured in the pastoral hymns of the Rig Veda"[16]. This had the salutary effect of protecting the rest of the population from the direct effects of war. SD Singh quotes the Rig Veda to emphasise that the caste system was not rigid "the growing specialisation of functions is clearly discernible in the Rig Veda where the three higher orders are specified, but there is little or no indication of an inflexible hereditary caste".[17] The whole society looked upon the Kshatriyas as the defender of the society and the state, and hence did not grudge the high influence and power which the Kshatriyas enjoyed. In the social hierarchy they were second only to the Brahmins. The Brahmins were teachers, philosophers and spiritual thinkers and were the repositories of the Vedic knowledge. This demarcation subsequently led to the promulgation of high levels of morals and ethics for war fighting.

Epic Period

The epic period is the period of the Ramayana and Mahabharata situated in the later Vedic period. Hermann Kulke and Deitmar Rothermund in their Book '*A History of India*' have used the findings of Painted Grey Ware to historically situate the epics between 1000 BC to 800 BC, the exact period being still a matter of historical debate. The Ramayana deals with the story of Rama the king of Kosala, while Mahabharata is the story of the war between the Pandavas and Kauravas who were the descendants of Bharata. During the epic age the primacy of the Kshatriya or the warrior class had become well established. Centrality of the king for warfare and administration had become well accepted.

His military function was inseparable from his royal obligation of protection of his people from invasion and anarchy. In the epics, wars were usually not fought for establishing supremacy; for this the path of Asvamedh Yagya[18] was followed. It was the earliest manifestations of establishing pan India supremacy in a unique way. The wars mentioned in the epics of Ramayana and Mahabharata were righteous conflicts, fought for establishing dharma or ideals of society. Swarna Rajgopalan while discussing the strategic thought process in the epics brings out that "both the epics revolve around dharma, the politics of family and the politics of honour; and conflict has more to do with restitution of rights than conquest or domination alone. The quest for suzerainty takes a ritual rather than a purely military form"[19]. Ram's killing of Bali and his subsequent battle with Ravana for getting his abducted wife Sita back was for establishing moral values and punishing the wrong in society.

The kings during this period were well versed in Niti (politics and administration) as well as in the art of warfare. They received training for this from an early age. In Ramayana, Rama and his brothers received their training from sages Vashistha and Vishvamitra. The Mahabharata explains in detail the military training received by the Kaurava and Pandava princes from their guru, Dronacharya. Apart from leading armies in battle the kings were also supposed to be skilled in the art of single combat using various weapons. If they were challenged by another warrior for a duel, they had to accept such a contest. Such encounters were always between opponents of equal status. This period reflects comprehensive military training of the warriors. This was also the period when detailed codes of ethics for war were enumerated. Indian historian B.K. Majumdar in his work on 'Military System in Ancient India' states that "the Epic literature holds before us an excellent military code, making a near approach to the laws of war as laid down in modern International Law".[20]

The importance of the military was well established. Bhisma in Mahabharata asserts that 'a king's roots are his treasury and his army'. "The epic makes out the army as one of the two prakritis (essential elements) of the early Indian state".[21] The military during this period was called 'chaturangbala' consisting of chariots, elephants, cavalry and foot soldiers. The warriors were also graded as per their war fighting abilities. The strongest of the warriors were called the Maharathis. They usually fought using chariots (rath in Sanskrit), which was the most prestigious war waging vehicle. B.K. Majumdar quotes the Adi Parva of Mahabharata to give the following composition of the army during the Mahabharata war[22]:

Unit	Chariot	Elephant	Horse	Foot Soldiers
Patti	1	1	3	5
Senamukha	3	3	9	15
Gulma	9	9	27	45
Gana	27	27	81	135
Vahini	81	81	243	405
Prtna	243	243	729	1215
Camu	729	729	2187	3645
Aneekini	2187	2187	6561	10935
Aksauhini	21870	21870	65610	109350

Each Aksauhini consisted of 10 Aneekinis, each of which was composed of three Chamus. Each Chamu was composed of three Prtanas which were in turn composed of three Vahinis and so on till the last element of Patti. In the Mahabharata war the Kauravas had 11 Aksauhini army (10 Aksauhini being contributed by their friends and allies) and the Pandavas had seven (six Aksauhini being contributed by their friends and allies).[23] Thus a total of close to three million soldiers fought in the Mahabharata war. There may be poetic exaggeration in the numbers, but the fact that it was a massive war fought over 18 days with most of the kingdoms of the period involved, is beyond doubt[24].

During this period the importance of a designated senapati, or commander in-chief, to lead the army comes to the fore. In the Mahabharata war different armies from different regions fought together. Therefore, a senapati was needed to ensure that the different components fought as a team. S.D. Singh in 'Ancient Indian Warfare' has amply brought this out; he explains that Duryodhana requests Bhisma to assume command as the first senapati of the Kaurava army and Dhrstadyumna becomes senapati for the Pandava army. The senapati used to decide the battle formation of the day, and he was responsible to exhort his warriors and individual commanders to fight as a team. S.D. Singh further quotes the Mahabharata to explain that the "status of the senapati was much coveted"[25]; after the death of Bhisma, Dronacharya took over as the Senapati and after his death, Karna took over thus maintaining continuity of command. The importance of command and control as a function of war was well understood and practised.

The interests of the army were well looked after. Repeated stress is laid on the importance of regular and punctual payment of wages and rations to the army;[26] irregularity in this could lead to disaffection or even rebellion.[27] "In the Sabha Parva of Mahabharata, Narada asks Yudhisthira if he pays his troops in advance before he marches, and if he supports the wives and children of men who lay down their lives for him, or undergo misery on his account."[28] There is ample reference of the utilisation of spies for intelligence gathering during the Epic age. Their main function was to gain entry into the enemy camp in disguise and obtain information about his plans and intentions. They were employed by Vibhishan to get information about Ravana's plans and by Ravana to get information about Rama's plans. The Epics also laid emphasis on conducting war in the proper seasons, thus respecting the weather prevalent in the subcontinent. The best season for going to war was the autumn and the spring, after the rains and before the start of heavy summers. This period was not marred by rains, was neither very hot nor very cold and had abundant supply of food due to the culmination of the harvesting season[29]. During the Epic period war fighting had fully developed and many aspects of military campaign as we understand them today were practised.

Pre Mauryan-Period (Sixth century BC – 323 BC)

Post epic period during the sixth century BC, there were four major kingdoms, Kosala (with capital at present day Ayodhya), Vatsa (near

Allahabad), Avanti (near Malwa region) and Magadha (near present Patna and Gaya); the present day towns mentioned are all in North and Central India. In addition to these there were other smaller kingdoms and few republics[30]. Out of these states the most prominent at a later stage became the kingdom of Magadha. Under the rule of Bimbisara, Magadh started its campaign to annex the neighbouring kingdoms and republics. After Bimbisara, his successor and son Ajatsatru continued with his expansion and by the end of his reign, Magadha had become the most powerful state. Ajatsatru's successor Sisunaga conquered and annexed most of the known kingdoms of North India at the time of the Buddha[31]. This was the period of consolidation of kingdoms in India, albeit by force The Nanda dynasty subsequently took over the Magadhan throne and became the most important and powerful kingdom of North India with a huge military. "The Nanda army was a powerful fighting machine, and the last king of the line kept in the field for guarding the approaches of his country, twenty thousand cavalry, and two hundred thousand infantry, besides two thousand four horsed chariots, and what was the most formidable force of all, a troop of elephants which ran upto the number of three thousand".[32] The famed strength of the Magadh Empire was one of the main reasons for Alexander's war weary soldiers to refuse further advancement into India and which made him decide to return back from the North West of the Indian subcontinent instead of continuing with his campaign of conquering India[33].

The lowest administrative unit during this period was the village or grama. The gramikas or the village headmen were probably appointed by the emperor. In the early days of the Magadhan monarchy the king appears to have kept in close touch with these village functionaries. Big assembly of thousands of Gramikas used to be held by Bimbisara. However, there is no evidence that the Nandas followed this example.[34] The consolidation of kingdoms during this period is an indication of continuous wars that would have been fought. The King was in direct control of his military as well as his administration. This unity of command led to the appropriate utilisation of resources for the military or for administration, as was required. The pre Mauryan period witnessed the territorial aggression of Magadh started by Bimbisar and followed by his successor Ajatshatru. It enabled Magadh to consolidate. Kosala checked this process briefly when it followed the same aggressive spirit. However, Magadh's aggression ensured its prominence. This was a period when aggression was the best form of defence. The annexation by Magadh of its nearby kingdoms proved that this was a period when being pacifist with a defensive military, could lead to subjugation by coercive states with powerful militaries. From this period in history India faced external aggression starting from Alexander (326 BC). This and subsequent period of history have unequivocally proven that survivability of a kingdom was dependent on an effective military and matching resources to support that military. This generally could be accomplished if the kingdom was sufficiently large to achieve both these objectives for a sustained period. The subsequent history of India would amply prove that whenever the Indian subcontinent had large empires it thwarted external aggression and whenever it had small fragmented kingdoms it got overrun by aggressors.

Mauryan period (323 BC to 185 BC)

The first real unification of the subcontinent happened under Chandragupta Maurya after the first invasion of India by any foreign power or ruler, which was Alexander. Not much authentic details are available about the early period of Chandragupta Maurya, but what is generally agreed to is that he started from a humble origin. Initially he captured the areas in the Punjab region before he moved on eastward towards Magadha. Here he defeated the Nanda kings and gained full control over Magadha. He was ably supported in all his endeavours by his brilliant mentor Chanakya, also known as Kautilya. By this time Chandragupta was able to completely remove all the remnants of the Greek invasion from the Indian subcontinent. One of the most decisive battles of Chandragupta's reign was his war with Seleucus Nicator who had succeeded to the eastern parts of Alexander's empire. In his attempt to re-establish the Greek sway,

Seleucus ran into Chandragupta and was comprehensively defeated. He ceded to Chandragupta almost entire Afghanistan south of the Hindukush including the present-day Baluchistan. In return he was presented five hundred war elephants by Chandragupta. After this victory Chandragupta ruled over the entire stretch from the Indus including the present-day Afghanistan to Magadha and Bengal in the east. In the south his sway extended till Mysore and even Tamil Nadu was under his influence.[35] The political and military genius of Chandragupta is unparalleled. He was a "great soldier who had liberated one part of his country from an unpopular dynasty and another from foreign yoke. The first architect of an empire embracing the greater part, if not whole of India, Chandragupta had a military comprising 600,000 foot soldiers, 30,000 cavalry, 8000 or 9000 elephants".[36] He set out to accomplish the unity of India, but did not venture beyond the sub-continent. The statement of the Greek writer Arrian who apparently quotes from Megasthenes[37] that "a sense of justice, they say, prevented an Indian king from attempting conquest beyond the limits of India"[38] perhaps reflects "one of the fundamental principles of Mauryan foreign policy as laid down by the founder of the line and upheld by his successors".[39] There are no records of his army indulging in unnecessary massacre or loot. Prof Nilkanta Shastri has quoted Greek historians Megasthenes (present in India during Chandragupta Maurya's period) and Arrian to describe this period: "in times of war the soldiers are not allowed to molest the husbandmen or ravage their land. This does not seem to be an idealised picture, but a matter of general practice and common knowledge in ancient India"[40]. Even Alexander indulged in large scale massacre of his enemies during his conquests (most notable being the massacre at Massaga or Maskavati). Unarguably, Chandragupta Maurya was one of the greatest and the most successful military leader India has ever produced. He began without any kingdom or army and by the time he left his empire, he was ruling over an area which has been surpassed only by his grandson Ashoka (because of the great empire he inherited from his grandfather). Chandragupta Maurya's successor

Bindusara further expanded the Mauryan Empire in peninsular India.

The Mauryan Empire reached its zenith during the rule of one of the greatest kings of India, Ashoka, son of Bindusara. He is not considered the greatest because he ruled over the largest kingdom the Indian subcontinent has seen but because of the path that he followed after his Kalinga victory. It was the first military campaign which Ashoka undertook after being crowned as a king. As mentioned in the thirteenth rock edict of Ashoka, the Kalinga war (256 BC) was fought eight years after his anointment as king. He "deplores the slaughter, death and deportation of people involved in the conquest of an unconquered country, and affirms that 150,000 men were deported, 100,000 were slain in battle, and many times that number died due to injury".[41] At the heights of his power he renounced war. As per Prof Nilkanta Shastri the Mauryan lineage had a total of nine kings, but none of Ashoka's successors were as illustrious as the first three rulers of the dynasty. The empire declined and disintegrated by 185 BC.

The Mauryan Empire had a large standing army, which enabled it to become the largest empire of India. According to Megasthenes it consisted of 6,00,000 infantry, 30,000 cavalry and 9000 elephants. He has not mentioned about chariots, but Diodorus and Curtis mention about 2000 of them. There were superintendents (adhyakshas) set over each of the four sections and they were charged with the duty of procuring the necessary supplies and keeping the men, animals and machines in proper trim.[42] Art of war was well understood and practised. Organisation, equipment and administration of the military were carried out by six Boards having five members each. The Boards did not have any command function but functioned as advisors to the heads of each of the arms. The detailed administration of the military was looked after by the Commissariat department. It was responsible for provisioning of stores, weapons, rations for men and animals, equipment and other requirements. It also trained and supplied non-combatants like grass-cutters, bandsmen, carpenters, masons, smiths and labour required for duties in the military camps.[43] The chief army officer was the Commander-in-Chief. He was supposed to be skilled in all forms of warfare. He was responsible for the strength of the military, its discipline and its actions during war. Thus, from those times the military had an elaborate fighting and supporting structure. According to Megasthenes the number of soldiers in the country was next to only the farmers. Soldiering was a popular, honourable and remunerative profession[44].

Chandragupta had considerably increased his elephant corps. It was one of the main reasons for his spectacular success in creating one of the most extensive empires. He also did not do away with his chariots. This is in spite of the defeat suffered by Porus at the hands of Alexander, where his elephants and chariots were found wanting in the face of Alexander's cavalry. Chandragupta had the genius to recognise his own requirements and differentiate them from what others possessed. There was an elaborate bureaucratic system to look after the administration of the empire. It kept itself informed and managed detailed and accurate information on the human and material resources of the country. The king was responsible for both the civil and military administration and there was no struggle for resources between the two. Resources were utilised as the situation required. The success and the extent of the empire is a testimony to the military might that existed at that time. VA Smith in his book 'The Early History of India' has remarked "The military organisation of Chandragupta shows no trace of Hellenic influence. It is based upon ancient Indian model and his vast military was merely a development of the considerable army maintained by the kingdom of Magadha".[45] Kautilya in his advice to the emperor kept close to the fundamentals of Indian tradition wherein he stated that political power must command the support of the sacerdotal power besides having the sound advice of experienced statesman at its disposal. The power of the king was not absolute. The duty of the state and the king to its people was clear and it in no way conflicted with fulfilling the requirements of maintaining a military which was capable of protecting the empire and its interests. There was complete understanding and cohesion between the military and civil responsibilities of the king. The invasion of Alexander had proved that Indian kings could not remain content with maintaining a military which could provide protection only from nearby kings. The threat had moved beyond the immediate neighbourhood. They had to be prepared for facing invasions from forces whose strength and fighting capabilities they did not know. Advised by Chanakya and implemented by Chandragupta, the Mauryan Empire achieved and maintained such a military capability.

The mention of Mauryan Period would be incomplete without looking at Kautilya's treatise on statecraft, the *'Arthshastra'*. Dealing with the entire book is a research in itself and out of context here, but a brief mention of few aspects would be prudent. Kautilya gave to the welfare of the citizens the first place in all considerations of policy; the good of the people and their sustained happiness were the main ends for which an elaborate administrative system was created. He did not by any means overlook the supreme importance of the presence of an able, energetic and good monarch for the proper functioning of that system. Absence of such monarchs has often led to the collapse of huge empires. Kautilya's ideal of good governance is best seen from his exhortation to the king to place the happiness of the people above his own personal comfort, and (the king must) feel that his happiness consists in their wellbeing.[46] In Book VI, Kautilya mentions that the elements of sovereignty are, "the King, the Minister, the country, the fort, the treasury, the army and the friend".[47] By 'friend' he means friendly countries. He goes on to enumerate the best qualities of each of the elements. Almost all great empires of the past were the result of the best kings and their armies, supported by the treasury. Similarly, all downfalls of big empires were the result of a weak king and a weakened army. The elements mentioned here are the true determinants of the national power of a country. They, in their best of forms, will ensure greatness and prosperity of a nation. The importance of each of these is as relevant today as it was then. It also signifies the importance of the character of the people or the country in contributing to the greatness of the nation. Chanakya has elaborated on the problems which can inflict the military and about which a king should guard against. He has further enumerated on the enlisting, training and maintenance of morale of the military. Harmony among the officer class is one of the important factors to ensure the effectiveness of the military. In his chapter on 'Relating to War' he describes in detail the various actions and factors that affect preparation for war and subsequently waging of war. The *Arthshastra* is a complete treatise on all aspects of statecraft and is an evidence of the intellectual greatness of its author. It had such a profound influence on statecraft and military doctrine that it was followed with respect and unquestioningly by teachers of statecraft. But subsequent history of the Indian subcontinent shows that not many kingdoms implemented it.

Post Mauryan Period (180 BC to 250 AD)

The post Mauryan age of India is marked by the existence of many small and medium sized kingdoms. Magadha continued to be an important seat of power. However, there was no pan-India empire to oppose the invasion of the Indian subcontinent. During this period invasion into India was first carried out by the Greek Demeritus. He was opposed by Pushyamitra and defeated by him. However, Pushyamitra was content to keep him out of his kingdom but the North West frontiers of the Indian subcontinent were occupied by the Greeks. The Greeks were replaced by the Sakas who were finally replaced by the Kushans. The Sakas and Kushans were nomadic tribes who were displaced from their areas (Bactria in Central Asia) by other nomadic tribes and they moved south; finding little resistance they created their kingdoms and merged into India. Being nomadic and without a base they adopted the local religions, customs and traditions. Their assimilation in the Indian culture was to such an extent that their subsequent rulers had names of Vasudeva (other name of Shri Krishna). They modelled their military on the Mauryan pattern. Some of their important officials were designated mahasenapati, dandanayaka, senagopa (army commander), gulmika (formation commander), arakshadhika (guard), asvaraka (sowar/trooper) and bhatomanushya (probably common soldier). In the civil administration an important official was the 'Strategos' (military governor), a designation borrowed from the Indo-Greeks, who was the head of both the civil and military administration in the province.[48] After the Mauryan Empire the Kushan empire was the largest. The most powerful king was Kanishka I. The Kushan Empire extended from present day Afghanistan up to Madhya Desh and possibly included Bihar. The progress of the Kushans into central India was stopped by the Satvahanas. They were the major military power in the Dakshinpatha. Their empire expanded the most under Gautamiputra Satkarni who had an army comprising 100,000 infantry, 1000 elephants and a modest cavalry of 2000 horses. The mountainous terrain of the Deccan in which they operated did not favour the cavalry. The Satvahans had a system of Military Governors who were also called Strategos like in the Kushan syatem. District administrators were called Senapatis and they combined the functions of commanders of civil and military resources within their jurisdictions.[49] This unity of command at the district level ensured correct utilisation of resources and protected their western borders from the continuous threat of the Sakas. By the beginning of the fourth century foreign domination in India had reduced. The Kushan Empire was restricted to Western Punjab and most of the Indian subcontinent was ruled by small kingdoms or republics.

Gupta Age (250 CE to 550 CE)

Around four centuries after the Mauryan Empire emerged one of the most important empires to have ruled over India. Geographically, it was smaller than the Mauryan Empire but this period in Indian history is referred to as the golden period of India. It was the last empire of this size before India was overrun by invaders. India achieved its zenith, socially and culturally, during this period. The military strength developed during this period prevented India from being overrun by the Huns at a time when Attila had threatened Europe and Rome. The Gupta Empire started with Chandragupta I, but it expanded from a small kingdom to an empire from the time of his successor Samudragupta. Samudragupta initially consolidated his empire in the northern areas before launching his campaign into southern India. He conquered entire Bengal and moved through Orissa along the coast and crossed the Godavari defeating all the kings enroute. He extended his southern conquest up to Nellore and Kanchi. Samudragupta defeated a coalition of Pallava kings headed by Vishnugopa and Hastivarman. His southernmost conquest was of King Dhananjaya of Kusthalpura near river Kusasthali which has been identified with Kuttalur near Pollur in Tamil Nadu. On his return march he conquered some of the kingdoms on the western coast like Kaurala (Keralaputra or Madura of the Cheras), Kottura in Coimbatore district, Pallaka (Palghat) on the Malabar Coast and Devarashtra (Maharashtra).[50] Having returned back he conquered the remaining hostile states in the north which surrounded his kingdom. When Samudragupta took over his father's kingdom and its military, it was no larger or bigger than the many kingdoms surrounding it. After becoming the King, he transformed his military into one of the most formidable fighting machines of that time rivalling that of Chandragupta Maurya. The fact that Samudragupta did not lose any battle that he fought is a testimony to his military skills, his organisational capability and the might of his military. His campaigns across varied terrains like the plains of the north; across mountains in the eastern coast and the deltaic regions of the south is an indication of his military brilliance both as a strategist and at the tactical level. Apart from being a great military leader Samudraguptawas also an able statesman and a farsighted administrator. He was also a poet himself and a man of learning. Not only did his military genius enable the country to assert itself politically but his reign also heralded the flowering of a new era of intellectual, artistic and cultural brilliance. This was the age of India when, after almost 300 years of fragmentation and foreign domination, the country was politically united under the rule of a powerful monarch. The elements of sovereignty – the King, the country, the treasury and the military (as mentioned by Kautilya in his *Arthashastra)* – all peaked in their individual capabilities to form a great empire. Repeatedly, history keeps on proving that the greatness of a kingdom depends upon how the king handles his kingdom and his military. Samudragupta was succeeded by his equally brilliant son Chandragupta II, who also came to be known as Vikramaditya, a name which is folklore in India. Vikramaditya further expanded the empire. His campaign in western India was a protracted one in which he seems to have operated from the Malwa region. It resulted in the removal of the remaining elements of Saka or Kushan kingdoms in India. Inscriptions on the Mehrauli pillar in Delhi indicate that the emperor, "having crossed in warfare the seven mouths of the river Sindhu, conquered the Vahilka".[51] This implies that "Chandragupta's army had to fight for a crossing over the Sindhu; that the river was crossed in the region of its delta and the campaign ended across the Hindukush, after the capture of Baktria or Balkh".[52] Vikramaditya defeated both the Sakas and the Kushans and freed the subcontinent from foreign dominations. During this period the Gupta Empire was at its zenith. The whole of the western, northern and eastern parts of the country and some parts of the Deccan were under the Gupta Empire. Vikramaditya was followed by his successor Kumaragupta. His reign was peaceful and the boundaries were kept intact. The power and glory of the Gupta Empire was at its peak towards the end of Vilkramaditya's and the early period of Kumargupta's reign. Near the end of the reign of Kumaragupta an unspecified tribe, the Pusyamitras, posed a grave threat to the empire. They were crushed by the successor prince Skandagupta. Skandagupta was another worthy successor of the Gupta Empire. One of his most outstanding achievements is his defeating of the Huns, when they tried to ravage India at the same time as another branch of the Huns were doing so in Europe under Attila. Skandagupta confronted the Huns in the Punjab region. "Skandgupta inflicted such a crushing defeat on the barbarians that they did not attempt another raid into the country for well over half a century".[53] Skandagupta during his reign had arranged efficiently for the defence of his territories, through scrupulous selection of his viceroys, governors and commandants of army. However, neither "Kumaragupta nor Skandagupta after him took care to guard the north western regions of India and soon foreign invasion led to the destruction of Bactria and Afghanistan as recorded by Chinese historians".[54] Skandagupta was the last great king of the Gupta Empire, and after his death the empire declined in strength and disintegrated.

The sphere of influence of the Gupta Empire was much larger than the geographical area which it directly controlled. The military department was the most important department of the period. There were a number of Mahasenapatis or Baladhikarnika under the king and it is quite possible that their armies were posted in different parts of the empire. Mahadandanayaks appear to have been the subordinates of Mahasenapatis. The military had different quartermasters in different places, the seals of some of whom have been found. The police department had its own chief called Dandapasadhikarnika.[55] As per the Basara seal inscription (clay seal discovered at Basara, among the ruins of the ancient Vaishali city in present day Bihar), of the Gupta period there was an appointment called Ranabhandagaradhikarana. During this period a distinction was made between the military budget and the civil budget. Ranabhandagaradhikarana was the member in charge of military finance.[56] Another very important office during the Gupta period was that of the Mahasandhivigrahika or the 'Minister of War and Peace'. He was a very high ranking official and used to accompany the king to the battlefield to assist him in matters of war and peace. This officer worked in close cooperation with the king and the military department. He was responsible for planning of campaigns, collection of intelligence – both military and diplomatic – and general supervision over the preparedness of the military. This was perhaps the busiest office in the early Gupta period, when Samudragupta and after him Chandragupta II were engaged in their campaigns in the north and south. This department decided which kingdoms were to be annexed to the Gupta dominions and which were permitted to remain as feudatory states. The Mahasandhivigrahika had a number of Sandhivigrahikas under him to assist in his work.[57] The concept of Mahasandhivigrahika was a novel one; it combined the functions of diplomacy and war. Diplomacy and war are two sides of the same coin; both are used for furthering state interests. This important aspect of statecraft was understood by the Gupta Kings almost 1700 years ago. The civil administration was handled by the Kumaramatyas; they were the ministers in attendance to the royal governors.

The military expenditure of the state was a little more than 50% of the total expenditure of the state. This was not felt as a burden since defence and protection were the most fundamental among the functions of the state.[58] The Gupta kings had an elaborate administrative and military set up. There was complete cohesion between the administrative functions and the military functions of the state. The separation of budget for the military ensured that all requirements of the military were met. The traditional rules about the duties of the kings and high ideals placed by semi-religious works of the past ensured that the king followed the right path. Indian historian Radhakumud Mukherjee opines that the Gupta Empire resulted in the material and moral progress of the country as it was able to provide political stability during the period. "Peace and prosperity secured by the Gupta Empire led to a rich and remarkable development of art, literature, philosophy and science".[59] The administrative system of the Guptas ensured that "people were virtuous, rich and prosperous; cities were teeming with population. The poor and sick were offered relief in hospitals and charitable institutions."[60] Brilliance of ideas, compassion for the people and individual greatness marked the Gupta age. B.K. Majumdar aptly sums up the Gupta period "with the fall of the Guptas in about 550 AD, a brilliant period of ancient India, a period of political excellence, military glory and cultural progress, ended".[61]

Post Gupta Period

Post Gupta period the only empire of some significance was that of Harshvardhan (590 – 647 CE) of Thaneswar. His empire extended from the Punjab to Northern Orissa and from the Himalayas to the banks of the Narmada. He started with an army of 5000 elephants, 20,000 cavalry and 50,000 infantry and subsequently increased it to 60,000 war elephants and 100,000 cavalries.[62] Historians have concluded that "upto the end of the seventh century ancient India's military tradition and organisation remained substantially unbroken in theory, although in practice and in detail traces of weakness were fast appearing".[63] After the decline of Harsha's empire, India was divided upto the Deccan into three major powers: the Pratiharas of western India, the Palas of

Eastern India and the Rashtrakutas of the Deccan area. The influence of each of these empires increased or decreased depending upon the personal capabilities of their kings. All three empires had large military forces at their disposal and the structure of the military remained the same as before.[64] Between them these three empires continued to try and establish their supremacy over each other. They never looked to the west and it was during this period that the Arab invasion of Sind (712 C.E.) happened. The military strength of these kingdoms prevented the Arab expansion into central India; however, there was no effort from them to contest the invasions in western India.[65] Mahmud of Ghazni raided and plundered India 16 times between 990 to 1030 CE. This was followed by raids by Ghori from 1192 to 1230 CE. These raids were religious raids against, the 'infidels' (both Mahmud of Ghazni and Ghori considered Hindus as infidels)[66]. This was also the time when Islam was surging into Europe. The invasion of India on its western and north–western borders during this period exposed the subcontinent to the phenomenon of loot and plunder of the common population after war. This was a new happening in war for India.[67]

Southern India beyond the Deccan,from the sixth century AD was dominated by the dynasties of the Chalukyas and the Pallavas. The most powerful Chalukya kings were Pulakeshin I and his successor Pulkeshin II. Pulakeshin II expanded his empire into Gujarat and Malwa regions and prevented Harshavardhan from expanding his kingdom in the south. The Chalukyas were defeated by the Rashtrakutas. During the same period the area around Tamil Nadu was dominated by the Pallavas. The Chalukyas and the Pallavas were rivals and constantly fought each other. Narasimhavarman was a prominent Pallava king who defeated Pulkeshin II. The Pallavas subsequently declined and were replaced by the Cholas. The Pandyas were another kingdom based at Madurai belonging to the same period. The Cholas became the dominant power of South India from the ninth century AD after they defeated the Pallavas. They expanded their influence by the tenth century to include the whole of southern India except the Chera kingdom of Kerala. Rajaraja I was a prominent king of the Chola dynasty. The Chola empire reached its zenith under his son Rajendra I. He conquered Sri Lanka and ventured into north India against the Pala kings. He also sent successful naval expeditions to the Maldives and subsequently to Sumatra and Malaya peninsula. It is an example of the naval prowess of India during the period. The Chola empire had deep influences in Southeast Asia during the eleventh century. The Chola kingdom "became the symbol of southern classicism, and the cultural levels achieved at that time became the benchmarks for southern culture in general".[68] It was one of the important political structures of India. The Chola empire was organised on sound principles of administration and management and had a good bureaucratic structure to support it. However, it declined by 1200 AD. The next powerful kingdom of South India, the Vijayanagar Empire emerged in AD 1346. It attained its zenith under Krishnadevaraya (1509-30) who practically ruled over entire South India. Like earlier Indian empires, the king was the central authority who looked after the administration as well as the military, resulting in unity of command for correct distribution of resources. The Vijayanagara Empire declined after the death of Krishnadevaraya.

Mughal Era (1526 to 1761)

Towards the end of the medieval period, the most prominent empire of India was the Mughal Empire. Before this the history of North and Central India is the history of many raids into India for looting, plundering and massacre. The Indian subcontinent was divided into many regional kingdom and principalities, which were governed by parochial and unimaginative rulers satisfied with their own indulgences. The society had feudal bureaucracy and was caste ridden and they proved to be no match for the incoming marauders. This period eventually led to the establishment of the Delhi Sultanate comprising many dynasties. The sultanate period lasted for about 300 years. During this period the ruling dynasties kept changing, viz. Slave dynasty (1206-90), Khilji dynasty (1290-1320), Tughlaq dynasty (1320-1413), Sayyid dynasty (1414-51), and Lodhi dynasty (1451-1526). "The account available of this period is by chroniclers who showed a keen sense of history and wrote detailed accounts of the day to day happenings and political upheavals. Their primary objective in doing so was, of course, the glory of Islam; they took keen pride in the military exploits of an amir ul momnin who attempted to transform dar ul haram to dar ul Islam by the conversion of infidels to the faith".[69] Many Indian historians like KS Lal, JL Mehta, Iswari Prasad, Satish Chandra and others are of the opinion that even though these writings have resulted in a detailed account of the period but they appear to be exaggerated (effort by the chroniclers to please their patrons). From the viewpoint of studying military prowess and socio military structures it would be fruitful to focus on the Mughal period (1526 to 1761), especially the period of Akbar. This was the period when the internal upheavals in the society were the least. Sir Wolseley in his book *'Cambridge History of India'* has remarked, "with all his faults, Akbar was the first of the Muslim sovereigns of India to conceive the idea of dealing impartially with all his subjects... It may also be said that he was the last".[70]

The Mughal Empire under Akbar (1556–1605) included the whole of north India and parts of the Deccan. It was one of the biggest centralisations of the Indian subcontinent after the Gupta Empire. It was a period marked by good governance and it contained elements of administration of the previous ruler of the area, Sher Shah. During his reign of fifty years Akbar built an empire, vestiges of which lasted till the British rule in India. As a king, Akbar was independent in his thinking; he treated all his subjects equally and did not refrain from opposing the orthodox Islamic scholars of his kingdom who tried to prevent him from doing so. All the power of the state was vested in the king. Apart from being the head of state he was the chief of the military. Some of the important functionaries of the administration were as follows:

- Wazir / Diwan: He was an expert in revenue affairs and was responsible for all income and expenditure.
- Mir Bakshi: He was the head of the military department and a warrior. All military appointments were made through him. He was also the head of the intelligence and information agencies of the empire.

- Mir Saman: He was in charge of logistics, stores and royal workshops and also looked after the imperial household.
- Qazi: He was in charge of the judicial department.
- Sadr: He was responsible for all charitable and religious endowments.

Before Akbar's rule, the position of Wazir was an all-important position in the Mughal governance system; its origin being from the Central Asian and Timurid traditions. The various heads of departments functioned under him. He was the principal link between the administration and the ruler. Akbar reduced the power of the Wazir and effectively made him responsible only for revenue from being the principal adviser of the king. By this he ensured that centralisation of power was only at the level of the king. The various departments had separate heads. For military appointments and promotions, the ruler acted on the advice of the Mir Bakshi. Once the emperor had accepted the recommendation it was sent to the Wazir/Diwan for implementation. Thus, during Akbar's reign, the Wazir/Diwan and the Mir Bakshi were on par and checked each other.[71] The two most important departments of the empire – the military and the administration/ revenue – were given equal importance and were each handled by professionals from their respective fields.

Akbar could acquire and retain a large empire because of his efficient and strong military. His was a professional military based on the Mansabdari system. In this every officer was assigned a mansab (rank). The lowest mansab was commander of 10, and the highest was commander of 7000 for the nobles. The rank had two parts, Zat and Sawar. Zat denoted the personal rank and the salary of the official and Sawar denoted the number of cavalrymen he was supposed to maintain. There were three categories in every rank. The Mansabs who were in the first category had to maintain as many numbers of Sawars as his Zat rank. The second category Mansabs had to maintain half or more Sawars as his Zat rank and the third category had to maintain less than half. The Mansabs used to ensure that the Sawars whom they recruited were good and fit to perform their duties. The contingent of every Mansab was periodically inspected by the emperor. The rule for the Mansabs was that for every Sawar that they had, they had to maintain twice the number of horses. Apart from cavalrymen, bowmen, musketeers, sappers and miners were also recruited in the contingents. The Mansabdar also had to maintain elephants, camels, mules and carts. The salary for the soldiers was included in the salary that was paid to the Mansabdar and he in turn was responsible for paying the soldiers; he was paid either in cash or by assigning a jagir to him. Officers holding ranks below 500 Zat were called Mansabdars, those from 500 to below 2500 were called Amirs, and those holding ranks of 2500 and more were called Amir-i-umda, or Umda-i-azam. Promotion from one rank to the next was possible as was demotion. The Mansabdars were supposed to maintain their entire contingent from their salary and they were paid handsomely. They formed the highest paid service in the world at that time.[72] Akbar was another brilliant example of Chanakya's elements of sovereignty being at their best, leading to a great empire. After his death the military administration deteriorated.

Post Mughal Period

After the decline of the Mughal Empire the only two empires of some significance were the Maratha Empire and the Sikh Empire, before India was overrun by the British. The Maratha influence at its zenith was upto the banks of the Indus in the North West, and from Delhi in the north to Srirangapatnam in the south.[73] The Maratha Empire was founded by Shivaji in 1674 (year of his coronation as Chatrapati or King). After Shivaji, the empire expanded rapidly under the Peshwas of Pune. This expansion suffered a major setback when they were defeated at Panipat by Ahmad Shah Abdali of Afghanistan; however, they quickly recovered. They also had a strong navy which reached its pinnacle under the Maratha leader Kanhoji Angre. After a century of being a dominant power, internal struggles between the various Maratha chiefs weakened them and they ultimately conceded to the British in 1819 when they were defeated at Pune. The rise and fall of the Maratha Empire provides very valuable lessons. The Marathas were an aggressive military power in the sense that they tried to expand their dominion as much as possible. Surendranath Sen in the preface of his book, *'The Military System of the Marathas'* has opined that the Maratha Empire was primarily a military organisation and its civilian institutions were closely connected with its military system. During the period of Shivaji, when the Maratha Empire was in its infancy, the military was governed by a central monarchy. The army which gave an expression to the ideals and aspirations of the state, was an institution which was directly controlled by the central authority, the king. It was a homogenous body commanded by regular officers who obeyed the central authority. During the Peshwa period, after Shivaji's death, this changed. The various Maratha leaders started having their own armies and they would come together to fight when summoned by the Peshwa.[74] This worked initially but subsequently led to infighting between the individual chiefs when the central authority weakened. It also led to differences in training and discipline in the various individual armies. They were more disciplined when compared with the Mughals (who were on the decline), but were less cohesive and disciplined when they faced the British. The Maratha leaders failed to correctly analyse the British and their military strength in terms of equipment and discipline. Their strategy of continuing to fight as they fought with the Moghuls and other Indian kings, without adapting to the changing circumstances, proved to be their undoing, when faced with the British.

The Sikh Empire was another Indian empire which rose during the same period. Initially, it started as a resistance to religious persecution against the Moghuls under Guru Gobind Singh. Later on, it rose to become an effective empire under Ranjit Singh. It extended from the hills beyond the Indus to Ladakh and from the northern banks of the Sutlej to Kashmir. On three sides it was surrounded by the British, but it held its own.[75] Ranjit Singh made all efforts to modernise his army as he correctly anticipated that the main threat to his empire were the British who were technologically superior. The Sikh Empire effectively prevented any incursion into India from the North West after Ahmad Shah Abdali's raid into India when he had defeated the Marathas at Panipat in 1761. After the death of Ranjit Singh, in the absence of any effective leader, the military strength and discipline of the Sikh Empire started to erode and they were finally defeated by the British (first British- Sikh war in 1845-46 and the second in 1848-49).

Lessons from History

The past provides lessons for the present and guidance for the future. India's political and military history offers many strategic lessons. These lessons when synchronised with the present concept of nation states and world order, can be as relevant today as they were in the past. Conflicts between states due to various reasons have happened in the past and are as prevalent today. These conflicts, which were limited to diplomacy and military in the past, have expanded to include many other domains like economic, cyber and information arenas. The basic competition between states for control of resources and dominance, nevertheless, remains the same. This competition, needless to say, will always tilt towards the state having better national power, and as importantly, the will to use that power to secure a favourable outcome. Having better national power is directly related to the resources that a nation has. This in some measures is related to the geography and the size of the state.

Bigger States with Better Resources have Better Survivability

Post the Epic period, starting from the sixth century B.C., political consolidation started in India. During this period inter-state rivalry was common and led to states having militaries as per their envisaged threat requirements. The smaller states, however, could not maintain large and powerful militaries due to lack of resources. The invasion of Alexander reinforced the importance of having a strong military. When faced with a bigger and superior military like that of Alexander's, the states crumbled. This changed when the Mauryan Empire was established. It had the resources and consequently maintained a military which successfully fended off all threats. This was true for all the major empires of the Indian subcontinent. These empires declined when their militaries declined. This lesson is as applicable today. A nation with adequate resources can afford a strong military which is a critical component of national power. A nation can enjoy complete sovereignty only if it is either protected by its own military or has an alliance with some other state with a powerful military. Increased dependence of nations on each other, international treaties and world organisations have changed the dynamics of inter-state relations but the underlying importance of military power and its dependence on a nation's resources still remains good. A corollary to the above postulate is that smaller states would always be either in the sphere of influence or be completely aligned with some great power. This holds important lessons for India while dealing with its neighbouring states. Bigger states with powerful militaries will have more influence in world affairs. This was true in the past and is as relevant today.

Strategically Assertive States Ensured Peace for Their Citizens and had Better Survivability

The biggest empires of the Indian sub-continent were the Mauryan, Gupta, and the Mughal Empire of Akbar. A common factor of these empires was that they displayed aggressive pursuit of their interests and established almost pan-India kingdoms. Indian history is testimony to the fact that these empires successfully fended off external aggressions due to their strong military capability. The success of coercive states attempting to establish pan-India kingdoms, started with the rise of Magadh under Bimbisar followed by Ajatshatru, culminating in the creation of the Mauryan Empire. States which could not match these assertive pursuits by hegemonic states were annexed. Indian history also brings out the bitter truth that smaller states were the bane of India; it got overrun by invaders whenever it was divided into small states. Coercive states led to political consolidation and when it combined with exceptional leadership it created great empires. It is equally true that the big empires of India at their zenith, did not attempt out of Indian-subcontinent conquest like Alexander did, inspite of having very powerful militaries. Therefore, does Indian history prove that in the Indian context certain amount of assertiveness is essential in pursuit of national interest? Probably it does. This 'certain amount' cannot be quantified and would be defined by the context of geo-political situation existing at a particular time; for example, the invasion of Alexander had created such a situation, necessitating the creation of a large empire with a powerful military.

The state has two components, the citizen and the state (comprising all the elements that govern the state). History proves that states that had assertive intent for protecting their interests and the capability in terms of military power to match that intent ensured that their citizenry remained peaceful. A peaceful society leads to progress and development in all spheres. Alternately, states which were pacifist in their intent were sooner than later defeated and subjugated. For assertive States the fight was always at the border or beyond their border and hence the people of these states remained peaceful. Conversely, for a pacifist state the fight entered the State and both the people and the state were affected. After Ashoka, the Mauryan Empire followed a pacifist approach and slowly it led to its decline, due to decline of its military capability. The same was true of the Gupta Empire after the reign of Kumaragupta. Is this true today? Indian history teaches this valuable lesson that in the Indian context a pacifist approach to statecraft invariably led to decline. It is the responsibility of the state to ensure peace for its citizens so that society can progress and this is possible only with a display of an aggressive intent by the state to secure its interests. It does not mean indulging in unnecessary war, but it certainly means the display of intent to use the whole of national power of the state to achieve national objectives.

Conclusion

The Indian sub-continent has witnessed the great empires of Mauryas, Guptas and that of Akbar. It also witnessed numerous prominent empires like Satvahanas, Harshavardan, Cholas, Vijaynagar, Marathas, Sikhs and many others. An elaborate military and an administrative structure to support such a military existed in the empires of India since ancient times. An empire of the size of the Mauryan Empire was created in India as early as 320 BC. This, and subsequent empires, are testimony to the military and strategic thought that existed in India since then. The *'Arthashastra,'* an elaborate treatise on statecraft, was written in India during the Mauryan period and many expositions contained in it are as relevant in the present as they were in those times. Chanakya's elements of sovereignty even today can be used to evaluate the effectiveness of a nation by analysing the individual elements. The importance of integrating diplomacy and military for a coherent approach to statecraft was recognised and practised by the Gupta Empire millennia ago in India. The founders of the Mauryan and Gupta Empires created formidable military institutions which ensured they never lost a war. This military might, rooted in ancient Indian concepts, ensured societal peace and progress. The military was the biggest enabler of a peaceful society. An important lesson from Indian history is that the sub-continent was protected from external aggression whenever it had assertive empires which dominated the sub-continent. Political stability ensured peace and development during these periods. *Indian history emphatically delivers this valuable message that if the state wants to ensure a peaceful and prosperous society then it is imperative for it to acquire the requisite national power to enable it to aggressively pursue its national interests.* The military history of India, which spans millennia created a strategic culture which is distinctly Indian. The next chapter will attempt to understand the strategic culture of India and its influence on the Indian strategic thought process.

Notes

1. George K Tanham, *Indian Strategic Thought - An Interpretive Essay*, (RAND, USA, 1992), p. 2, at https://www.rand.org/content/dam/rand/pubs/reports/2007/R4207.pdf, accessed on February 17, 2020.
2. Maj Gen Gurcharn Singh Sandhu, *A Military History of Ancient India* (New Delhi: Vision Books, 2000), p. 20.
3. For more on this refer Jaswant Singh, *Defending India* (Bangalore: Macmillan India Limited, 1999).
4. For detailed reading on the early history of India refer Hermann Kulke and Dietmar Rothermund, *A History of India* (London: Routledge, Taylor and Francis Group, 2002), pp. 16-45.
5. For more on the time period of the Indus valley civilisation and archaeological findings refer, Robin Cunningham and Ruth Young, *The Archaeology of South Asia,*

From Indus to Ashoka, c. 6500 BCE to 200 CE (New York: Cambridge University Press, 2015).

6. Tim Dyson, *A population History of India, From the First Modern People to the Present Day,* (Oxford, UK: Oxford University Press, 2018), p. 8.
7. Sarvdaman Singh, Ancient *Indian Warfare with Special Reference to the Vedic Period* (Leiden: E.J. Brill Publications, 1965), p. 135.
8. Ibid., p. 136.
9. Aitareya Brahmana I.14 as quoted by Sarva Daman Singh, Ibid.
10. Ibid., p. 137.
11. Ram Sharan Sharma, *Aspects of Political Ideas and Institutions in Ancient India* (New Delhi: Motilal Banarsidass Publishers Private Limited, 1996), pp. 106-109.
12. Ibid., p. 112.
13. Rig Veda X. 166.4 as quoted by Ram Sharan Sharma, Ibid., p. 114.
14. Hermann Kulke and Deitmar Rothermund, *A History of India, 3rd edition*, (London, Routledge, 1998), p. 39.
15. Atharva Veda XIX. 31.12-13 as quoted by Sarv Daman Singh, n. 7, p. 142.
16. Sarv Daman Singh, n. 7, p. 141.
17. Rig Veda VIII. 35. 16-18, as quoted by Sarv Daman Singh, n. 7, p. 138.
18. In the Asvamedh Yagya a sacrificial horse was let loose and whichever territory the horse wandered, the king of that territory had to accept the supremacy of the king conducting the yagya or had to challenge him to a fight. For detailed description refer Subash Kak, *The Asvamedh, The Rite and its Logic* (Delhi: Motilal Banarsidass Publishers Pvt Ltd, 2002).
19. Swarna Rajgopalan, "Grand Strategic Thought in the Ramayana and Mahabharata," in Kanti Bajpai, Saira Basit and V. Krishnappa, ed., *India's Grand Strategy - History, Theory, Cases*, (New Delhi: Routledge, Taylor and Francis Group, 2014), pp. 32-33.
20. Bimal Kanti Majumdar, *The Military System in Ancient India*, (Calcutta: Firma K.L. Mukhopadhyay, 1960), pp. 40-41.
21. Maj Gen GS Sandhu, n. 2, p. 131.
22. B.K. Majumdar, n. 20, p. 55.
23. The Mahabharata-Research, "Military Academy", http://mahabharata- research.com/military%20academy/index.html, accessed on November 19, 2019.
24. For detailed information on all the kingdoms who participated in the Mahabharata war and their co-relation with present geography refer C.V. Vaidya, *Epic India* (New Delhi: Asian Educational Services, 2001). p. 19, and H.C. Raychaudhuri, *Political History of Ancient India* (Calcutta: University of Calcutta, 1923), pp. 31-81.
25. Mahabharata, 7.5.15 as quoted by SD Singh, n.7, p. 147.
26. Mahabharata 3.16.21,22 as quoted by SD Singh, n. 7, p. 149.
27. Mahabharata 2.5.39 as quoted by SD Singh, Ibid.
28. Ibid., p. 149.
29. For more on this refer Maj Gen GS Sandhu, n. 2, pp. 137-138.

30. There were few states in India like the Yaudheya, Malavas, Sakyas, Vaishali and others which were non-monarchial or republics. They may not have been like the present-day republics, the governing of the state in them, resided in a finite number of aristocratic classes. For more on this refer A.S. Altekar, *State and Government in Ancient India* (Delhi: Motilal Banarsidass, 1984), pp. 109-138.
31. For detailed reading on this period and the kingdoms refer Prof HC Raychaudhuri, Political *History of Ancient India* (Calutta: University of Calcutta, 1923).
32. J.W. M'Crindle, *Invasion of India by Alexander the Great as Described by Arrian, Q. Curtis, Diodorus, Plutarch and Justin*, (Westminister: Archibald Constable and Company, 1896), pp. 221-222.
33. Ibid. Indian historians are unanimous in their understanding that the king Agrammes mentioned by the Greeks in M'Crindle's work was the Nanda king.
34. Prof HC Raychaudhuri.,"India in the Age of the Nandas" in *Age of the Nandas and Mauryas,* ed., by K.A. Nilkanta Sastri (Banaras: Motilal Banarsidass Publishers and Booksellers, 1952), p. 22.
35. Prof K.A. Nilkanta Sastri, "South India and Ceylon" in *Age of the Nandas and Mauryas,* ed., by K.A. Nilkanta Sastri (Banaras: Motilal Banarsidass Publishers and Booksellers, 1952), p. 255.
36. J.W. McCrindle, *Ancient India as described by Megasthenes and Arrian* (London: Turner and Company, 1877), p. 139. Available online at http://cslrepository.nvli.in//handle/123456789/7044, accessed on March 12, 2020.
37. Megasthenes was a Greek envoy in Chandraguta's court. He is supposed to have travelled extensively during Chandragupta's times and recorded his observations in the book 'Indica'. The original book is lost but his writings survive in later Greek and Latin works.
38. Ibid., p. 204.
39. Prof HC Raychaudhuri, "Chandragupta and Bindusara" in *Age of the Nandas and Mauryas,* ed., by K.A. Nilkanta Sastri (Banaras: Motilal Banarsidass Publishers and Booksellers, 1952), p. 156.
40. Prof Nilkanta Sastri, "India in Early Greek and Latin Literature" in *Age of the Nandas and Mauryas,* ed., by K.A. Nilkanta Sastri (Banaras: Motilal Banarsidass Publishers and Booksellers, 1952), p. 114.
41. Prof Nilkanta Sastri, "Asoka and his Successors" in *Age of the Nandas and Mauryas,* ed., by K.A. Nilkanta Sastri (Banaras: Motilal Banarsidass Publishers and Booksellers, 1952), p. 210.
42. Prof K.A. Nilakanta Sastri, "Mauryan Polity" in *Age of the Nandas and Mauryas,* ed., by K.A. Nilkanta Sastri (Banaras: Motilal Banarsidass Publishers and Booksellers, 1952), p. 188.
43. Maj Gen GS Sandhu, n. 2, p. 232.
44. Prof K.A. Nilkanta Sastri, n. 42, pp. 184-188.
45. Vincent A. Smith, *The Early History of India*, (Oxford: Clarendon Press, 1924), p. 153. Available online at https://archive.org/details/in.ernet.dli.2015.283155/page/n1/mode/2up, accessed on March 13, 2020.

46. Prof Nilkanta Sastri, n. 24, p. 190.
47. Kautilya, *Arthshastra*, trans. R Shamasastry (Bangalore: Government Press, 1915), p. 362. Available online at https://archive.org/details/ArthashastraOfChanakyaEnglish_201506/page/n17/mode/2up, accessed on December 26, 2019.
48. Maj Gen GS Sandhu, n.2, p. 308.
49. Ibid, p. 309.
50. Radhakumud Mookerji, *The Gupta Empire* (Delhi: Motilal Banarsidass, 1989), pp. 22-23.
51. RN Dandekar, *A History of the Guptas* (Poona: Oriental Book Agency, 1941), p. 81.
52. Maj Gen GS Sandhu, n. 2, p. 333.
53. Ibid, p. 335.
54. Dandekar, n. 32, p. 115.
55. Ibid., p. 255.
56. VR Ramchandra Dikshitar, *War in Ancient India* (Madras: Macmillan and Co Limited, 1944), p. 208.
57. Raghunath Rai, *A history of the Gupta Age* (Amritsar: Lajpat and Company, 1965), pp. 200-201.
58. Dikshitar, n. 57, p. 210.
59. Dr AS Altekar, "The Administrative Organisation" in R.C. Majumdar, ed., The *Vakataka – Gupta Age* (Banaras: Motilal Banarsidass Publishers and Booksellers, 1954), p. 271.
60. A.S. Altekar, n. 55, p. 271.
61. B.K. Majumdar, n. 20, p. 125.
62. R.C. Majumdar, "Harsh Vardhana and His Time" in R.C. Majumdar, ed., History *and Culture of the Indian People Vol III – The Classical Age* (Banaras: Motilal Banarsidass Publishers and Booksellers, 1954), p. 108.
63. B.K. Majumdar, The *Military System in Ancient India* (Calcutta: Firma, 1960), p. 95.
64. For more reading on these kingdoms refer V.A. Smith, The Early History of India (Oxford: Oxford University Press, 1924), pp. 392-397.
65. For detailed reading on the military history of this period refer Hermann Kulke and Dietmar Rothermund, *A History of India* (London: Routledge, Taylor and Francis Group, 2002), pp. 105-112.
66. For more on these raids refer Stanley Lane-Poole, *Medieval India under Mohammedan Rule* (London: T Fisher Unwin Ltd, 1903). Available online at https://www.rarebooksocietyofindia.org/book_archive/196174216674_10152591985846675.pdf
67. Ibid.
68. Burjor Avari, *India: The Ancient Past* (London: Routledge, 2007), p. 229.
69. JL Mehta, *Advanced Study in the History of Medieval India* (New Delhi: Sterling Publishers Pvt Ltd, 1979), p. 1.
70. Kishori Saran Lal, *Studies in Medieval Indian History* (Delhi: Ranjit Printers and Publishers, 1966), pp. 237-238.

71. Satish Chandra, *History of Medieval India (800-1700)* (Delhi: Orient Blackswan Pvt Ltd, 2014), pp. 240-241.
72. Ibid., pp. 237-238.
73. Surendranath Sen, *Military System of the Marathas* (Calcutta: The Book Company Ltd, 1928), p. 1.
74. Ibid, p. 4.
75. AF Rudolf Hoernle and Herbert A Stark, *A History of India* (Cuttack: Orissa Mission Press, 1909), p. 144.

3. India's Strategic Culture

Asato ma sad gamaye
Tamso ma jyotir gamaye
Mrityor ma amritam gamaye
Lead us from - delusion to truth
darkness to light
death to immortality

– 'Brihadaranyaka Upanishad'

India is an ancient culture. As per contemporary history, Indian culture can be traced back to approximately 7000 BC, with the beginning of the Indus valley civilisation. Indian history after the Indus valley period, can be divided into various phases such as the Vedic and Epic periods followed by periods of various empires. Archaeological and documentary evidence is available for the post Epic periods; whereas the Vedic and Epic periods have been analysed and understood based on various ancient works like the Vedas, Upanishads, Puranas, Epics of Ramayana, Mahabharata, etc. India has a rich military history which spans millennia. This military history of India has spawned a strategic culture which is uniquely Indian in characteristics.

India has civilisational continuity.[1] This continuity which is characterised by cultural factors, beliefs, value systems, ethos and ethics, is likely to have led to its conditioning along a strategic pattern. Societal and strategic behaviour at various points in Indian history have been shaped by the external stimulus prevailing at that time; but has there been throughout, a commonality of underlying culture, beliefs and values, which shaped its response? This underlying culture (assuming it exists) is not only a characteristic of societal behaviour but also characterises the strategic behaviour of India. It permeates Indian history and is what makes India distinctive. The strategic culture of India is not a determinant. It would to some extent determine the response but the response would be modulated by a number of other factors. But strategic culture would definitely help in understanding how the stimulus is perceived and what its conditioned responses are. If a country understands its 'Strategic Culture', it understands its own strengths and weaknesses. It would be able to better align its administrative and security organisations to maximise its strengths and take care of its weaknesses.

The aim, therefore, would be to understand the strategic culture of India and its shaping due to the continuity and underlying commonality of India's culture. It would encompass understanding its evolution, analysing beliefs and values which have transcended time and have affected Indian strategic thought through history. The analysis would be limited to understanding the society's approach to war and would not go into the tactical aspects of battle. The scope would be limited to history before the British rule in India. The period from the British rule onwards would be covered in the next chapter. The concept of strategic culture in academia evolved and gained traction in the late nineties.

Concept of Strategic Culture

The concept of strategic culture was introduced by Jack Snyder in 1977 for a Rand Corporation conducted study about a limited nuclear war between USA and USSR. He argued that Soviet response would be fashioned by what he termed as Soviet strategic culture. He postulated that this strategic culture would affect all Soviet decision making and is unique to the country. The academic field of strategic culture evolved as a means of trying to understand the strategic choices of nations. The study of strategic culture was taken forward by many scholars such as Ian Johnston, Colin Gray, Ken Booth, David Jones and others. Ken Booth gives credit to Snyder for coming up with the concept of strategic culture; "the notion that different nations have distinctive ways of thinking and behaving on war and peace issues has been long understood, but it rarely has if ever been exposed to systematic scholarly examination"[2]. As per Ken Booth "the strategic culture of a nation derives from its history, geography and political culture, and it represents the aggregation of the attitudes and patterns of behaviour of the most influential voices".[3] He further states that the strategic culture of a nation represents its traditions, values, attitudes and behaviour. Ken Booth takes the concept of strategic culture to a level where he asserts that it characterises and defines a society. Though he further clarifies that strategic culture is not deterministic, "it helps shape but does not determine how a nation interacts with others in the security field".[4] This is plausible as the concept of strategic culture cannot be equated with a scientific theory (which can accurately forecast a future outcome based on inputs) to predict a nation's behaviour in the strategic dimension. However, what strategic culture does is, it "characterises state behaviour by rooting strategic choice in deeply historical, formative ideational legacies".[5] There are divergent views on the efficacy of strategic culture as a tool to analyse and predict a state's behaviour, but there is unanimity that strategic culture operates at the sub-conscious level and plays a fundamental role in shaping the strategic choices available to a state. The concept of strategic culture is a useful tool in analysing and understanding Indian strategic thought.

The concept of strategic culture has gone through more than three generations of evolution.[6] Some social scientists, like Colin Gray, have considered strategic culture as more deterministic. As per him "strategic culture should be approached both as a shaping context for behaviour and itself as a constituent of that behaviour".[7] He further amplifies by stating "one can think of strategic culture as being 'out there' as a rich and distilled source of influence which might 'cause' behaviour"[8]. The importance of strategic culture in influencing the strategic thought process is now well established. There is general consensus among political scientists that even though strategic culture may not be completely accurate in either determining or explaining a State's strategic behaviour, nevertheless it greatly influences the strategic thought process of the state. Understanding strategic culture enables one to understand oneself.

However, to understand strategic culture what are the components of history that needs to be focussed upon? As per Gray; "culture or cultures comprises the persisting (though not eternal) socially transmitted ideas, attitudes, traditions, habits of mind, and preferred methods of operation that are more or less specific to a particular geographically based security community that has had a necessarily unique historical experience".[9] Applying the concept of strategic culture in the Indian context it can be safely assumed that the strategic culture of India is the summation of its traditions, values, socially transmitted ideas, persistent attitudes, and behaviour, more specifically in the strategic context. Grey uses Iain Johnston's work 'Cultural Realism' to make the point that "strategic culture may comprise more a litany of canonical idealised beliefs than a set of attitudes, perspectives, and preferences that are operational as real guides to action".[10] India is an ancient civilisation. In spite of it being subjected to many invasions and colonisation by the British, there is continuity of culture, values and traditions. In light of the above argument any assertion about India not having a strategic culture would not stand scrutiny.

Indian's culture is not homogenous; rather it is heterogeneous comprising a host of traditions, ideas, beliefs and value systems. Nonetheless strategic ideas and beliefs of the Indian society which have displayed certain continuity about them from the Vedic age are important determinants of India's strategic culture. AL Basham in his work about Indian culture '*The Wonder that was India*' presents the argument that unlike Greece, Egypt and Mesopotamia; in India "traditions have been preserved without a break down to the present day".[11] He supports his argument by stating that Greece, Egypt and Iraq came to know about the culture of their forefathers, only after being enabled by the advent of archaeology; their present society being completely disconnected from its ancient past.[12] Whereas in the case of India, "the earliest Europeans to visit India found a culture fully conscious of its own antiquity – a culture which indeed exaggerated that antiquity and claimed not to have fundamentally changed for many thousands of years".[13] He further goes on to state that "India and China have, in fact the oldest continuous cultural traditions in the world".[14] One may not agree with Basham's claim about the exaggerated antiquity of Indian civilisation (Indus Valley civilisation dates back to 7000 BC) but the 'continuity' in Indian civilisation adequately comes to the fore in his elucidations. In the case of India, the inference that traditions, values and belief systems show certain continuity from its ancient past is well founded. In 2006 US Department of Defence commissioned a study on India's strategic culture. It was conducted by Rodney W. Jones. As per Jones:

> "India's strategic culture is not monolithic, rather is mosaic-like, but as a composite is more distinct and coherent than that of most contemporary nation-states. This is due to its substantial continuity with the symbolism of pre-modern Indian state systems and threads of Hindu or Vedic civilisation dating back several millennia. Embedded in educated social elites, the consciousness of Hindu values has been resident in essentially the same territorial space, namely, the Indian subcontinent. This continuity of values was battered and overlaid but never severed or completely submerged, whether by Muslim invasions and Mughal rule, the seaborne arrival of French and Portuguese adventurers and missionaries, or the encroachment of the British Empire – with its implantation of representative political institutions and modern law."[15]

Most studies on India's strategic culture like by Kanti Bajpai, Kajari Kamal, Rashed uz Zaman, Leibig and others are overwhelmingly dominated by Kautilya's '*Arthshastra*'. *Arthshastra* is by any yardstick the most complete treatise on statecraft to originate in India. It is also representative of the wisdom of ancient India that existed before it was written and to which it refers in its elucidation. But considering India's vast culture and tradition, concentrating only on the '*Arthshastra*' would amount to overlooking the other sources of influence on India's strategic culture. Epics like the *Ramayana* and *Mahabharata* are part of India's folklore and have played an important role in shaping the ethos of India. *Bhagavad Gita*, a part of the epic *Mahabharata*, is a discourse on the battlefield between Shri Krishna and Arjuna. It is considered as one of the greatest philosophical treatises of India. What distinguishes it from other philosophical texts is the fact that the setting of this discourse is the battlefield of Kurukshetra and it is upon Shri Krishna to motivate a demoralised Arjuna for war; to fight for the right cause and for one's duty to society. S Jaishankar, India's External Affairs Minister has brought out in his book '*The India Way*', that Shri Krishna guides Arjuna to undertake his responsibility irrespective of the difficulty of its consequences; "India's national security would have been significantly better if that had been more widely appreciated and practised".[16]

To understand India's strategic culture, all aspects of its culture and traditions which are likely to affect the strategic thought process would need to be considered. Therefore, it would be prudent to go back into history and ancient Indian writings and start at the very beginning with the concept of kingship in India. As would be brought out subsequently, King was the singular institution which had the maximum effect on the strategic culture of India. While doing so it would be as important to focus on the fact that in ancient India the method of preserving knowledge and imparting it, was the oral tradition method. "The outstanding feature of the oldest Indian education and Indian culture in general, especially in the centuries BC, is its orality".[17]

India's Strategic Culture - Evolution

Before looking at the origin of the institution of king it would be imperative to have a basic understanding of the various books of ancient India. It would not be totally correct to refer to them as books because there were no written books in ancient India especially in the Vedic and the Epic periods. "It is the system of **oral tradition** by which India has built up her culture through the ages; the uninterrupted ideal succession by which knowledge is conserved and transmitted".[18] Indian historian Radha Kumud Mookerji brings out, that because of this very reason the books of knowledge were known as '*Sruti*', (what is heard). The knowledge of ancient India which we refer today as books was transmitted by mouth from person to person. "Knowledge did not then exist in the form which could be stored up in a library like household furniture, for knowledge was the furniture of the mind, while the teacher himself was the living and walking library of those days".[19] He further explains that the creation of 'mantra' (hymn) or 'sutra' was done to maximise meaning by compressing it within minimum of words. The oral tradition may also have led to knowledge remaining contemporary with milieu as the teacher was not bound to some written text but could interpret and contextualise knowledge to his period. The oral culture of India is probably one of the important reasons for continuity of tradition, culture and ethos inspite of widespread destruction of historical and educational resources caused by invasions during the medieval period.[20]

Sources of Knowledge

The oldest and the most important repository of knowledge in India are the Vedas. The four Vedas of India are Rig Veda, Sama Veda, Yajur Veda and Atharva Veda. Each Veda consists of four parts; Samhitas, which consist of hymns to various gods; Brahmanas, which provide instructions on conduct of rituals; Aranyakas, which provide a guide to rituals meant for forest-dwellers and hermits; and Upanishads, which contain the philosophical message of the Vedas. The Upanishads are also known as Vedanta which literally means the end of the Vedas.[21] Historians widely differ on the period when the Vedas were created with the period ranging from 2000 BC to 1000 BC. There are the two great epics, Ramayana and Mahabharata. Apart from these there are the Puranas which can be broadly classified into three groups, Brahmaa Purana, Vaishnava Purana and Shaiva Purana. These three groups contain many other Puranas. The Vedas and the Upanishads, also known as 'Sruti' constituted the main source of Knowledge and all later works derived heavily from them or were their interpretations. Another important genre in ancient Indian works were the Dharmashastras or the Dharmasutras. They were written by many sages like Gautama, Apastamba, Baudhayana and Vasistha. In addition to these another Grihyasutra by Manu, (Manava Dharmashastra also known as Manu Smriti) reflect the customs and traditions followed in ancient India.

Upinder Singh cites Indian historian Kane to situate the Dharmashastras in between 600 to 300 BC.[22] The British made these Dharmashastras, the basis for formulating law in India for all non-Muslims starting from 1772.[23] India was also influenced by the teachings of Jainism and Buddhism and in the later periods by Islam and Sikhism.

The first three portions of the Vedas mainly comprise hymns devoted to various gods and religious rituals. The Vedas mention a total of 33 gods also known as devas each personifying natural phenomena. No god is superior to the other. The god that is invoked in a particular hymn is accorded the highest importance at that instance. The Vedas reflect polytheism with no deference to any particular god. Some gods are mentioned more than others.[24] It is the Upanishadic part of the Vedas that have profoundly influenced the philosophical evolution of India. When George Tanham in his essay on the Indian Strategic thought comments "the Hindu concept of time, or rather the lack of a sense of time – Indians view life as eternal present, with neither history nor future - discourages planning"; he is talking about the philosophy of India. He further says "Hindus consider life a mystery, largely unknowable and not entirely under man's control. In this view, fate, intuition, tradition and emotions play important roles, but how much and when is never clearly known. Man's control over his life is thus limited in Hindu eyes, and he cannot forecast or plan with any confidence".[25] These remarks reflect his understanding or rather the lack of it, about the philosophical culture of India. The Hindu way of life has been considered by many western thinkers to be fatalistic. Therefore, a little exposition on the Upanishads (fountainhead of Indian philosophy) and the philosophical traditions of India is essential.

Philosophy of the Upanishads

The Upanishads[26] represent the end portion of the Vedas and therefore like the Vedas their origin cannot be apportioned to any particular individual. They represent evolution of ideas over centuries and dwell on the concept of the 'ultimate reality' and man's relationship with it. As per Upinder Singh they fundamentally deal with the concept of 'Brahman' (not to be confused with the Brahmin caste or the God Brahmaa[27]) and 'Atman'. "A major concern of Upanishadic thought is to explore and explain their meaning and mutual relationship. The Upanishads also deal with the practice of meditation and yoga".[28] Suren Navlakha in his introduction for Max Mueller's translation of the Upanishads says that "Brahman is the absolute reality, changing and featureless self-existent and alone. But Brahman is also this world, the phenomenal world of change and manyness".[29] Upinder Singh quotes the Taittriya Upanishad to state that "Brahman is that from which all beings are born, that by which they are sustained, and that into which they enter on death". Upinder Singh says that even the Upanishads find it difficult to completely describe Brahman; she quotes the Kena Upanishad to say "the gods themselves were not able to understand Brahman, and even those who think they have understood it have not".[30] She goes on to describe Atman as the "ultimate reality within the self of an individual. Atman is the knowing subject within us, which sees but is not seen, hears but is not heard, comprehends but is not comprehended, knows but is not known".[31] Paul Deussen in 'The Philosophy of the Upanishads' says that Brahman is the cosmic principle of the Universe and Atman is the physical. He says that:

> "Brahma the power which presents itself to us materialised in all existing things, which creates, sustains, preserves, and receives back into itself again all worlds, this eternal infinite divine power is identical with the atman, with that which, after stripping of everything external, we discover in ourselves as our real most essential being, our individual self, the soul. This identity of the Brahman and the Atman, of God and the soul, is the fundamental thought of the entire doctrine of the Upanishads. It is briefly expressed by the great saying 'tat tvam asi', 'that thou art' (Chandyoga Upanishad 6.8.7.f)".[32]

Suren Navlakaha reiterates the same, and adds that "this central doctrine of the Upanishads is the cornerstone of Vedanta philosophy, which is also faithfully shared by two other celebrated works, the

Bhagavad Gita and the *Brahma Sutras*".[33] The Vedic rituals and hymns mentioned in the initial sections of the Vedas get subsumed in this actuality; all the gods or divinities mentioned, are within us in the form of the Atman which represents the ultimate reality 'Brahman'. Navlakha says "this renders the Vedic sacrifices and the rituals for invoking them, somewhat redundant or meaningless".[34] The ultimate path is Self-realisation. The diversity of India comes to the fore. Polytheism transforms into the ultimate monotheism. Interpretations of the Upanishadic philosophy were propagated by Shankar in the 8th – 9th century and by Ramanuja in the 10th – 11th century.

In Bhagavad Gita, Shri Krishna expounds the same philosophy to Arjun, while motivating him to follow his Kshatriya-dharma. He also tells Arjun about the doctrine of 'karma' or action. He propounds that a man can never renounce karma or action, because even in renunciation there is the 'action' of renunciation.[35] He advises Arjun to follow the path of 'nishkama karma', 'action which is not bound to the outcome', because when a man does that, he frees himself from emotions of the outcome and can fully concentrate on the karma or action.[36] Motivated, Arjun fights the war and wins it. A philosophy which motivated a demotivated and demoralised warrior to fight and win can hardly be fatalistic. George Tanham was way off the mark in his judgement when he opined on a culture which evolved such philosophies and a strategic culture which is based on it.

Influence on the general populace

The Vedas were not widely read by the masses, but the two epics Ramayana and Mahabharata are widely amalgamated in the culture and traditions of India. So were the teachings of Mahavira and Gautama Buddha. The teachings in these ancient books have permeated the length and breadth of India in some form or the other but mainly in the form of folklores. The messages and stories in these books, mainly the epics, were kept alive by ballad singers in society and in households, by the stories narrated by the elders to children. The Ramayana and Mahabharata have been quintessential aspects of Indian thought and culture over the centuries. Historians like Brajdulal Chattopadyaya and Suvira Jaiswal believe that the Ramayana has been popular in India right from the fifth and sixth century CE and the Bhakti Movement of the fifteenth and sixteenth century reinforced the popularity of the epics among the masses. The Epics have inspired art, dance, narratives, writings and moral values in the entire Indian subcontinent. Stories from the epics are narrated even today to differentiate the right from wrong. Such is the appeal of these books that when these two epics were televised as serials on television in India, the roads would be deserted during their transmissions. As Robert Goldman a distinguished professor of Sanskrit at the University of California notes, "few works of literature produced at any time have been as popular and influential as the great and ancient Sanskrit epic poem, the *Vālmīki Rāmāyaṇa* which has entertained, moved, enchanted, and uplifted untold millions of people in India and much of Southeast Asia".[37]

Concept of Kingship

Returning back to the concept of kingship in ancient India, it is found that the institution of king was given divine support by rooting its origin in divinity. Indian historian V.R. Dikshitar in his work '*Hindu Administrative Institutions*'; explains that the divine theory of the origin of kingship is found in the Mahabharata and the Puranas. A.S. Altekar in '*State and the Government in Ancient India*' supports it and further asserts that the Buddhist work '*Dighnikaya*' also supports the same concept. Dikshitar explains by quoting the Shanti Parva of the Mahabharata that the main aim of the institution of king was to prevent anarchy, and protect the people. He quotes the Aitareya Brahmana (part of Rig Veda) to establish that another reason for the origin of kingship was war. In the war between Devas and Asuras, the Devas lost because they did not have a leader; "through our lack of a king they conquer us, said the gods, 'let us make a king'. They made Soma king and with him as their leader they conquered all quarters".[38] Another Indian historian Upinder Singh in her book '*Political Violence in Ancient India*' quotes from the Mahabharata about kingship in ancient India "a land without a king is weak; it is overrun by barbarians (*dasyus*); the social order of the *varṇas* is overturned; free men are enslaved; livelihoods perish, and there is famine; life is unsafe because theft, plunder, and rape are rampant; there are no sacrifices of Vedic study. If there were no kings, humankind would perish".[39] Thus, the king was necessary to provide military leadership and to protect the state from anarchy. The Shanti Parva and Anusasana Parva of Mahabharata extensively deals with the duties and responsibilities of the king, during a dialogue between Yudhisthir the eldest Pandava prince with his grandfather Bhisma; who is lying on his deathbed in the battlefield of Kurukshetra.

Kingship in India originated out of military necessity and for preventing anarchy; therefore, it was only logical that the king had onerous duties and responsibilities towards his people. He was the upholder of 'Dharma' (Indian historian Kaushik Roy describes dharma as not being the same as religion. He states that dharma was a guiding principle for morality, a code of conduct which operated at the personal level, the level of society and at the cosmic level[40]). The dharma of the king was 'Raj-dharma'. Historian AS Altekar in his work '*State and the Government in Ancient India*' states that the king, apart from being a provider of security, was also regarded as the servant of the people. Another notion of kingship was that it was like a trust; the kingdom was not the private property of the king and the king was only a trustee to take care of the kingdom.[41] Ancient India placed exacting responsibilities on the king. The development of kingship happened in a manner which inherently guarded against despotism. It in no way implies that despotic rulers did not exist but the system was hostile against such rulers and they could not claim sacerdotal approval.[42] Upinder Singh says that in ancient India, violence by the people against an unjust and violent king was justified. She cites the Mahabharata to state "dharma abandons the king who tolerates unrighteousness. A king who goes by the advice of wicked men who do not follow dharma strictly, is a slayer of dharma and should be killed by the people".[43] She quotes from the Anusasana Parva of Mahabharata; "A cruel king, who does not protect his people, who robs them in the name of levying taxes, is evil incarnate and should be killed by his subjects. A king, who, after declaring 'I will protect you', does not protect them, should be killed by his people coming together, as though he were a mad dog".[44] In the same Anusasana Parva it is further amplified "the subjects should arm themselves to slay that king who does not protect them, who simply plunders their wealth, who confounds all distinctions, who is ever incapable of taking their lead, who is without compassion, and who is regarded as the most sinful of kings".[45] Ancient India, in spite of associating divinity to the king, justified people's action against a tyrant king even to the point of regicide. The important point to note here is that this action against the tyrant is by the people; the Mahabharata exhorts the **people** to come together, arm themselves and slay the king; the army or the Senapati (general) is not called upon for undertaking this act. It was not the army's responsibility to ensure that the king remained just and fulfilled his responsibilities to his people; the role of the army was protection of the state and not to interfere in its functioning. An army which had no role in the state's internal politics is an ancient Indian dictum.

Indian historian Dikshitar in '*Mauryan Polity*' has brought out that the end aim of the Mauryan state like the "established tradition of the land was the moral and material welfare of the citizen". He further states that as per ancient Indian traditions "the king could not be and was not a lawmaker. The law is eternal and based on the Dharmashastras of the Shrutis and he was to act as per the law prescribed by these lawgivers".[46] Kautilya has described in detail the duties and responsibility of the king in *Arthshastra* Book I. Kautilya uses the Vedas as the source for deriving his concept of the king's dharma and his duties towards his subjects. The concept of Rajdharma was also followed by the kings of the Gupta Empire (250 AD to 550 AD) as brought out by RN Dandekar in '*A History of the Guptas*'; Dandekar writes that "general study of the Gupta inscriptions bears ample testimony to the high standard of perfection in several aspects of national life attained under the regime of the Guptas, who's ideal was the propagation of peace, prosperity and happiness among the people".[47] The fundamental sources of Knowledge (Vedas), for deriving the concept of Raj-dharma and duties of the king, remained the same and hence similar ideals for the king continued even subsequently in history; it may not have been followed in the same spirit by subsequent kings but they always remained as the guiding precepts.

The interpretation of the various sources of Knowledge (Vedas, Puranas, and others) for the king was done by the Purohit. He was from the Brahmin varna (caste) and the king was dependent on him for guidance on matters of dharma. The purohit provided the sacerdotal authority to the king and there was interdependence between the two. In the Vedic period two institutions 'Sabha' and 'Samiti' provided checks on the king. The king had to regularly consult them and in fact he was appointed by them. They ceased to exist by the period of the Epics when kingship became hereditary. However, the interdependence of the purohit and the king remained. Thus, it is found that since its evolution, the institution of kingship in India did not have absolute authority. It was bound by a code of conduct (Rajdharma) and it had defined responsibilities. It may not have been followed by all kings (despotic kings are part of Indian history) but they were aberrations rather than the norm. AS Altekar cites the example of king Veena who was killed by the sages because of his tyrannical behaviour. He also gives the example of kings like Nahusa, Sudasa, Sumukha and Nimi; who were tyrants and who lost their lives because of the anger of their people.[48] The normal was clearly laid down by ancient India and reiterated from time to time in various treatises like *Arthshastra* and Kamandaka's *Nitisara*.

Dharma

Dharma was the socio-political and philosophical foundation of ancient India. It was derived from the sources of Knowledge (Vedas) as mentioned earlier. Since transmission of knowledge was done orally the interpretation of dharma could have been done so as to always have it contemporary to society.[49] Jawaharlal Nehru the first Prime Minister of India defines dharma in '*Discovery of India*' as "an ethical concept which includes the moral code, righteousness and the whole range of man's duties and responsibilities".[50] In the foreword of their book 'India's Grand Strategy' Arvind Gupta and Professor Sven G.

Holtsmark, Director, IFS, Oslo, say that "the Indian tradition of strategic thought emphasises the concept of *dharma* – a set of rules that bound the ruler and the ruled alike".[51] Dharma as a concept defined the duties and responsibilities of various social structures in such a manner that it led to betterment and coordinated functioning of society thereby reducing anarchy. Swara Rajagopalan in '*India's Grand Strategy*' says that "Dharma is both the ideological foundation and the purpose of the political community, which is intended to end the state of anarchy and restore and protect dharma".[52]

There is no English equivalent of the word dharma. It neither signifies religion nor does it signify rights; the closest would be 'conscience' with a sense of duty and responsibility for betterment of society. It was functional at various levels, from the individual to the various strata of society. At times dharma is ambivalent. In Mahabharata the eldest Pandava prince Yudhistir, losing his brothers and wife in gambling was correct as per the existing rules but it was 'adharma' (opposite of dharma) as it was bad for society. There were various dimensions of dharma. At the individual level it defined responsibilities of a father, mother, son, daughter, wife, brother, sister, or any relationship that binds a family. In Ramayana, Ram fulfils his dharma of being a son by going to the jungle instead of being crowned as a prince; his wife Sita fulfils the dharma of a wife and his brother Laxman the dharma of a brother by going to the jungle with him. At the social level, it defined the social responsibilities of the various varnas or castes. The dharma of the Brahmin varna was to perform various rituals and have understanding of the various sources of Knowledge (Vedas, Puranas, Upanishads, etc). The dharma of the Kshatriya (warrior class) was to protect society.

Upinder Singh, while describing kingship in the Mahabharata, states that "the epic makes a powerful attempt to relate kingship with a morality and duty that is peculiar to the political sphere – *rāja-dharma* (the dharma of the king)".[53] Dharma is discussed in detail in the Mahabharata. Shri Krishna reminds Arjuna of his dharma as a warrior in the Bhagavad Gita. The Mahabharata discusses in detail the Kshatriya dharma (code of conduct of the warrior). The Mahabharata places the dharma of the king or 'Raj-dharma' above all other, as it was a necessity, for protection as well as for maintenance of order and stability in society. Thus, dharma prevented anarchy in society by providing a code of conduct which was derived from the various sources of Knowledge. It was the foundation on which orderliness of society was built. It provided legitimacy to an act. Therefore, dharma was placed on the highest pedestal in India. When the choice was between dharma and other social norms or laws, dharma prevailed. In the Mahabharata, Shri Krishna advises the Pandava princes to violate the ethics of war in certain instances, to ensure that dharma triumphs in the best interest of society.[54] Dharma was one of the most important pillars on which not only the culture but also the *strategic culture* of India was based. The concept of Kshatriya dharma and Raj-dharma elevated warfighting from being a brutal act to providing it legitimacy as an act of protecting society and preventing anarchy. Warfighting shifted from being a personal act to becoming a social act for the good of society.

Torkel Brekke in his essay '*The Indian Tradition*' ascribes thc same importance of dharma to other religious traditions that originated in the sub-continent; "Buddhists, Jains, and Sikhs have shared a vision of politics according to which the world should be ruled according to *dharma* and in which war (*yuddha*) must be fought according to *dharma*".[55] The idea of dharma permeates the Indian thought process and in its various interpretations, is an integral part of Indian culture from the ancient to the present. Whenever the Indian soldier fights 'last man last bullet', one of the many reasons may be that he is following his dharma as a soldier. War is brutal and it brings out the extremes of human emotions in the form of violence, rage, anger, hatred and barbarism. These emotions were conditioned in India to a certain extent by the concept of dharma when applied to war. By the Epic age ancient India had evolved an elaborate code of ethics for war.

Ethics of War

Historian Sarv Daman Singh in his research on 'Ancient Indian Warfare' says that the phase of the Upanishads holds a very important significance towards the development of ethics for war. It marked a momentous stage in the development of moral consciousness. This period indicated a departure from unnecessary violence and movement towards morality. To support his claim, SD Singh quotes the Chandogya Upanishad wherein stress is laid on ahimsa or non-violence together with austerity, charity and truth in speech. "The Brihadranayaka Upanishad places law and justice (dharma) higher than ksatra (power): dharma is the ksatra of the Kshatriya; therefore, there is nothing higher than dharma. A weak man thus hopes to defeat a strong man by means of justice, as one does through a king".[56] By the period of the Epics, code of ethics in war had become institutionalised. As per Torkel Brekke, Indian tradition as mentioned in the epics of Ramayana and Mahabharat, circumscribes war and warfare with rules and norms. Historian BK Majumdar opines that the Epic and the Puranic literature of India contain an excellent code of ethics of war which can be compared to modern international law. Some of the rules quoted by him citing the Mahabharata and Puranas are as follows:

- "A warrior in armour should not fight a Kshatriya without a coat of mail.
- Fight should be between equals.
- Poisoned arrows and barbed wire should not be used.
- A suppliant enemy after he has laid down his arms should not be killed. Prisoners of war should be treated well.
- The Puranic literature forbids clearly seizure or destruction of enemy's property except under grave necessity. Properties of non-combatants and private individuals enjoyed immunity from seizure and destruction in war."[57]

SD Singh cites the Mahabharata; "in the Sabha Parva the sage Narada asks the Pandava prince Yudhistir if he cherishes with paternal affection the foe who has surrendered from fear, or who has sought asylum, vanquished in battle. A Kshatriya should defend his enemy if entreated with joined hands".[58] War is a brutal activity, the ethics of war as enumerated in the Epics helped in softening the edge of conflict. There are instances in the Mahabharata where these ethics were violated. Upinder Singh in her analyses of war in the Mahabharata asserts that the violations of the code of ethics were commented upon and receive censure.[59] There are attempts to justify these violations which is proof that these violations digressed from the accepted norms. Shri Krishna advises the Pandava princes at various important occasions to violate these codes to ensure victory; these are instances where dharma clashes with the code of ethics and it is important that dharma triumphs and hence the codes could be violated. The Mahabharata war is about the victory of dharma, it is about dharma-vijaya. Victory of dharma was more important than anything else as it was dharma that stood between society and anarchy. Thus, it is found that inspite of the ethics of war being propagated, the most important end objective was the establishment of dharma in society. Mahabharata establishes that a righteous war fought for the larger good of society, could involve digressing from the code of ethics. The Pandava princes represented the good for society and therefore it was imperative that they win even if it required violating the ethics of war. The importance of dharma is summed up in the Mahabharata statement "Yato Dharma stato Jayah" (where there is dharma there is victory).[60]

Another important factor which contributed to ethics in war fighting was the Kshatriya varna (caste) of ancient India. There are references of this varna along with the Brahmin varna even during the early periods of Vedic society. The main purpose of the Kshatriya varna was war fighting and hence the main objective of their dharma, the Kshatriya-dharma was to provide protection to society. As per historian Ramchandra Dikshitar, the evolution of the Kshatriya varna led to "cut and dry distinction of the civil population from the military and the equally clear distinction between the civil and military functions of the state".[61] Upinder Singh brings out another aspect of Kshatriya-dharma and Raj-dharma. She quotes the Mahabharata to connect the outer and the inner battle which has to be fought by a warrior. "Bhishma tells Yudhishthira that a king must first conquer himself and then his enemies. The battle within has to be fought in the mind - alone, sans weapons, without the support of allies or kin. Winning this battle helps attaining victory over enemies in the outer war".[62] The wars that were waged following the code of ethics were dharmayuddha.

Types of War

The two main types of war in ancient India were dharmayuddha also known as prakasayuddha and kutayuddha. Dikshitar defines dharmayuddha as war waged using the principles of dharma (Kshatriya-dharma); "a just and righteous war which had the approval of society".[63] Kaushik Roy says that dharmayuddha could only be started for a just reason, was to be waged in accordance with rules and regulations, at a place and time previously decided and where the combatants were bound by ethics of warfare. Kutayuddha on the other hand was free from ethical constraints, the only aim being to win by all means. Kutayuddha involved covert actions, trickery, deceit, raids, misinformation, tactical retreats and other such actions undertaken during war.[64] Kaushik Roy further asserts that the ethics of war evolved from the concept of dharmayuddha to minimise the sufferings caused by war. Although both these types of war are mentioned in the ancient Indian texts, both the epics Ramayana and Mahabharata propagate and recommend dharmayuddha over kutayuddha. As mentioned earlier, in spite of many instances of the ethics of war being violated in the Mahabharata, it was essentially a war fought for the protection of dharma, dharma-vijay. Thus, it is found that dharma-vijay inspite of overlapping with dharmayuddha and the code of ethics, is actually greater than them. Kautilya in 'Arthshastra' advises that if the king is strong and if he has taken all precautions for his victory then he should indulge in dharmayuddha, whereas against a stronger enemy it is better to resort to kutayuddha.[65]

Continuity of Concepts – The March of Strategic Culture

Did Indian society continue following the ethics of war subsequent to the Epic age? This is what the Greek historian Arrian (of Roman period) had to say about war during the Mauryan period. "In times of war the soldiers are not allowed to molest the husbandmen or ravage their land: hence while the former are fighting and killing each other as they can, the latter may be seen close at hand tranquilly pursuing their work – perhaps ploughing, or gathering in their crops, pruning the trees or reaping the harvest".[66] Upinder Singh quotes another ancient Greek historian Diodorus mentioning about an unusual Indian practice; "both sides of those warring kill each other in battle, but they leave those farming unharmed as the common benefactors of all, and they do not burn the lands or cut down the trees of those fighting against them".[67] This was in an empire which emerged in the aftermath of Alexander's invasion of India. Kaushik Roy quotes Hanson to say that "Alexander's signal contribution (to war) in Hansons' view was to pursue the defeated enemy force to destruction. Thus, elimination, and not defeat of the enemy armies, was Alexander's aim".[68] The concept of dharma and ethics of warfare in India preached exactly the opposite and it is found that the Mauryan Empire under Chandragupta Maurya followed it.

Kaushik Roy while describing the battle between Alexander and Porus at Hydapses argues that, instead of waiting for Alexander at the chosen battlefield, had Porus attacked Alexander when the later had just crossed the river, the outcome of the war would have been different. Instead of an aggressive approach Porus preferred a defensive stand. Here we find that Porus was engaging in dharmayuddha, a battle of force on force. An aggressive stance and kutayuddha may have changed the course of the battle. This was an Indian king's penchant to follow dharmayuddha. Kaushik Roy draws another important inference from this battle when he cites Greek historians to say that the Greeks suffered a much higher casualty at Hydapses than they had suffered at Persia (Alexander's campaign against Persian emperor Darius III) whereas the Indians suffered much lesser casualties than what the Persians had when they lost to Alexander. Thus, it is found that the military effectiveness of a small Indian king and the fighting ability of the Indians were much better than the Persian army under Darius III.[69]

Kajari Kamal in her article on the Strategic Culture of India says that Kautilya is a proponent of expansion of the state by conquest of territory; the underlying principle behind it being the concept of *yogakshema* (stability of the state) and ensuring the safety and security of the people.[70] Kautilya deviates from the past (during the epic period dharmayuddha was given preference over kutayuddha) because he does not lay stress on following only dharmayuddha. He advises the king to follow either dharmayuddha or kutayuddha to ensure victory. He follows the principle of Shri Krishna where establishing dharma or welfare of society is more important than following ethics of war. With Kautilya as advisor, the Mauryan empire became the formidable power that it was. The roles of Shri Krishna in Mahabharata to ensure Pandava victory and Kautilya's role in creation of the Mauryan Empire, highlight the importance of a master strategist for the success of the state.

The Mauryan emperor Asoka deviated from the ethics of war (not harming non-combatants during war) in his Kalinga conquest. He deported 1,50,000 persons as prisoners, to be used as cultivators. After this war Asoka renounced war and involved himself in the practice and preaching of Buddhism. In another significant event the last king of the Mauryan dynasty Brihadratha was assassinated by his general, Pusyamitra Sunga. This is the only chronicled instance of a general overthrowing his king to usurp power in ancient Indian history.[71] Kaushik Roy calls it "a rare case of a military coup in the history of India".[72] The next such recorded incident of military coup happened during the Islamic Sultanate rule at Delhi.

In the post Mauryan period an important literature which influenced statecraft and strategy was Manu's *Manava Dharmashastra* also known as Manu Smriti. Upinder Singh ascribes the period 200 BC to 200 CE to it and this places it after the *Arthshastra*. Manu in his work, places great emphasis on the concept of dharma. Kaushik Roy says that unlike Kautilya, Manu over-emphasises the role of dharma in statecraft. "Manu is a strong critique of Kautilya's kutayuddha. He advises that the king should always act without guile".[73] He has similar views as Kautilya on many aspects like the responsibilities of the king and importance of an efficient army; nevertheless, he remains steadfast in propagating dharmayuddha as a means of waging war. This was a period when India was subjected to invasions by the Greeks, Sakas and Kushans. During this period Indian political thinkers should have propagated the importance of winning either by dharmayuddha or kutayuddha, as the prime concern should have been to stop the invaders. Instead, it is found that following dharmayuddha, became the guiding principle. The means was given more importance than the end result. This was a defining turn of path for India's strategic culture from what was promulgated in the *Arthshastra*. Hereinafter it is found that the stress on dharmayuddha is a continuous underlying thread in Indian military history. No explanations are available as to why *Manu Smriti* was preferred. Manu in his work has emphasised the dominance of the Brahmin caste in society. The Brahmins as purohits were the interpreter of dharma for the king and were also his main advisor. It is probable that the importance and superiority ascribed to the Brahmins (in Manu Smriti) may have been a reason for them favouring *Manu Smriti* over other texts of statecraft for their advice to the king. The influence of Manu Smriti was seminal. Patrick Olivelli in *The Law Code of Manu* says that Manu Smriti remained pre-eminent throughout the Middle Ages and medieval works cite Manu more than any other text.[74] It was one of the first Sanskrit texts to be translated in English by Sir William Jones in 1776 and adapted as the basis for formulating laws to govern India by the British.[75]

Historians are unanimous that the Gupta Empire saw a revival of Brahminical Hinduism. RN Dandekar says that "the most popular sect of Hindu religion, patronised in the Gupta period seems to have been Vaisnavism (following God Vishnu)".[76] Manu's *Manava Dharmashastra* must have been the central treatise of statecraft as Manu stressed on the dominance of the Brahmin caste who were offered state patronage during the Gupta period. The Gupta kings, following the teachings of Manu and Kautilya, built an army which made them almost invincible. The strength of the army was such that it enabled them to follow the concepts of dharmayuddha. Dandekar says that "Samudragupta in his southern conquest followed the ideals of dharmavijaya. He employed the policy more of conciliation than aggression and annexation".[77] He does not contest Samudragupta's win over the kings of the south (all historians unanimously agree with it), but implies that Samudragupta was content with establishing his supremacy and did not indulge in annexation and extermination. Pravarsena I (a Vakataka king who was contemporary to the Guptas) is described in inscriptions as a righteous victor, 'dharma vijayin'.[78] The Gupta period reflects the following of dharma in various aspects of life including in strategy. Their mighty military empowered them to do so. The founders of the Gupta Empire never lost a war.

As brought out earlier, the effect of Manu's treatise was long-lasting. Kaushik Roy cites Kane to inform that "an inscription by a Valabhi king dated 571 CE states that the rules made by Manu were obeyed by this king".[79] The concept of dharmayuddha was again stressed by the ancient Indian author Bana who wrote '*Harshacharita*', the treatise about Harshavardhana's empire. "By waging dharmayuddha says Bana the just ruler should become the sovereign of the earth bound by the four oceans".[80]

The next important treatise on statecraft was Kamandaka's *Nitisara*. Different historians have offered different periods for the composition of *Nitisara*. Kaushik Roy has cited various historians like PV Kane, D Devahuti, PC Chakravarti, Keith and Upinder Singh to arrive at a date for the Nitisara. He assumes that "Kamandaka's *Nitisara* belongs to the post-Harsha and pre-Islamic Turkish period".[81] This places *Nitisara* after the work of Bana. *Nitisara* follows most of the precepts of *Arthshastra*. Kamandaka considers Kautilya as his guru (mentor). As per Upinder Singh, Kamandaka theorises war as the last resort. Kamandaka lists the various reasons for waging war. As per him the outcome of war is uncertain, so the king should use all methods at his disposal to avoid war and these methods include the use of kutayuddha to gain advantage and avoid war. Thus, unlike Kautilya, Kamandaka does not advise using kutayuddha for winning war, instead he propagates using kutayuddha to avoid or minimise the effect of war. Upinder Singh says that Kamandaka "argues persuasively to avoid war. While Kautilya urges caution in war, Kamandaka's reservations are stronger".[82] Kaushik

Roy agrees with Upinder Singh and says that "Kamandaka discourages a risk-taking strategy for the vijigishu (king). Here one can discern the influence of Manu's, Manav Dharmashastra on *Nitisara*".[83] If Kaushik Roy's period of the *Nitisara* is accepted, then this was the period when north India was dominated by three powers, the Gurjar Pratihar in the west, Palas in the east and Rashtrakutas in the Deccan region. The Arab invasion of Sind happened in 712 AD. The Gurjar Pratihars prevented the Arabs from expanding in the north and the Rashtrakutas prevented their expansion in the south; thereby limiting the Arab influence to Sindh.[84] There was continuous tussle for supremacy between these three powers which ultimately led to their considerable weakening by mid-tenth century, leaving northern and western India open for invasion and plundering by Mahmud of Gajni. As per Kaushik Roy and Upinder Singh "treatises like Kamandaka's *Nitisara* not only reflected contemporary political reality but also shaped the political discourse". The ideas of political theorists were absorbed and expressed in poetry, drama, didactic stories, and so on and reached a wider audience".[85] They thus become intrinsic to India's strategic culture. Another Indian treatise of the 9th – 10th century was '*Kathasaritsagar*' by Somadeva. Somadeva in his work warns the "Indian kings not to attack the north-west India as that region is dominated by mlechchas (Indian term for foreigners). The mlecchas did not obey the normative model of dharmayuddha as laid down by Manu".[86] This statement proves that Indians during this period also mostly followed the dharmayuddha norms of war as laid down by Manu; it also brings out that the invaders followed no such ethics. Here it is found that the advice is to avoid fighting the invaders because of this and not to change own way of conducting war (rigidity to follow Manu Smriti) to ensure victory.

The Turkish invasion of India began from 900 CE. It changed the nature of warfare in India. A country which had revelled in the practice of dharmayuddha was exposed to a form of warfare involving destruction and plunders which affected the common citizenry as much as the warriors. The Turks who invaded India followed the concept of al-harb-khada, which meant following deception in war. The Rajputs who faced them were followers of dharmayuddha. "The principal Rajput culture was chivalry, which was an essential element of Kshatriya-dharma".[87] They preferred death over abandoning their Kshatriya-dharma. Indian historian KS Lal observes that even during this period when India was subjected to loot, plunder and abduction, the Rajputs did not indulge in harassment of civil population or abduction of women during war.[88] When Muhammad Ghori invaded India, he faced the Rajput king Prithviraj Chauhan. Stanley Lane Poole while writing about the encounter between the Turks and the Rajputs says "the Turks were well acquainted with the fighting of the Central Asians but in the Rajputs they encountered a soldiery second to none in the world, a race of born fighters who fought to the death and many of whose principalities never submitted in more than name to Muslim rule".[89] In this battle Chauhan defeated Ghori; who again attacked after a year. During the second battle instead of aggressively encountering his enemy, Prithviraj asked Ghori to turn back without fighting and save his soldiers. Ghori used deception, accepted the offer and agreed to suspend hostilities. He then attacked early before daybreak, when the Rajputs had not even finished their morning ablutions and were not ready for war, and defeated them.[90] An Indian king's folly of following dharmayuddha while not being prepared for it (by being asymmetrically superior), changed the course of India's history.

The Sultanate period was established after the raids of Ghori, by his slaves. The dynasties during this period were, Slave dynasty (1206-90), Khilji dynasty (1290-1320), Tughlaq dynasty (1320-1413), Sayyid dynasty (1414-51), and Lodhi dynasty (1451-1526). For historical data of the Sultanate period, most historians refer to Ziauddin Barani. considered as one of the best historians of the period for his work 'Tarikh- i-Firoz Shahi'. However, Barani had a strong bias against non-Muslims as is reflected in his other work 'Fatwa-i Jahandari' where he states that it was obligatory for a sultan to conduct jihad and Mahmud of Ghazni was praised for his jihad against the Hindus. As per Kaushik Roy, Barani advocated the "killing of 2-300,000 brahmins and that the rest of Hindus be given the option of death or Islam, however since such a thing may not have been possible, he recommended oppressing and disgracing Hindus".[91] Barani was not the only fanatic; there were others like Sayyid Ali Hamadani and Fakhr-i Mudabbir with similar views. Kaushik Roy further states that the army of an Islamic ruler fighting Hindus was known as laskar-i-Islam and the campaign was jihad. This bias against Hindus changed during the period of Akbar; all his subjects were treated as equals. However Akbar was an exception, for the other Mughals "the demands of Islam loomed large in the governance of a country where the majority of the subjects were non-Muslims".[92] The socio-political scene existing during the Sultanate period in India (described as the land of kufr by the Muslim conquerors) reflected this as described by Rajat Dutta "the traditional intersection between niti (policies based on legal precepts), dharma and rajdharma were broken and replaced by the notions of dar-ul Islam and jahandari as abiding principles of state action. The earlier consensus of a moral and transcendental order of things was now replaced by deep anxieties, founded in reality of subversion and sedition – fitna – in these subjugated lands".[93]

Most Indian historian like KS Lal, CV Vaidya, Mohammad Habib, Iswari Prasad and others hold the Indian caste system responsible for Indian defeat during this era.[94] The caste system of India had become rigid by this period. But this argument fails to account for the splendid rise of Maratha power in the same Indian society. However, Brahminism did play a role in shaping the political scene during this period. During the late BC and early CE years, in the intervening period between the Mauryan and Gupta empires, the Indian culture had displayed remarkable adaptability. The invaders were absorbed into the Indian culture. But during the medieval period, this adaptability was missing. KS Lal says that the rigidity forced by Brahmins on society was such that whenever Hindus who were taken prisoners by Islamic kings during war returned back, they were either forced to do severe penance or were not allowed back into the social system. These soldiers were thus not available for fighting in the battlefield again.[95] This was degeneration of a culture which had assimilated the Sakas and the Kushans completely into itself. Historian Satish Chandra disagrees that caste was responsible for Indian defeat; he holds that feudalism in society had weakened the military organisation. The rulers had to rely on the local chiefs who rarely acted in coordination and this weakened the military structure.[96] Perhaps both these factors contributed towards weakening the military system during this period. However, as argued earlier it can be inferred that to a certain extent Brahminism in Indian society was responsible for *Manu Smriti* (importance of dharmayuddha) being preferred over *Arthshastra* (importance of winning and using dharmayuddha or kutayuddha as dictated by the circumstances) in statecraft, after the decline of the Gupta Empire. This led to the strategic culture evolving in a manner where patronage of dharmayuddha became more important than winning the war. Kautilya's precept that dharmayuddha should only be resorted to if you are militarily strong and have ensured your victory, was forgotten. Vanity perhaps made every king believe that he was strong enough to follow dharmayuddha.

It is not that the militaries of the sub-continent did not have their ethical failings. Ashoka had resorted to capture of prisoners after the Kalinga war as mentioned in his rock edicts; similarly, the Marathas had their weak moment. When the Maratha army raided Bengal against Alivardi Khan in 1750-51 under the Bhonsalas of Nagpur, they indulged in loot and plunder.[97] However aberrations do not make the rule, and when the history being referred to is for a period of almost 4000 years, aberrations are likely to happen. There is an interesting anecdote about the behaviour of the Indian army under the British during World War II in Italy, as narrated by Capt Raj Mohindra (Retd) IN. In his words:

> "In 1967 I was an officer on board INS Brahmaputra. My ship was diverted to Taranto (Italy) owing to a coup against King Constantine in Greece our original destination. The ship berthed in Taranto in the early hours of a Sunday. There was no one there apart from the shore berthing party of a few men. As time went by, a large number of Taranto's residents, including several senior citizens started congregating near the ship. They carried placards welcoming the Indians to Taranto. It was a mystery to us as to why such a crowd

was building up. We were told that the news of the Indian ship's arrival was announced on the local radio. By the evening, the crowd had swelled. Several residents held placards inviting us to dinners, lunches and picnics. I was invited to dinner by the family of the late Ms. Ines Ghosh, the Italian wife of the late Surgeon Rear Admiral J.N. Ghosh of the Indian Navy. Ghosh met Ines in Taranto where he was a prisoner of war. There I heard heart-rending stories of World War II. They narrated how when the British 8th Army comprising British, Australian, Canadian, Indian and troops of other nationalities invaded southern Italy in July 1943. The soldiers from all armies except the Indian Army indulged in rape, molestation and plunder. One of the elderly ladies' present told us how she was being chased by two Allied soldiers when an Indian soldier intervened and protected her. He told them not to harm her because she was his sister! In another instance a posse of Indian soldiers voluntarily guarded an apartment building and prevented soldiers of the other Allied armies from entering it. There were numerous stories of heroism like this. These marvellous episodes bore testimony to the ethical standards and professionalism of the Indian Army."[98]

Ethical standards of war which date back to almost 4000 years! This incident reflects the continuity of the concepts of dharma, and ethics of war. Torkel Brekke has inferred from his study that even in contemporary India "the concepts of dharma and ethics have a lot to say for individual soldiers in their management of stress, in the formation of a sense of honour and duty in their service".[99]

Lessons from India's Strategic Culture – Dharma and Kingship

The concept of kingship in India ensured that the king was not supreme in his authority. He was obliged to follow the responsibilities laid down for him as his raj-dharma, which warranted that his main responsibilities were towards his people. The state and the king were upholders of law, not its legislators; that was the domain of dharma. The concept of dharma defined the responsibilities at the individual level as well as at the level of the society. This resulted in each functionary of the state including the military identifying its responsibility well, and since dharma was kept at the highest pedestal, following this responsibility or dharma was sacrosanct. This created a strategic culture in which the role of not only the military but of each element of the state was distinct and defined. This was amplified to a level where the responsibility of deposing a tyrant king lay with the people. The effect was that the state never became a military rule. The military's domain did not extend into the administrative functioning of the state. As per recorded history this strategic culture was broken only once during the end period of the Mauryan Empire, when Pusyamitra Sunga who was the Senapati (general) killed the king and usurped the throne. This incident received the highest condemnation from authors of statecraft as a base action and was never repeated in India except by the Muslim rulers of the Sultanate. Therefore, can it be inferred that the strategic culture of India by its concepts of dharma and kingship ensured that the Indian military remained non-interfering in state affairs? ***Non-interference of the military in state administration is a legacy of the strategic culture of India and Indian policy planners would do well to understand this tremendous inherent strength of India's strategic culture while framing policies on civil-military relations.*** The bogey of military coup which is a creation of western study does not fit into the strategic culture of India.

Lessons from India's Strategic Culture – Dharma and National Power

India's strategic culture shows a clear bias for dharmayuddha and against kutayuddha. This is in spite of the two biggest proponents of kutayuddha being Shri Krishna and Chanakya, their ultimate aim being the restoration of dharma for the good of society. Both Shri Krishna and Chanakya ensured that their protagonists (Arjun in Mahabharata and Chandragupta Maurya respectively) not only followed kutayuddha but also prepared well for their forthcoming war.[100] This brings out ***the importance of a master strategist for the state, and it is equally important that he is well versed in the art of conflict.***

The next important lesson comes from the Gupta Empire. The Gupta kings were dharmavijayin. But for being able to do so they created a military which ensured that they always remained victorious. The important lesson which comes out from this is the imperative requirement of military power (comprehensive national power in today's context). Indians, throughout history have never followed the principle of pursuing the enemy and eliminating them like Alexander. It is not a weakness; in fact, any civilisation should be proud of achieving such strategic culture greatness. But with this greatness comes the immense responsibility of becoming such a formidable power, that it can enable you to follow dharma and dharmayuddha and still be victorious, as achieved by the Gupta kings. Remaining weak or mediocre and aspiring to be morally superior by following dharmayuddha is a sure recipe for disaster as India's history has proved time and again. This is one of the most important lessons from the strategic culture of India. In the present milieu military power alone is not sufficient for a nation, though it is still the most important. Military power has been replaced by comprehensive national power. Therefore, the lesson from India's strategic culture is that ***India needs to acquire formidable national power to enable it to follow its cultural greatness, proclivity for which is an important trait of its strategic culture.***

Lessons from India's Strategic Culture – Philosophy

India's philosophy which originated in the Upanishads does not propound inaction. It is not fatalist or pacifist. In fact, it motivated a demoralised and dejected Arjuna to fight and win for the sake of dharma. This sublime philosophy is not a shield for the weak. Various strands of philosophies which subsequently developed from it, defined the original concepts in multitudinous ways. Buddhism and Jainism emphasised on non-violence, but at its very essence, the philosophy remained the same. Mahatma Gandhi developed the concept of ahimsa from it. The philosophy of the Upanishads and the various strands that developed from it, at its very core, addresses the individual. It was a concept focussed on the individual; about Brahman and Atman and how an individual can achieve his highest state by realising the Brahman in him. The philosophy itself was not a guidance for statecraft and for management of dharma in society. Indian philosophy exclusively addressed the individual and extending its realm into statecraft, for defining strategic culture and determining policies, may not be its correct understanding as attempted by many western thinkers like George Tanham.

Lessons from India's Strategic Culture – Importance of Institutions

In the post Epic period, India has witnessed three great empires of Maurya, Gupta and Akbar. The founders of these empires created institutions both military and administrative which not only empowered them to attain great power status but also enabled them to create a legacy which lasted many generations. The founders of these empires were not the only military geniuses that India had. After the Mauryan Empire, king Kharavela of Orissa created a powerful kingdom which lost its glory after him. Post the Gupta Empire, king Yashodharman of Kanauj defeated the Huna king Mihirkula and established a kingdom covering most of north India. However, after him his kingdom disintegrated. After Harshvardhan's empire, king Yasovarman of Kanauj and Lalitaditya of Kashmir were one generation military geniuses.[101] They were accomplished military leaders and achieved great success during their lifetime; but they proved to be unsuccessful institutional builders. Their military capabilities were their own and it disappeared after they were gone. This brings out the importance of creating empowered institutional structures. ***Powerful military institutions were the foundations of the great empires of India and they were supported by equally competent administrative structures***. Institutional military power cannot exist without an equally efficient administrative setup. Brilliance of these institutions have been the hallmark of the powerful empires of India. Herein lies a very important lesson for the civil-military relations of India – the cohesion of civil and military power for creating a great State.

Conclusion

India has witnessed the destruction and carnage that can be inflicted on its culture and society when its armies were outwitted by the Turks starting from the invasion by Mahmud of Ghazni. Indians did not lack courage or the will to fight, but that they were outwitted is a fact and the price paid was heavy in terms of plunder and destruction. It can be argued that it happened a millennium ago and that in today's civilised society and international world order such a thing may not happen. But is that the truth? Even in the present world order, one cannot argue against the importance of 'power' (comprehensive national power) for protecting own interests and consequently its centrality in international relations; it was true in the past and it is as true today. A central component of this power is the military. It is the pivot of comprehensive national power. This fundamental centrality of the military was accepted by the present prime minister of India Shri Narendra Modi when he addressed the nation from Ayodhya on August 05, 2020 quoting from the Ramayana, "bhay bin hoe na Preet" (fear is important for implementing friendship).[102]

India's military history brings out the fact that Indians at the individual level were among the best warriors. The culture that developed in India elevated ethical principles to a level, wherein it tried to tame the basest of human emotions even in war. The strategic culture that emerged, was common to the sub-continent and it was followed in the wars that happened between kingdoms here. This led to it getting reinforced over a period. When these ethical concepts encountered untamed human emotions of savagery in war, the thing that could have protected it viz, 'strength or power' in the required measure, was not available, leading to its defeat. For most periods in Indian history, Indian kings never tried to build formidable institutional military power which could have enabled dominance.

India's strategic culture needs to be looked at from an Indian frame of reference. The thread of ideas will have to be picked up from where they evolve. Picking up a concept or an idea intermittently and examining it from a modern frame of reference may lead to incorrect conclusions like

'Indians were pacifist' or 'India lacked a strategic culture'. Indians placed their strategy into the realm of ethical standards, and India's strategic culture needs to be viewed from this context. The imperative requirement of comprehensive national power for the success and preservation of such a culture is the most important lesson that emerges from the strategic culture of India. The path that India followed post-independence will be analysed against its strategic culture in the subsequent chapter. The next chapter will deal with the evolution of civil-military relations and Higher Defence Organisation of India from the British period onwards.

Notes

1. Historians like AL Basham and strategic culture theorist like Rodney Jones have substantiated the continuity in India's civilisation. For more on the concept of 'civilisation' in general and Indian civilisation in particular refer, Amit Kumar Sharma. "Elements of Indian Civilisation: A Sociological Perspective." *Indian Anthropologist* 33, no. 1 (2003): 71-92. Accessed January 9, 2021. http://www.jstor.org/stable/41919927. The idea of continuity of Indian civilisation has been dealt with in detail subsequently in the chapter.
2. Booth K. (1990) *The Concept of Strategic Culture Affirmed.* In: Jacobsen C.G. (eds) Strategic Power: USA/USSR. Palgrave Macmillan, London, p. 122, at https://doi.org/10.1007/978-1-349-20574-5_8, accessed on August 18, 2020.
3. Ibid. p. 121.
4. Ibid.
5. Alistair Iain Johnston, *Cultural Realism - Strategic Culture and Grand Strategy in Chinese History* (New Jersey: Princeton University Press, 1995), p. ix.
6. Ian Jhonston in *Thinking About Strategic Culture* states that the concept of Strategic Culture underwent through three generational ideas, first generation was in early 1980s, second in the mid-1980s and the third in the early 1990s.
7. Colin S. Gray, "Strategic Culture as Context: The First generation of Theory Strikes Back," *Review of International Studies* vol. 25, no. 1, 1999, pp. 49-69, at https://www.jstor.org/stable/20097575, accessed on June 17, 2020.
8. Ibid.
9. Ibid.
10. Ibid.
11. AL Basham, *The Wonder that was India* (New Delhi: Rupa & Co, 1954), p. 4.
12. Ibid.
13. Ibid.
14. Ibid.
15. U.S. Department of Defence, Defense Threat Reduction Agency Advanced Systems and Concept Office, USA, *India's Strategic Culture*, by Rodney W. Jones, 31 October

2006. At https://fas.org/irp/agency/dod/dtra/india.pdf, accessed on September 25, 2020.
16. S. Jaishankar, *The India Way - Strategies for an Uncertain World* (India: Harper Collins Publishers, 2020)
17. Hartmut Scharfe, *Education in Ancient India* (Leiden, The Netherlands: Brill, 2002), p. 8.
18. Radha Kumud Mookerji, *Ancient Indian Education* (Delhi: Motilal Banarsidass, 1969), p. xxxi.
19. Ibid.
20. For more on these invasions refer Stanley Lane-Poole, *Medieval India under Mohammedan Rule* (London: T Fisher Unwin Ltd, 1903).
21. For more understanding of the Vedas refer, Roshen Dalal, *The Vedas, An Introduction to Hinduism's Sacred Text* (Delhi: Penguin Books Ltd, 2014).
22. Upinder Singh, *A History of Ancient and Early Medieval India*, (Noida, India: Pearson, 2016), p. 259.
23. J. Duncan M. Derrett. "The Administration of Hindu Law by the British." *Comparative Studies in Society and History* 4, no. 1 (1961): 10-52. Accessed February 26, 2021, http://www.jstor.org/stable/177940.
24. Upinder Singh, n. 22, p. 195.
25. George K Tanham, *Indian Strategic Thought - An Interpretive Essay*, (RAND, USA, 1992), p. 50, at https://www.rand.org/content/dam/rand/pubs/reports/2007/R4207.pdf, accessed on February 17, 2020.
26. For detailed reading on the Upanishads refer, Paul Deussen, *The Philosophy of The Upanishads* (New York: Cosmo Classics, 2009).
27. As per Hindu religion God Brahmaa along with God Vishnu and God Shiva are responsible for creation, sustenance and destruction of the universe, Brahmaa being responsible for creation.
28. Upinder Singh, n. 22, p. 208.
29. Suren Navlakha, *Upanishads – Translation by Max Mueller* (London: Wordsworth Classics of World Literature, 2000), pp. xiii-xiv.
30. Kena Upanishad (2.1) as quoted by Upinder Singh, n. 22, p. 208.
31. Brihadaranyaka Upanishad (3.14.2-3) as quoted by Upinder Singh, n. 22, p. 209.
32. Paul Deussen, *The Philosophy of The Upanishads* (New York: Cosmo Classics, 2009), p. 39.
33. Suren Navlakha, n. 29, p. xxvi.
34. Ibid., p. xii.
35. Bhagavad Gita Ch. 3, shloka, 4-5. (Gorakhpur, India: Gita Press)
36. Ibid. Ch. 2, shloka 40-47.
37. Article by Raj Balkaran, A Walter Dorn, *Violence in the Valmiki Ramayana*, as cited in academic.oup.com site accessed on November 25, 2019.
38. Aitareya Brahmana I.14 as quoted by Sarva Daman Singh, *Ancient Indian Warfare with Special Reference to the Vedic Period* (Leiden: E.J. Brill Publications, 1965), p. 136.

39. Upinder Singh, *Political Violence in Ancient India*, (Cambridge: Harvard University Press, 2017), p. 60.
40. Kaushik Roy, *Hinduism and the Ethics of Warfare in South Asia from Antiquity to the Present* (Cambridge: Cambridge University Press, 2012), p. xiii.
41. AS Altekar, *State and Government in Ancient India,* (Delhi: Motilal Banarsidas Publishers, 1984), p. 97.
42. Ibid., p. 93.
43. Upinder Singh, n. 39, p. 76.
44. Mahabharata, 13.60.32–33, as quoted by Upinder Singh, n. 39, p. 77.
45. The Mahabharata, Vol XI Anusasana Parva, Section 61, translated by Pratap Chandra Roy, p. 66, available at https://www.holybooks.com/mahabharata-all-volumes-in-12-pdf-files/, accessed on February 12, 2021.
46. VR Ramchandra Dikshitar, *The Mauryan Polity* (Madras: Madras University Press, 1932), p. 91.
47. RN Dandekar, *A History of the Guptas* (Poona: Oriental Book Agency, 1941), p. 202.
48. AS Altekar, n. 41, p. 101.
49. Since Knowledge was transmitted orally, the teacher had the flexibility of situating his knowledge or its interpretation in the prevalent times so as to make it contemporary to society. This would not have been possible if this Knowledge was based on some rigid written text. This is corroborated by the fact that the Vedas or other sources of knowledge in India did not have a single source or author; knowledge kept on getting added or subtracted and remained contemporary. They represent knowledge acquired over a substantial period of time. For more on the education system and oral traditions of ancient India refer, Radha Kumud Mookerji, *Ancient Indian Education* (Delhi: Motilal Banarsidass, 1969).
50. Jawaharlal Nehru, Discovery of India (Delhi: Oxford University Press, 1994), p. 74.
51. Dr Arvind Gupta, and Professor Sven G. Holtsmark, 'Foreword', in Kanti Bajpai, Saira Basit and V. Krishnappa ed., *India's Grand Strategy: History, Theory, Cases,* (New Delhi: Routledge, 2014), p. x.
52. Ibid., p. 39.
53. Upinder Singh, n. 22, p. 65.
54. In the battle between Arjuna and Karna, Shri Krishna advises Arjuna to attack Karna when Karna was unarmed as he had got down from his chariot to extricate its wheel which was stuck in the ground. Similarly, he advises the Pandava prince Bhim to strike Duryodhana on his thighs with his mace; both these acts of the Pandava princes Arjuna and Bhim were against the ethics of war.
55. Torkel Brekke, 'The Indian Tradition', in James Turner Jhonson and Eric D Patterson, ed., *The Research Gate Companion to Military Ethics,* (Surrey, England: Ashgate Publishing Ltd., 2015), p. 422.
56. Upanishads as quoted by Sarvdaman Singh, *Ancient Indian Warfare with Special Reference to the Vedic Period* (Leiden: E.J. Brill Publications, 1965), p. 158.
57. Bimal Kanti Majumdar, *The Military System in Ancient India* (Calcutta: Firma K.L. Mukhopadhyay, 1960), p. 41.

58. Mahabharata as quoted by Sarvdaman Singh, *Ancient Indian Warfare with Special Reference to the Vedic Period* (Leiden: E.J. Brill Publications, 1965), pp. 161-162.
59. Upinder Singh, n. 39, p. 283.
60. Mahabharata as quoted by Sarvdaman Singh, n. 58, pp. 162.
61. Ramchandra Dikshitar, *War in Ancient India* (Madras: Macmillan and Company Limited, 1944), p. 5.
62. Mahabharata. 12.16.21; 12.69.4–5. as quoted by Upinder Singh, n. 22, p. 287.
63. Ramchandra Dikshitar, *War in Ancient India* (Madras: Macmillan and Company Limited, 1944), p. 59.
64. For more reading on the ways and means of kutayuddha, refer *Kautilya, Arthshastra, Book X, Chapter 3*, trans. R Shamasastry (Bangalore: Government Press, 1915), also refer the definition provided by Kaushik Roy, n. 35, p. xiii.
65. Kautilya, *Arthshastra, Book X, Chapter 3,* trans. R Shamasastry (Bangalore: Government Press, 1915), p. 525.
66. J.W.McCrindle, *Ancient India as Described by Megasthenes and Arrian*, (London: Trubner and Company, 1877), p.210, at https://wayback.archive-it.org/358/20060920132733/http://www.archive.org/details/AncientIndiaAsDescribedByMegasthenesAndArrian, accessed on September 17, 2020.
67. Upinder Singh, n. 22, p. 266.
68. Kaushik Roy, Warfare in Pre-British India, 1500 BCE to1740 CE (London: Routledge, Taylor and Francis Group, 2015), p. 32.
69. Ibid., p. 36.
70 Kajari Kamal (2018): Kautilya's Arthashastra: Indian Strategic Culture and Grand Strategic Preferences, *Journal of Defence Studies*, Vol. 12, No. 3, July-September 2018, pp. 27-54, available at https://idsa.in/jds/jds-12-3-2018-kautilya-arthashastra-kajari-kamal.
71. R Prsannan interviews Upinder Singh, "Ancient Indian rulers lost wars not because of non-violence but because of incompetent military", *The Week* (December 3, 2017) at https://www.theweek.in/theweek/leisure/ancient-indian-rulers-lost-wars-not-because-of-non-violence-but-incompetent-military.html, accessed on December 25, 2020.
72. Kaushik Roy, n. 68, p. 53.
73. Kaushik Roy, n. 40, p. 117.
74. Patrick Olivelli, *The Law Code of Manu* (Oxford: Oxford University Press, 2004), p. xvi.
75. Rachel E. Brule, *Women, Power and Property - The Paradox of Gender Equality Laws in India* (Cambridge: Cambridge University Press, 2020), pp. 59-60.
76. RN Dandekar, *A History of the Guptas* (Pune: Oriental Book Agency, 1941), p. 187.
77. Ibid., p. 49.
78. Upinder Singh, n. 39, p. 337.
79. Kaushik Roy, n. 40, p. 121.
80. Ibid., p. 129.
81. Ibid., p. 137.

82. Upinder Singh, n. 39, pp. 324-325.
83. Kaushik Roy, n. 68, p. 69.
84. Hermann Kulke and Dietmar Rothermund, *A History of India* (London: Routledge, Taylor and Francis Group, 2002), p. 153.
85. Kaushik Roy, n. 40, p. 144.
86. Ibid., p. 146.
87. Kaushik Roy, "Norms of War in Hinduism" in *World Religions and Norms of War*, ed. by Vesselin Popovski, Gregory M. Reichberg and Nicholas Turner (Tokyo: United Nations University Press, 2009), p. 42.
88. Kishori Sharan Lal, *Studies in Medieval Indian History* (Delhi: Ranjit Printers and Publishers, 1966), p. 121.
89. Stanley Lane-Poole, *Medieval India under Mohammedan Rule*(London: T Fisher Unwin Ltd, 1903). p. 50. Available online at https://www.rarebooksocietyofindia.org/book_archive/196174216674_10152591985846675.pdf
90. Jadunath Sarkar, Military History of India (Calcutta: MC Sarkar & Sons Pvt Ltd., 1960), pp. 33-35.
91. Kaushik Roy, n. 40, p. 171.
92. Ibid., pp. 170-171.
93. Rajat Dutta, "Indian History from Eighth to Eighteenth Centuries: Problems, Perspectives and Possibilities" in *Rethinking a Millennium – Perspectives on Indian History from the Eighth to the Eighteenth Century*, ed. by Rajat Dutta (Delhi: Aakar Books, 2008), p. 4.
94. Kishori Sharan Lal, n. 88, p. 114.
95. Ibid., pp. 118-119. KS Lal has explained the degeneration in the fighting capabilities because of the dogmatic approach that the caste system had attained, during this period.
96. Satish Chandra, History of Medieval India (Hyderabad: Orient Blackswan, 2007), p. 74.
97. PJ Marshall, The New Cambridge History of India II.2 (Cambridge: Cambridge University Press, 1987), p. 72.
98. Capt Raj Mohindra (Retd) IN, "When Italy opened its arms to Indian sailors" *The Hindu* (April 03, 2013) at https://www.thehindu.com/opinion/op-ed/when-italy-opened-its-arms-to-indian-sailors/article4573884, accessed on November 20, 2019
99. Torkel Brekke, n. 55, p. 423.
100. Shri Krishna had advised Arjun, the Pandava prince to carry out penance for acquiring power and celestial weapons for the Mahabharata war, much before the war was declared.
101. To read more about the history of these kings refer, Vincent A Smith, *The Early History of India* (London: Oxford University Press, 1924).
102. Pankaj Shah & Arshad Afjal Khan. "Bhoomi pujan of Ram temple symbolises second liberation day: PM Modi". *The Times of India,* (August 6, 2020) at https://timesofindia.indiatimes.com/city/lucknow/bhoomi-pujan-of-ram-temple-symbolises-second-liberation-day-modi/articleshow/77383097.cms, accessed on January 02, 2021.

4. Exploring India's Higher Defence Organisation and Civil-Military Relations

Quartered in snow, silent to remain. When the bugle calls, they shall rise and march again.

– 'Scroll of honour at the Siachen base camp'

The present governance structure as well as the structure of the military in India is a legacy of what it inherited from the British. The system of ministries and government departments and the staffing of these structures by the bureaucracy at the upper echelons is a continuation from the past. The Higher Defence Organisation (HDO) of India is also a relic from the past, but it has undergone major course-corrections first in 2001 when a Group of Ministers recommended significant changes in the management of defence, and second in 2019 with the creation of the post of Chief of Defence Staff (CDS) and Department of Military Affairs. The governance and military structures created by the British were for the sole purpose of consolidating their hold over India. The British Indian Army was the most important tool for enabling their rule. In both the World Wars the British extensively utilised the Indian Army for their military aims. Such was the importance of the Indian Army for the British Empire that "in December 1950, Attlee asked the Chief of the Imperial General Staff, Sir William Slim, how long it would take to create from the African colonies an army comparable in size and quality with the Indian Army".[1] The chapter will attempt to explore the Higher

Defence Organisation and Civil-Military Relations (CMR) of India as it evolved starting with the origin of the British Indian Army and trace the path that India followed in creating its present security architecture dealing with external security.

After independence the security institutions and structures that India created were largely influenced by two factors. First was the existing situation immediately after independence when the top hierarchy of the military was still manned by British officers and the civilian bureaucracy was comfortable with the British governance system; the second important factor was the thought process of the Indian political leaders after independence. India's security structure (dealing with external security), its HDO and its CMR emerged in this environment. Immediately after independence the country faced security challenges and thereafter India has had no respite on the external security front having fought major wars in 1947-48, 1962, 1965, 1971, 1999 and a major stand-off with China in 2020 which is still ongoing. Despite this, a major review of its security structure happened only in 2001. Apart from understanding the evolution of India's HDO and CMR, its path post-independence will also be analysed against the lessons of its strategic culture that has emerged in the previous chapter.

Evolution of the British Indian Army and its Control Structure

On January 11, 1613 the Mughal Emperor Jahangir gave permission to Captain Best, a representative of the East India Company then known as 'The Company of Merchants of London trading unto the East Indies' to start a factory at Surat. This was the beginning of British activity in India and the origin of the Bombay Presidency of the British. A trading centre was established at Masulipatam in 1625, which was later shifted to Armegaon where fortifications were also built. In 1634 Emperor Shah Jahan permitted the establishment of factories in Bengal and the construction of a fort at Piplee. Subsequently, the company acquired Madras in 1640 and built a fort 'Fort St George' there. This was the origin of the Madras Presidency.

These business establishments were guarded by European and Indian chowkidars (guards).

In 1662 the island of Bombay was handed over to King Charles II of England by the Portuguese king, as marriage settlement. The King maintained a garrison of soldiers on the island and it was governed by a Governor of the British Empire. The relations between the East India Company president who resided at Surat and the Governor became strained and also due to the island being non-profitable, on March 27, 1668, the King handed over the island of Bombay along with the garrison of soldiers to the Company. The garrison consisted of two gunners, 21 pieces of cannon, five officers and 193 non-commissioned officers and men.[2] This was the largest body of troops that the Company had and was the origin of the British Indian Army. In 1683 it was augmented by enrolling two companies of Rajputs each consisting of 100 men. In 1696 Fort William was constructed at Calcutta and it remained the headquarters of the army for the next 200 years. In 1708 the Company came to be known as the East India Company. The Company then formed three independent Presidencies at Calcutta, Bombay and Madras and the president of each also became the Commander-in-Chief of the military forces of the Presidencies. He was directly responsible to the directors of the company in England. In 1748, the post of Commander-in-Chief for all the Company's forces in India was created. His responsibility was co-ordination between the three Presidential armies whenever the need arose. In 1754 the Mutiny Act was passed by the British Parliament and it became the basis of military discipline in British India. It permitted British army regiments to be sent to India and also decreed that the British army officers were to be senior to the same ranking officers employed by the East India Company in India. This subsequently became a source of grievance between the British officers. This was the period when the military created by the British in India got modelled on the European pattern in the form of companies led by a company commander.[3] In 1757 the British won a decisive victory over the Nawab of Bengal and his French supporters at Plassey. In 1765 Robert Clive organised the Bengal army into three brigades, each commanded by a colonel and consisting of companies of artillery and infantry. By this period the East India Company had a standing army comprising European and Indian regulars. In the next 40 years the Company expanded its territorial acquisitions over most part of India. The areas of present-day Uttar Pradesh, Madhya Pradesh, Haryana and Punjab were controlled by the Bengal Presidency. As per Heathcote, during this period discontent in the officer class over pay and allowances was not uncommon and there were instances when officers resigned their commission over it.[4]

In 1773, the British Parliament passed the Regulating Act, by which the post of Governor General was created for India. He was to reside at Calcutta and the Presidencies of Bombay and Madras also came under his control. Warren Hastings was appointed as the first Governor General in 1774 and all the three presidency armies came under his control. He had a council of four members and the Commander-in-Chief was part of this council. There emerged opposing factions within the Council and the Governor General was not able to overrule majority decisions. Meanwhile at the Madras Presidency, a problem emerged between Governor Pigot and his Commander-in-Chief Fletcher which led to the dismissal and arrest of Fletcher by the Governor. Pigot was subsequently arrested by the acting C-in-C, Col. Stuart. Both Pigot and Fletcher died before the issue could be resolved from Britain. Pigot was replaced by Lord Macartney and subsequently Stuart became his C-in-C. The two had a fallout which led to the dismissal of Stuart by Macartney.[5] This was an indication that all was not well in the civil-military setup that the British had created and this was only exacerbated by the differences between the British and the Company's officers and soldiers.

In 1784 the India Act was passed which increased the powers of the Governor General and created a Board of Control in London comprising a secretary of state and five other members, whose decisions were binding on the Governor General.[6] This was the beginning of the intervention of the British Government in the affairs of the Company. In 1776 a Military Department was created to help the Governor General, exercise control over the armies. It was headed by a military member who was a military officer and dealt with matters concerning expenditure, pay and pensions, recruitment and other administrative issues. The military member was junior to the C-in-C and worked as an interface between him and the Governor General. This arrangement was created in all the three Presidencies. Mirroring this development, a Military Department was also created in the Company's office in London which coordinated with the military department of the three Presidencies.

By 1805 Sir John Cradock took over as the new C-in-C in Madras. In order to smarten up his army he created regulations banning personal ornaments and symbols which the sepoys had earlier worn; in addition, he also ordered trimming of moustaches and beards. Heathcote says that he tried to model the Indian soldiers in the British pattern. This was the period when Christian missionaries in India were involved in propagating their religion. Heathcote further adds that during the same period Tipu Sultan had indulged in forceful conversion of his subjects. This act of John Cradock was seen as an act of trying to impose the Christian religion and that compounded Tipu's earlier behaviour. In 1806, in Vellore, the sepoys refused to wear the new dress and in July 1806 mutiny broke out over religion. Sepoy mutinies had happened earlier too but they were over military grievances of pay and conditions of service. In this mutiny approximately 500-600 sepoys were killed.[7] John Cradock was recalled to Britain after this incident and activities of Christian missionaries were discouraged.

By 1823 the Company rapidly expanded the British Indian army to keep pace with its territorial gains in India. Sind was controlled by the Bombay Presidency. The Bengal and Madras Presidencies had eight regiments of cavalry each and the Bombay Presidency had two. The Bengal, Madras and Bombay Presidencies had 60, 54 and 24 battalions respectively. By 1824 the regiments became corps and the battalions became regiments.[8] The next major changes in the control structure of the military happened by the Charter Act of 1833. The administration of India was to be headed by a Governor-General in Council which would be responsible for the entire civil and military administration of India.

The C-in-C of Bengal became the C-in-C of all the British forces in India. By this act, four independent Presidencies were created; the two at Bombay and Madras were to have a Governor and a council of three members. A Military member, who was an army officer, was made part of this council and his responsibility was to advise the Governor on matters related to the army as the C-in-C was generally away on campaigns. The other two new Presidencies to be created were Agra and Bengal. The act was modified in 1835 and Agra came to be headed by a Lt. Governor; the Governor-General of India continued to function as the governor of Bengal. By 1857 a Punjab Frontier Force was created under the Bengal Presidency to look after Punjab area.

The singular event that changed the character of the British rule and the British Indian Army was the rebellion by the Indian soldiers against their British masters in 1857, also known as the sepoy mutiny.[9] It was a brutal massacre on both sides. An after-effect of this rebellion was the India Act enacted by the British Parliament in August 1858, by which the governance of India was taken over from the East India Company by the British government. The military of the East India Company became the military of the British Empire. The representative of the British government in India became the Governor General also known as the Viceroy. He was now the head of the government in India. The C-in-C of Bengal became the C-in-C of all India military forces. He had an army headquarter to support him in his functioning. The Council Act of 1861 created a council of five members to assist the Governor General in his functioning. The C-in-C was an extraordinary member of this council. The Military member who was part of the earlier Governor's Council continued to be part of the new council and in addition the Military department was placed under him. In 1864 the military accounts department of the three Presidencies were merged into the Military department of the Governor General of India. By 1886 the various military departments of the Presidencies were also merged into the military department of the Government of India. In 1896 the Presidential armies were abolished; the unified British Indian Army was divided into four commands of Punjab, Bengal, Madras and Bombay. Each of them was placed under the command of a Lieutenant General. The Military department of the Governor General was responsible for all the four commands. The Military Member in charge of the military department functioned directly under the Governor General. The departments of ordinance, accounts, transport and supply were handled by the military department and the Military Member became the link between the Viceroy and the C-in-C with all proposals of the C-in-C being routed through him.[10] This was the nascent beginning of the present Ministry of Defence.

Kitchener took over as C-in-C in 1902. He brought out several reforms in the army which erased the hangovers of the presidential armies and shaped the unified Indian army. Meanwhile the military department had increased its importance and power and the military member, though junior to the C-in-C, decided on matters related to the military especially logistics, independently of the C-in-C. Kitchener recommended the abolishing of the military member and the military department and its amalgamation into army headquarter. He suggested that the C-in-C should be the sole advisor to the Viceroy on military matters. Viceroy Curzon objected to these proposals as he wanted to have the freedom of an alternate opinion on military matters apart from the C-in-C. This is referred to as the Curzon-Kitchener dispute. The British government sided with Kitchener and the military department was split into two, with an army department (comprising personnel, mobilisation and logistics) functioning under the C-in-C and a military supply department under a military officer of the rank of Major General. Curzon resigned in 1905 and in 1909, the military supply department was subsumed in the army department and the post of the military member was abolished. The C-in-C now became all powerful with him being the only military advisor in the Viceroy's council. He wore two hats; he was the C-in-C as well as the army member in charge of the army department. The role of the C-in-C was an operational role and the role of the army member was the role of a functionary of the Government of India. The staff of the army department consisted of a secretary, who like the other departments was a secretary of the

Government of India. This post of the secretary of the army department was held by an army officer of the rank of Major-General. A military finance department was created with the accounts department of the military placed under it; it was made responsible for all the financial matters of the military. The military finance department was placed under a Financial Adviser who functioned under the Finance Member of the Viceroy's Executive Council. It also functioned in conjunction with the army department.

The secretaries of the Government of India used to brief the Viceroy. The army secretary was a military officer junior to the C-in-C. In 1919 Esher Committee was set up to suggest reforms in the British Indian Army after the First World War. The committee recommended that the post of the army secretary should be tenanted by a civilian officer as in the current arrangement two military officers were briefing the Viceroy; the C-in-C as well as the army secretary. The proposal was accepted and from 1921 the army secretary post was held by a civil officer functioning under the C-in-C. Esher committee also recommended merging the army headquarters and the army department; however, this proposal was not accepted as it was contended that both the departments were working under the C-in-C, hence coordination between the two was achieved. In 1933 the army department became the defence department and the army secretary designation was changed to defence secretary. This army department was responsible to deal with the affairs of the Royal Indian Navy (RIN) and the Royal Indian Air Force (RIAF) also. Flag officer Commanding (FOC) was the chief of the RIN and Air Officer Commanding (AOC) was the chief of the RIAF. Both AOC and FOC were subordinate to the C-in-C. In 1942 the responsibilities of the C-in-C were again split. He was made responsible for war and became the War Member in the Viceroy's Council. The post of Defence Member was recreated as part of the Viceroy's Council, and it was held by an Indian, Sir Feroze Khan Noon. The setup of the Viceroy's Council was back to what existed before the Curzon-Kitchener dispute except that the military member was now known as the defence member and he was an Indian. In 1946 an interim government of Indians took over, with

Jawaharlal Nehru as Vice-President. Sardar Baldev Singh became the defence member; the post of war member was abolished and the C-in-C was placed under the defence member. India gained independence on August 15, 1947 with this setup of the Indian military and its control structure.

Analysis of British institutions – CMR in British India

The British had a very uneasy relationship with India. Invaders before them had either plundered India and went back or they had chosen India as their home and amalgamated into the Indian society. The Britishers were different, they did neither. They exploited and stayed on to continue doing so.[11] Indian culture was completely different from theirs. Their understanding of Indian society was from a prism of their own. All institutions built by the British and actions taken by them, either in India or in Britain affecting India, were with the singular aim of consolidating their hold on one of their most profitable colonies. Jon Wilson in *India Conquered* says that "the British imperial regime in India was ruled by doubt and anxiety from beginning to end. The institutions, mistaken as means of effective power were ad hoc measures to assuage British fear".[12] The economic and cultural exploitation of India by the British has been vividly described by Shashi Tharoor in his book *An Era of Darkness.*[13]

Military muscle was initially acquired by the British traders as a means of protection, which expanded into the ability to influence battle between local kings. This military muscle was then subsequently enhanced to develop a capability to acquire territories through force and then the military power to win over a sub-continent. The end result was that a trading company of Britain was able to acquire a state for itself. The institutions that the British developed were for the sole purpose of consolidating their power and they evolved from their knowledge of their own culture and society. At the top of the governmental hierarchy was the office of the governor and on the military side it was the C-in-C. Throughout the British rule in India the relationship between the two generally remained frayed. In the Madras Presidency the governor,

Pigot sacked his C-in-C, Fletcher and put him under house arrest. He himself was put under arrest by the next acting C-in-C, Stuart. Both died in prison. General Stuart was sacked by another governor, Lord Macartney. In the Bengal Presidency Harry Velrest who was Governor General Clive's successor, had a fall out with General Richard Smith. Another governor Lord Macartney almost created an armed conflict between the Company's army and the British troops, who also served with the Company. Governor Hastings and his C-in-C, Barker had an uneasy relationship, with both trying to undercut each other's authority.[14] However inspite of differences between the governors and the C-in-Cs, no C-in-C tried to seize overall control of the administration; as per G.J. Bryant this was because "they all wished to return to Britain as respectable members of the society".[15] The dispute between them was overcome by making the Governor General all powerful; however the Curzon-Kitchener dispute that happened in 1905 demonstrated that the Governor and the C-in-C never reconciled with each other. This was the legacy that India inherited on independence.

Security structure post-independence – Evolution

After India became independent the post of the defence member became the Defence Minister and the defence department became the Ministry of Defence (MoD). The C-in-C of British era was now only the commander of the army, the institution that was part of the government was the MoD. The FOC Navy and AOC Air Force were made independent commanders of their service with their own headquarters and responsible directly to the Defence Minister. Like all other ministries of the government the functioning of the MoD became the responsibility of the Secretary (Defence Secretary). During this period Lord Ismay was the Chief of Staff to the Governor General in India. He was entrusted with role of devising a Higher Defence Organisation (HDO). On his suggestions a series of committees were set up to manage defence. At the apex was the Defence Committee of the Cabinet (DCC), comprising the Prime Minister (who also held the External Affairs portfolio), Home Minister, Defence Minister and

Minister for Information and Broadcasting. The three Service Chiefs and the Defence Secretary were required to attend all the meetings of the DCC and therefore inspite of not formally being a member of it the Service Chiefs were accountable and had access to the highest governmental decision-making body on national defence. The DCC was provided secretarial services by the Military Wing headed by Joint Secretary (JS) (Military) which functioned under the Cabinet Secretary. However, later this was shifted to the MoD to function under the Defence Secretary.

At the level of the Defence Minister was the Defence Minister's Committee (DMC), with him as the chairman and the three Service Chiefs, Defence Secretary and Financial Advisor of the MoD as member. The DMC was effectively the executive arm of the government responsible for managing the country's defence. Then there was the Chiefs of Staff Committee (COSC) comprising the three Service Chiefs. The chairmanship of the COSC was rotational with the Service Chief who had been longest in the committee becoming its chairman. During this period the Army Chief was a four-star rank while the other two Service Chiefs were three-star. This was a legacy of the British rule and was subsequently changed to all three holding four-star ranks. The responsibility of the COSC was inter-service co-ordination. Two sub-committees were created to service the COSC, the Joint Planning Committee (JPC) and the Joint Intelligence Committee (JIC). The JPC was to undertake joint military planning for the COSC with a staff of its own, which never materialised. The JIC was to provide the COSC and the JPC with intelligence on issues that affected national security. The JIC was chaired by a Joint Secretary from the Ministry of External Affairs and had members from MoD and MHA besides the directors of intelligence of the three services. Apart from these two committees, Joint Training Committee and Inter-Service Equipment Policy Committee were also constituted.

The authority of the service chiefs to attend the DCC meetings was contested by the then Defence Secretary HM Patel. The explanation given was that the service chiefs then were British officers and they should not be attending meetings on issues concerning India's defence. His objection was accepted and since then the access of the service chiefs was restricted to only the DMC.[16] This provision was never revoked even when Indians took over as service chiefs. HM Patel was associated with the partition of the armed forces and the events confirm that he had more say on matters of defence than the service chiefs. The service chiefs at the onset of independence were British officers and therefore the political leaders of that time could get inputs only on the civil aspect of the civil military equation from Indians. Subsequent history has proved that the inputs of the Defence Secretary to prevent the Service Chiefs from attending the DCC, was not in the best security interests of the country. The Service Chiefs were higher in protocol to all the secretaries which changed in 1963, when the Cabinet Secretary was made higher in protocol than the service chiefs. Ayesha Ray in *The Soldier and the State* opines that "the recommendations of the COSC were subject to approval or rejection by a small number of officials in the MoD, therefore the COSC exercised very little powers".[17]

Defence Secretary HM Patel on 27 May 1952 wrote to the Chairman COSC General KM Cariappa about a proposal to designate the service headquarters as attached offices of the MoD, and sought his response. Inspite of Gen Cariappa expressing strong objections to it and seeking a discussion on the proposal, on July 07, 1952 the Cabinet Secretariat informed him that the govt had approved the proposal. The service headquarters became attached offices and they were now responsible only for providing technical inputs as required from them and for implementing policies issued by the MoD. In 1955 the nomenclature of C-in-C for the service chiefs was changed to Chiefs of Staff. In 1961, the Allocation of Business (AoB) / Transaction of Business (ToB) Rules were promulgated. As per these rules all the businesses of the Government of India were to be transacted by various ministries and departments. These ministries were to function under an elected Minister who was the overall incharge of the ministry. Below the minister the functions of each ministry was to be transacted by the Secretary of that ministry; for the MoD it was the Defence Secretary. The three services were not given any direct responsibility in these rules and they were to function as attached offices of the MoD. Their access to the government was only through the MoD. The military which as per Kautilya's *Arthshastra* is one of the seven elements of sovereignty (others being king, minister, country, treasury, fort and friends) of the state, was effectively separated from the executive arm of the government. Thus, largely, the security structure that independent India started functioning with was whatever it inherited from the British with additional bureaucratic supervision thrown in over the military.

Analysis of the post-independence (upto 1962) security structure

Indian leaders before independence had seen the military and the Indian Civil Service furthering the interests of the British Empire. Jawaharlal Nehru in his book *The Discovery of India* called the ICS a close and well-knit corporation, "they ran India, they were India and anything that was harmful to their interests must of necessity be injurious to India".[18] India inherited such structures, which had been fashioned by the British for their basic purpose of ruling India. The purpose of the military was to deal with any uprising within the country and to aid the British in fighting their wars. After independence both these objectives had changed; however, the Indian leaders largely continued with the security structure that they had inherited. A big reason for this was that the top echelon of the military that India inherited at independence was still British, and Indian leaders did not have the benefit of genuine Indian advice. During a DCC meeting on December 20, 1947, during the on-going conflict with Pakistan, the Prime Minister, Jawaharlal Nehru suggested that if militarily required, India should strike deep inside Pakistan. This was immediately vetoed by Governor General Mountbatten and the British generals.[19] This demonstrates that the advice that the Indian leaders got during this period from the British military brass working for India, was not always in Indian interests. There was another important factor which influenced decision making. Nehru in *The Discovery of India* accepts that the Congress adhered to the principle of non-violence in its struggle for independence, but he adds that the requirement of the military for external defence and internal disorder was never questioned. However, he acknowledges that "non-violence did have a powerful effect on our thinking in many ways and it made the Congress favour disarmament and a peaceful solution of all international, as well as national disputes".[20] History shows that this thought process may have influenced his strategic decisions as the Prime Minister of India.

Patrick Blackett was a British experimental physicist who won the Noble prize for physics in 1948. He was also the scientific adviser to many generals during the Second World War. Pandit Nehru met him in January 1947 and sought his help "to Indianize the military, meaning both its command structure and its weapons production and supply". Robert S. Anderson quotes Blackett (interview given in 1967) about the deep influence which the British government system had on Indians;

> "Indian officials and advisors were thinking purely from a Whitehall (British governance system) angle. There was an appalling psychological dependence on every word that Whitehall speaks. I understand in the beginning, in 1948, there was very little time and experience to think for yourself. But a great many of your problems are due to imitative adoption of Whitehall habits."[21]

The above quote illustrates the enormous influence which 150-200 years of colonialism had on the Indian thinking. It had negated 3000-4000 years of Indian strategic culture. The effect of this negation was the most on the Indian security structure. Blackett made another comment on the Indian thought process of that time; "he perceived an Indian predisposition to adopting the solutions developed elsewhere to problems which were not theirs".[22] As per Anderson, Blackett had advised Nehru to prepare India's military to fight an adversary of the size of Pakistan and not build its capability for fighting Russia or a western power, he did not consider China in his calculations.[23]

Jawaharlal Nehru had deep knowledge of Indian history as revealed in his book *The Discovery of India*, therefore the importance of the military for the protection of the state was not lost on him; but his conditioning in non-violence and his idealistic approach to geopolitics perhaps shaped his outlook in not attempting to fully realise the military potential of India. As per Jaswant Singh, India's former defence minister, the perfect complement to Jawaharlal Nehru's idealist approach to geopolitical affairs was Sardar Vallabhbhai Patel's realist approach.[24] It ensured Indian success while dealing with the remnants of the princely states in India, like Junagadh and Hyderabad. Inspite of the country dealing with many socio-economic problems during this period the inability of India to maintain control over entire Jammu and Kashmir by liberating its parts from Pakistani occupation should have been a reality check for India, about the importance of the military for the nation. However, the Kashmir war was followed by the military's success in Hyderabad, and Junagadh. This may have led the Indian leaders to believe that the military capability that India had, was all that the nation needed for its security. Jawaharlal Nehru in one of his letters to Blackett (written in September 1948), while thanking him for his contributions to India, praised the Indian army for its actions in Hyderabad and expressed the opinion that war risk over Kashmir had subsided and there was no possibility of a war with Pakistan.[25]

In 1950 the Korean crisis happened. Jawaharlal Nehru throughout maintained a non-aligned stand during the crisis. He tried to mediate between the USA and USSR to resolve the crisis. Throughout this period, he was a very vocal supporter for the recognition of PRC as the legitimate government of China and its admission to the United Nations.[26] The diplomatic aims of India during this period were without any corresponding support of national power especially military power. This absence of requisite military power became glaringly obvious when the Chinese military entered Tibet. As per Lezlee Brown Halper and Stefan Halper, the Indian Prime Minister had hoped that the Chinese would resolve their problems with the Tibetans peacefully, like he had hoped for a peaceful resolution of the Korean crisis. After the Chinese invasion of Tibet, Pandit Nehru was faced with a fait accompli for which he had no solution. The Indian political and bureaucratic system had not prepared its military to provide options for national strategic interests; consequently "India did not have the capacity to resist the Chinese invasion or to provide effective assistance to the Tibetans".[27] Patel's views on this development expressed to the foreign secretary were "the Chinese advance into Tibet upsets all our security calculations. Hitherto, the danger to India on its land frontiers has always come from the North-West. Throughout our history we have concentrated our armed might in that region. For the first time, a serious danger is now developing on the North and North-East side".[28] Inspite of such adverse strategic occurrences for India's security, no efforts were taken to reassess the country's security structure and the role of its armed forces in the strategic decision making process of the country. In fact, the opposite happened, in 1952 the service headquarters were designated as attached offices of the government, thereby isolating them from the security evaluation and decision-making structure of the country. The AoB and ToB rules of 1961 indicated a classical bureaucratic approach to statecraft and kept the most important organ of the state, its military, out of the government decision making structure.

International relations and diplomacy were handled by the diplomatic corps through the system of ambassadors and their inputs to the Prime Minister; however, the military chiefs could access the political leadership only when they were consulted by the government which was usually only in case of contingencies, and hence the experts of national security were outside the Indian decision making and consulting process. This is because, as brought out earlier, the Service Chiefs had no access to the DCC and the Service headquarters had become attached offices of the MoD and hence could provide inputs only when asked for. Assessing the Chinese threat, Indian diplomacy moved and tried to secure Indian interests by entering into relevant treaties with Nepal, Sikkim and Bhutan[29]; but India immediately after independence did not create a security structure which could do the same to enable its military to face future national security requirements.

The only institution for external security was the MoD. India did not have an institution or a structure which could analyse the country's security environment and provide strategic solutions or options to the government. The MoD neither had the capability or the expertise for it. Ayesha Ray in her book *The Soldier and the State in India* sums up the pre 1962 (India China war) period as India having an "isolated military and a dysfunctional defence policy".[30] Shiv Kunal Verma has been quoted by Anit Mukherjee in his analyses of India's CMR in *The Absent Dialogue* stating that "Nehru's biggest failing was the virtual destruction of his own military thanks to his deep rooted insecurities".[31] Shiv Kunal Verma may not be totally correct in blaming the first Prime Minister of India for the path that India chose for its military. The responsibility will have to be of the entire political class of that period for the path that India followed.

India followed a colonial structure and forgot its strategic culture where the security of the state was the most important function of its ruler and the enabler of this responsibility was the military. As per India's strategic culture the two most important functions of the state were protection of its people and their welfare. They both are related and dependent on each other and one is not at the cost of the other. Late K Subrahmanyam in his introduction for Jaswant Singh's book *Defending India* has stressed that "security, stability and development are symbiotically related and have to be addressed as an integral whole".[32] Every tool that the state uses, including diplomacy, is for the achievement of these two objectives. That the Indian state failed to follow its strategic culture was evident in its lack of military preparation to face the Chinese threat and consequently its defeat in 1962 by the Chinese.

The debacle of 1962

Indian leaders' reluctance to build up the military power of India and to create security structures which could fulfil the country's requirements led to it not having military options for the strategic problems that it faced. It is not that this became evident only after the Chinese invasion of Tibet; India had failed to reach a solution for the

Pakistani occupation of Jammu and Kashmir which was essentially a military problem caused by forced occupation of its parts by Pakistani forces. Chinese aggression in Tibet exacerbated the threats that India faced and this, coupled with a hostile Pakistan, presented a security dilemma to the Indian state right after its independence. By 1959 China had refused to accept the McMohan line as a boundary between India and China; a boundary which got created essentially in 1950 with the Chinese invasion of Tibet. In 1959-60, Army headquarters presented to defence minister, Krishna Menon, an assessment that unless the army was considerably upgraded both in terms of men and material, India would not be able to face Chinese aggression. The army chief Gen Thimayya, on not getting a suitable response from the Defence Minister, broached the topic with the Prime Minister. The Defence Minister on learning about it castigated the army chief; this led to Gen Thimayya sending in his resignation to the Prime Minister, which he subsequently withdrew on being persuaded by him.[33] Professional military advice was not accepted by the Defence Minister and consequently an under prepared army faced the Chinese aggression in 1962. To deal with the 1962 crisis an Emergency Committee of the Cabinet (ECC) comprising the Prime Minister, Defence Minister, Home Minister, Finance Minister and Foreign Minister was created. The ECC based its decisions on inputs from a Committee of Secretaries consisting of Cabinet Secretary and Secretaries of Defence, Finance, Home and Foreign Affairs. The Committee of Secretaries obtained its inputs from senior military officers who were called by them for briefing about the progress of war.[34] That the ECC in the initial period of the war obtained its inputs from the Committee of Secretaries rather than the Service Chiefs themselves points to the fact that 150-200 years of colonisation had triumphed 4000 years of strategic culture to create a situation where professional military advice could not have been more distanced from the executive head of the nation.

The 1962 debacle led to the removal of the Defence Minister and the retirements of the Army Chief and the Defence Secretary. The debacle cannot be viewed only as a result of individual failures, instead it was failure of a security structure where professional advice was sought by the executive element of the government only during execution of war. The defeat of 1962 did not lead to any major changes in the security set-up of India. The control of JIC was shifted from the COSC to the Cabinet Secretariat. "There were no operational or hierarchical changes which could strengthen the decision-making apparatus of the Indian Higher Defence Organisation"[35]. The Prime Minister, Jawaharlal Nehru took over the responsibilities of defence on November 01, 1962 and started the practice of holding a meeting with the service chiefs and the various secretaries to monitor the war.[36] YB Chavan who became the new Defence Minister after Krishna Menon continued with Nehru's practice. With his adept handling of the Defence Ministry, he was able to win over the confidence of the military as well as the bureaucracy. The debacle of 1962 however led to major expansion, logistical improvements and modernisation of the military. The wars of 1965 and 1971 were fought with the same structure but with much better coordination. The Prime Ministers of India during the wars of 1965 and 1971 interacted directly with the military leadership inspite of there being no organisational structure enabling such an interaction. An issue which created a mistrust in the political structure about the military was the possibility of the military's intervention in the functioning of the government especially after the military coup in Pakistan in 1958.

Spectre of Military Intervention

As per western theories of Civil Military Relations (CMR), one of the basic questions of CMR was how to prevent the military from interfering in the administration of the state.[37] As brought out by Peter Feaver, protection from the military is the foundation of the Civil Military construct. In India's case as argued by Steven I Wilkinson in his *Book Army and Nation*, the military's propensity to interfere in the State's functioning was a given because of the structure of the Indian Army.[38] The inferences of these studies were largely based on western societies.[39] This issue was examined in depth in the previous chapter based on a study of the Strategic Culture of India. It was found that because of the way in which India's strategic culture evolved, the dharma of the military as an instrument of the state was only the protection of the state; it had no other role. This is backed by almost 4000 years of strategic culture and military history. India's military did not need a lesson in being non-interfering in the administrative affairs of the state; to use hyperbole it can be said that it is steeped in its genes. But did India's policy makers take note of this while framing institutions and policies? India forgot its past and tried to learn every concept and idea from the West.

R Chandrasekhar in his book on the CMR of India mentions that in January 1961 when Krishna Menon was the Defence Minister, the then Chief of Army Staff (COAS) Gen Thimayya ordered the movement of a brigade from Ambala to Delhi which was reported as a coup attempt and the movement of the brigade had to be cancelled.[40] Lt Gen Harbaksh Singh in his memoirs *In the Line of Duty – A Soldier Remembers*, recalls that in June 1964, he was slated to be posted as Army Commander of Eastern Army Command which was changed to Western Army Command. The reason as per him for this was that the MoD suspected that the COAS Gen Chaudhuri and Army Commander, Western Army Command Lt Gen SJ Manekshaw were planning a coup against the government.[41] In March 1966, Defence Minister YB Chavan, on being directed by the Prime Minister Smt Indira Gandhi, had a detailed discussion with the COAS Gen Chaudhuri on the circumstances in which the army can try to seize power from the civil authority.[42] The apprehension then was that the President may order the army to do so; the COAS in his discussions with the Defence Minister had denied about such a possibility by the Indian Army. In January 2012, two army units were slated to move towards Delhi as part of an army exercise, reportedly at the behest of the COAS Gen VK Singh. This was reported by the agencies to the government as an attempt for military coup. The Defence Secretary met the Director General of Military Operations (DGMO) and told him to stop the movement of the units, which was followed by the army.[43] The incident was reported by the Indian Express as an event which spooked the civil establishment at New Delhi.

The bogey of a military coup has been consistently played up by the 'agencies' and this has resulted in a phobia being created in the minds of the politicians against the military. Since independence the bureaucracy has kept itself between the military and the political leadership and this persistent fear of military coup helps in maintaining this divide and preventing the integration of the military with the government. A recent work on the subject is by Steven I. Wilkinson.

Wilkinson in his book *Army and the Nation* has attempted to understand as to why the Indian military did not interfere in the governments functioning whereas in Pakistan military coups happened. He starts with the premise that because the Indian army was ethnically structured it was very prone to indulging in military coups. He bases this argument, on studies by Morris Janowitz and Horowitz; their inference being "armies with high internal cohesion will have greater capacity to intervene in domestic politics".[44] He concludes by accepting that inspite of India not changing its military structure substantially, the Indian military has stayed away from interfering in the state's administration and he credits the CMR of India, broad based character of the Congress party, reorganisation of Indian states on linguistic bases, caste based reservations, and many other factors, for preventing military coups.[45] He does not provide a convincing answer to his fundamental question. The foundational argument of the book utilises theories which are derived by studies conducted in different parts of the world and they are superimposed on the Indian society to draw the conclusion that the Indian military because of being structured along ethnic lines by the British, should have also interfered in the states functioning, as in Pakistan.[46] Therefore his basic postulate that the Indian military should have been prone to coups because of its structure is questionable. It completely ignores India's own 4000-5000 years of strategic culture and the shaping that has resulted from it as covered in the previous chapter. There is a requirement for the political system of the country to understand the strategic culture of India. The military is one of the finest institutions of the Indian State and is not a British creation but a legacy of almost four millennia of strategic culture and military ethos beginning from the Vedic period. India needs to understand its inherent strength and utilise it in building up its institutions. India never attempted a complete overhaul of its defence set-up that it inherited from the British; however, some changes in the structure were attempted.

Attempts for Change

In 1966 an Administrative Reforms Commission (ARC) was setup by the Government of India under the chairmanship of Mr Morarji Desai (a prominent leader of the Congress Party and a Member of Parliament), to look into the aspects of administrative reforms. This Commission formed two teams to look into defence issues one headed by Nawab Ali Yavar Jung (a diplomat) and the second by Shri SN Mishra (leader of the Congress party and Member of Parliament). The Ali Yavar Jung committee brought out that "the subordination of the military to the civil power should be in political and not bureaucratic sense".[47] The Mishra committee supported this view and stated that "the principle of civilian control over the Services should not be civil servants' control but political control".[48] One of the recommendations of the first ARC which could have impacted the three services was as follows:

> "The heads of non-secretariat organizations which are integrated with the Secretariat should function as the principal advisers to the Government in the respective areas and should enjoy a status appropriate to the nature of their duties and responsibilities. They may retain their present designations. It is not necessary to confer on them a formal ex-officio Secretariat status."[49]

As per this recommendation the three Service Chiefs while retaining their designations could have become the principal advisers to the government for defence, however the three service-headquarters were already designated as attached offices of the MoD and hence as per bureaucratic interpretations, this recommendation did not apply to the military. The committee also recommended the creation of the post of Chief of Defence Staff (CDS), however there were disagreements between the various members on this.

The apex decision making body on defence matters, the Defence Committee of the Cabinet (DCC) had changed into the Emergency Committee of the Cabinet (ECC) during the 1962 India - China conflict. After the recommendations of the first ARC, a new Cabinet Committee on Political Affairs (CCPA) was created in 1969. It had the Prime Minister as its chairman and included the Defence Minister, Home Minister, Finance Minister and the External Affairs Minister. After the establishment of the CCPA, the ECC ceased to exist. The CCPA became the highest body to deal with national security issues. The Service Chiefs had no representation in the CCPA. In fact, earlier in 1963 the Cabinet Secretary was elevated to a higher status than the Service Chiefs. Four thousand years of strategic culture of India was ignored wherein the military was the most important instrument of the state, directly controlled by the highest administrator of the state – the king; and an intermediary in the form of bureaucracy was created between the military and the political decision-making authority of the country. The effect was that the political authority did not have the benefit of direct strategic advice on issues facing the country. The sphere of India's strategic thought and international relations were dominated by diplomacy and did not have the benefit of military inputs and advice. This was in a country where 1700 years ago the Gupta Empire had integrated military and diplomacy to create a powerful instrument of the state for strategic decision making. The military was consulted during crisis, in 1965 the Prime Minister directly interacted with the military and similarly in 1971 the Prime Minister regularly interacted with the Service Chiefs and accepted their advice; but this was personality based and not institutionalised as no institution for such an interaction existed.

An organisation called Defence Planning Staff (DPS) headed by Director General Defence Planning Staff (DGDPS) was created in 1986 to assist the Chiefs of Staff Committee (COSC) in its functioning. It was an inter-ministerial organisation with representatives of MoD, Defence Finance, Ministry of External Affairs (MEA) and Defence Research and Development Organisation (DRDO). The DGDPS was a Lieutenant General rank officer with the post being held by the three Services in rotation. The function of the DPS was to carry out threat assessment and analysis, evolve military aims, formulate joint operations concept, recommend balanced force levels to achieve military aims, joint training and joint logistics management, coordinate 15/20 years perspective plans and closely interact with defence production, R & D, industry and finance.[50] R Chandrasekhar in *Rooks and Knights* states that "the efficiency of the DPS was hamstrung by lack of coordination between the three Services towards various issues".[51] He further states that the DPS as an organisation was originally intended to be a Strategic Planning Committee headed by the Defence Minister with various Secretaries and Service Chiefs as its members, but was downsized as a support organisation to the COSC.[52]

The Sixth Parliamentary Standing Committee on Defence in its report of March 1996, had enquired from the MoD about "ways and means to enhance the level of interaction and ensure better coordination amongst the Service Headquarters, the Ministry and other Government agencies and departments".[53] The MoD reply stated, "MoD draws heavily on the professional and technical expertise of the Service Chiefs for all defence related matters, including long term perspective planning. Integration beyond this point would be fraught with the drawbacks of losing out on independent in-depth analyses and re-evaluation of proposed policies".[54] In-depth analyses and re-evaluation of proposed defence policies by generalist bureaucrats, in a system wherein bureaucrats rarely tenant five-year tenure in the MoD! It showed the reluctance on the part of the MoD to involve the military (the specialist) in the national security policy framing process.

The National Security Council (NSC) was setup in August 1990 by the government to develop an integrated approach to national security policy making. A Strategic Core Group (SCG) was also created to assist it, headed by the Cabinet Secretary. PS Raghavan has stated that this committee met only once in October 1990 and did not meet after that.[55] A task force was setup in 1998 under the chairmanship of late KC Pant, who was the then Deputy Chairman of the Planning Commission, to recommend a suitable structure for a holistic approach to India's national security. Based on the recommendations of this commission, the government constituted a NSC in April 1999. The NSC had the Prime Minister, Defence Minister, Home Minister, Finance Minister, External Affairs Minister and Deputy Chairman of the Planning Commission as its members. The stated purpose of the NSC was to promote "integrated thinking and coordinated application of the political, military, diplomatic, scientific and technological resources of the State to protect and promote national security goals and objectives".[56] The SCG was renamed as Strategic Policy Group (SPG). A National Security Advisory Board (NSAB) was also created to render advice to the NSC on national security matters that were referred to it. A post of National Security Advisor was created and the then Principal Secretary to the Prime Minister, Brajesh Mishra was given this additional responsibility. A National Security Council Secretariat (NSCS) was formed to assist the NSC, SPG and NSAB in discharging their responsibilities. Apart from this a major review of the defence setup happened after the Kargil conflict.

Post Kargil Reforms

Post Kargil war in 1999, a Kargil Review Committee (KRC) headed by K Subrahmanyam was setup. The task of the committee was to "review the events leading up to the Pakistani aggression in the Kargil District of Ladakh in Jammu & Kashmir; and, to recommend such measures as are considered necessary to safeguard national security against such armed intrusions".[57] As per late Brig Gurmeet Kanwal the KRC, inspite of having a very limited charter, carried out a comprehensive review of the challenges and shortcomings in the national security management. PS Raghvan cites the KRC report and states that it recommended "a thorough review of the national security system in its entirety; more effective tasking, evaluation and coordination of intelligence agencies; strengthening of their technical capacities; improved border management structures and procedures; and better civil–military liaison mechanisms".[58] After the submission of the KRC report the government constituted a Group of Ministers (GoM) in April 2000. The GoM was headed by Shri LK Advani who was the Home Minister, and it had the Defence Minister, Finance Minister and the External Affairs Minister as members. The mandate of the GoM was "to review the national security system in its entirety and in particular, to consider the recommendations of the KRC and formulate specific proposals for implementation".[59] The GoM created four task forces, one each for review of intelligence apparatus, internal security, border management and management of defence. The task force reports were forwarded to the concerned ministries for their comments before the finalisation of the recommendations.

One of the critical observations of the KRC concerning management of defence, as mentioned in the GoM report, was that the armed forces headquarters are only attached offices and consequently are outside the apex governmental decision-making structure. KRC recommended a comprehensive overhaul of the apex decision making structure and interface between the MoD and the Service Headquarters with an aim to locate the Service Headquarters within the government.[60] The GoM report inferred that the Service Headquarters are referred to as attached offices only for administrative reasons and the perception that they do not participate in policy formulation is erroneous. To remove this perception, it recommended that the Service Headquarters be redesignated as 'Integrated Headquarters' of the MoD.[61] It also recommended delegating administrative and financial powers from the MoD to the Services and strengthening of the decision-making structure within the Services. It recommended enhancing the financial powers of the Defence Minister and the Finance Minister to enable faster procurement. All these recommendations were implemented. However as stated by Anit Mukherjee, merely re-designating the Service Headquarters as Integrated Headquarters did not fundamentally resolve the problematic relationship between the MoD and the Services.[62]

The GoM in its recommendations for management of defence recommended the creation of the post of Chief of Defence Staff (CDS) and Vice-Chief of Defence Staff (VCDS). The CDS was to function as the single point of military advice to the government, exercise administrative control over India's strategic forces (dealing with nuclear weapons), ensure jointness in the Services and enhance the effectiveness of the Services through intra and inter Service prioritisation. The proposal for creation of CDS was not accepted by the government however the proposal for creation of VCDS was accepted and it was created as Chief of Integrated Staff to the COSC (CISC). On the recommendations of the GoM, the Defence Planning Staff and JS (Military) were merged to create Integrated Defence Staff (IDS). IDS was to function as the secretariat for the CDS, however in the absence of the CDS it functioned under the CISC.

Recognising the importance of the Andaman and Nicobar Islands the GoM recommended the creation of a Joint Andaman and Nicobar Command (ANC), which was accepted. It also recommended the creation of a Strategic Forces Command (SFC) to manage all strategic forces, and a Defence Intelligence Agency (DIA) to co-ordinate the functioning of the different intelligence agencies of the three services. The GoM also recommended that the Defence Secretary be the 'Principal Defence Advisor' to the government and functionally be equivalent to the Service Chiefs and the CDS, irrespective of the Warrant of Precedence. These recommendations were accepted.[63] In addition to the above the GoM had recommended the setting up of an Indian National Defence University (INDU), which is under the implementation process. On the recommendations of the KRC and GoM, a National Technical Research Organisation (NTRO) was created as a nodal agency for providing electronic and other technical intelligence.

The recommendations of the KRC and the GoM and the implementations of the recommendations of the GoM was the first major overhaul of the security apparatus of India. It created significant reforms in the system. As per PS Raghavan these decisions "form the foundation of the current national security management system and were the first comprehensive review of the country's security mechanisms in their entirety and the first (and only one) to be made public".[64]

Ten years after the GoM recommendations on management of national security, the government appointed a task force led by Mr Naresh Chandra, a career bureaucrat, to review the progress of the implementation of the proposals of the GoM. The Naresh Chandra Task Force (NCTF) had 13 members and was given six months to submit its report. After the report was submitted, it was circulated to various ministries of the government for their inputs. The recommendations of the NCTF are not available in the public domain. As per late Gurmeet Kanwal, the NCTF recommended the establishment of a permanent Chairman for the COSC, since the post of CDS had not been created. Recommendations also included the creation of three joint commands viz. Special Operations Command, Aerospace Command and Cyber Command. As per him the task force also recommended "the establishment of a Bureau of Politico-Military Affairs to deliberate on security issues having foreign policy implications".[65] As per R Chandrasekhar the NCTF recommended that the Service Headquarters be designated as government departments under the MoD with specific role enumerated in the Allocation of Business (AOB) and Transaction of Business (TOB) Rules, 1961; with the responsibility of the defence of India being shifted to the Armed Forces from the Defence Secretary, as is the present case. It also recommended posting of military officers into the MoD to increase its professional expertise which is seemingly lacking in the present set-up.[66] Chandrasekhar says that the recommendations of the NCTF were examined by the government. The MoD opposed the recommendation of a permanent Chairman of COSC; it was also against posting of military officers in the MoD, their argument being that the present system was working well. Chandrasekhar has stated that senior Defence Ministry officials confidentially expressed apprehensions that "such a move would not be in the overall interests of either national security nor of the Services, as military officers are at no stage formally trained to execute government responsibilities"; their concern being that the "command structure of the armed forces prevented rational concerned decision making".[67] This lack of understanding by the bureaucracy of the MoD expresses everything that ails the MoD-Military relationship. Late Jaswant Singh in his book *Defending India* has aptly described this relationship as "prejudices layered by bureaucratic upmanship with damaging consequences"; he amplifies, "Defence Ministry, in effect, becomes the principal destroyer of the cutting edge of the military's morale; ironic considering that the very reverse of it is their responsibility. The sword arm of the state gets blunted by the state itself".[68]

An important reform which greatly impacted the functioning of the MoD and the Civil Military relations, was undertaken by the government in end 2019 by the creation of the post of Chief of Defence Staff (CDS) and its enabling structure Department of Military Affairs (DMA). As brought out earlier the requirement of the post of CDS was first brought out by the First Administrative Reforms Commission in 1966 and was later stressed upon by the Kargil Review Committee and the GoM recommendations.

Chief of Defence Staff and the Department of Military Affairs

On December 31, 2019 the government undertook one of the most significant defence reforms by creating the post of CDS and the establishment of DMA. The creation of the CDS and the DMA has resulted in a paradigm shift in the way the Ministry of Defence (MoD) operates. The DMA is predominantly staffed by personnel from the military. A large amount of the control that was exercised on the army, navy and the air force by the Department of Defence (DoD) in the MoD, has been transferred to the DMA. The Department of Defence (DoD) in the MoD headed by the Defence Secretary will now be responsible for defence policy, capital procurements and will have under him the Defence Acquisition Council (DAC) which is the approving body of the MoD for capital procurements.[69] As per AoB Rules 1961, Defence Secretary continues to be responsible for the defence of India. The CDS will be responsible for the revenue budget of the MoD. By designating the CDS as Secretary of the DMA, the government has made the CDS an executive functionary of the government. For the first time, because of the creation of the DMA, the Indian military has been integrated with the MoD at the decision making level of the government. This is expected to lead to better coordination in the military's functioning and reduction in friction between the civil and the military.

Conclusion

The British came to India as traders. They initially started with a security organization for the protection of their trade; however, due to the prevailing political and security environment in India they soon expanded and built an army which was the beginning of the British Indian Army. It was the institution by which the British not only consolidated their hold over India but also used them to fight their wars everywhere else in the world. The governance structures and the military structures that they created was with the sole aim of controlling India. The civil and military structures had a very uneasy relationship between them. Their sole purpose was to consolidate the British hold over India. The CMR during the British rule in India should be viewed from this perspective.

After independence, India inherited the governance and security structures from the British, and with minor changes adapted it. It was the probably the best that could have been done immediately after independence. As brought out by Robert Blackett, this was a period when Indians displayed a penchant for everything British. However, not reviewing governance and security structures subsequently, especially as India faced security challenges immediately after its independence, set India on the wrong path to safeguard its national security. This was also the period when India led by its first Prime Minister tried to utilise diplomacy as the primary means for achieving national security on the external front. This led to India not developing its military potential to the extent required. The path that India followed for developing its security structure also led to a bureaucratic stranglehold over the military and it getting isolated from the decision-making apparatus of the government. This culminated in the debacle of 1962.

After 1962, India expanded its military and modernized it; however, the HDO and consequently the civil-military relations remained the same. The Prime Ministers of India, both during 1965 and 1971 war, interacted directly with the Service Chiefs even though no formal structure enabling such consultations existed. It was solely up to the discretion of the Prime Minister to call for such consultation. Another important factor that has been utilised to maintain a wedge between the military and the political executive is the bogey of a military coup. This has been raised by vested interests from time to time to create a fear of the military. This bogey of a coup is inconsistent with the strategic culture of India.

Post the 1999 Kargil war, a comprehensive review of the security setup was carried out which resulted in significant changes. Inter-service organisations like the IDS, ANC and Strategic Command were created. It brought about much needed overhaul in the intelligence system by creating institutions like the DIA and NTRO. The Service Headquarters were re-designated as integrated offices of the MoD. However, the relationship of the Service Headquarters with the MoD and consequently CMR remained the same. This has undergone a substantial change with the establishment of the post of CDS and more importantly with the creation of DMA in end December 2019. Management of the military has now shifted from the DoD to the DMA in MoD and has resulted in the integration of the military with the MoD. It is likely to significantly alter the CMR field in India. The next chapter will critically analyse the existing security architecture of India dealing with external security.

Notes

1. John Newsinger, "War, Empire and the Atlee Government 1945-1951", *Race & Class 60(1)*. (2018), available at https://journals.sagepub.com/doi/full/10.1177/0306396818779864, accessed on March 04, 2021.
2. Government of India, *The Army in India and Its Evolution*, (Calcutta: Superintendent, Government Printing, 1924), p. 3.
3. TA Heathcote, The Military in British India (Great Britain: Manchester University Press, 1995), pp. 28-29.
4. Ibid, p. 41.
5. Ibid, pp. 47-48.

6. Ian Barrow, *The East India Company, 1600 – 1858* (Cambridge: Hackett Publishing Company, Inc. 2017), p. 63.
7. Heathcote, n. 3. pp. 61-63.
8. Ibid, p. 74.
9. For detailed reading on the Indian rebellion of 1857 refer, Saul David, *The Indian Mutiny* (London: Penguin Books, 2003).
10. Lt Gen S.K. Sinha (Retd), *USI National Security Lectures - Higher Defence Organisation* (New Delhi: United Services Institution of India, 1991), p. 12.
11. The exploitation of India by the British was actually akin to plunder, so much so that colonial rule has come to be associated with the word plunder. See https://dictionary.cambridge.org/dictionary/english/plunder.
12. Jon Wilson, *India Conquered* (London: Simon and Schuster, 2016), p. iv.
13. Shashi Tharoor, *An Era of Darkness – The British Empire in India* (New Delhi: Aleph Book Company, 2016).
14. Bryant, G. J. "Civil-Military Relationsin Early British India, 1750-85." *Journal of the Society for Army Historical Research* 83, no. 334 (2005): 131-51, at http://www.jstor.org/stable/44231169, accessed January 6, 2021.
15. Ibid, p. 149.
16. R Chandrashekhar, *Rooks and Knights, Civil – Military Relations in India* (New Delhi: CENJOWS, Pentagon Press, 2017), p. 35.
17. Ayesha Ray, *The Soldier and the State in India* (New Delhi, Sage Publications, 2013), p. 37.
18. Pandit Jawaharlal Nehru, *The Discovery of India* (Delhi: Oxford University Press, 1994), p. 292.
19. Wg Cdr (Dr) R. Venkataraman, *India's Higher Defence - Organisation and Management*, (New Delhi, KW Publishers, 2011), p. 84.
20. Pandit Nehru, n. 16, p. 445.
21. Robert S Anderson, "Patrick Blackett in India: Military Consultant and Scientific Intervenor, 1947-72. Part One." *Notes and Records of the Royal Society of London* 53, no. 2 (1999): 253-73 at http://www.jstor.org/stable/ 532210, accessed on January 17, 2021.
22. Ibid. p. 268.
23. Ibid. p. 265.
24. Itty Abraham, How India became Territorial - Foreign Policy, Diaspora, Geopolitics (Stanford, California: Stanford University Press, 2014), p. 122.
25. Anderson, n. 19, p. 265.
26. Lezlee Brown Halper & Stefan Halper, *Tibet an Unfinished Story* (Oxford: Oxford University Press, 2014), p. 102.
27. Ibid., p. 107.
28. Ibid., p. 109.
29. Itty Abraham, *How India became Territorial - Foreign Policy, Diaspora, Geopolitics* (Stanford, California: Stanford University Press, 2014), pp. 127-128.

30. Ayesha Ray, n.15, pp. 39-40.
31. Anit Mukerjee, The Absent Dialogue (New Delhi: Oxford University Press, 2020), p. 64.
32. Jaswant Singh, *Defending India* (Bangalore: Macmillan India Ltd, 1999), p. xix.
33. Jairam Ramesh, "Was Krishna Menon thinking of a coup against Nehru? COAS Gen Thimayya had privately said this", *The Print*, (January 13, 2020) at https://theprint.in/pageturner/excerpt/krishna-menon-thinking-of-coup-against-nehru-coas-thimayya-privately-said-this/348690/, accessed on March 03, 2021.
34. Wg Cdr (Dr) Venkataraman, n. 17, p. 99.
35. Ibid., p. 103.
36. RD Pradhan, *Debacle to Revival – YB Chavan as Defence Minister* (New Delhi: Orient Longman, 1999), p. 18.
37. As discussed in the first chapter. For more on this refer David Pion Berlin, "Foreword" in *Who Guards the Guardians and How, Democratic Civil-Military Relations,* (Austin: University of Texas Press, 2006), p. ix, and Peter D Feaver, "Civil – Military Relations," *Annual Review of Political Science, 1999.* 2:1, 211-241.
38. Steven I. Wilkinson, Army and the Nation (Ranikhet, India: Permanent Black, Ashoka University, 2015), p. 3.
39. Refer Peter D Feaver, "Civil – Military Relations," *Annual Review of Political Science, 1999.* 2:1, 211-241.
40. R Chandrashekhar, n.14, p. 63.
41. Lt Gen Harbakhsh Singh, In the Line of Duty – A Soldier Remembers (New Delhi: Lancer Publishers & Distributers, 2000), p. 323.
42. AG Noorani. "Our Secrets in British Archives". *Frontline*, (February 28, 2003) at https://frontline.thehindu.com/books/article30215704.ece, accessed on February 12, 2021.
43. First Post Staff. "Retired General confirms report that UPA feared coup in 2012". *Firstpost*, (February 21, 2014) at https://www.firstpost.com/india/retired-general-confirms-report-that-upa-feared-coup-in-2012-1401793.html, accessed on February 17, 2021 also refer Shekhar Gupta, Ritu Sarin, Pranab Dhal Samanta. "The January night Raisina Hill was spooked: Two key Army units moved towards Delhi without notifying Govt" The Indian Express, (January 10, 2016) at https://indianexpress.com/article/news-archive/web/the-january-night-raisina-hill-was-spooked-two-key-army-units-moved-towards-delhi-without-notifying-govt/ accessed on February 17, 2021.
44. Steven I. Wilkinson, Army and the Nation (Ranikhet, India: Permanent Black, Ashoka University, 2015), p. 3. Morris Janowitz and Horowitz have based their inference on studies done in Africa, Middle East and Burma.
45. Ibid., pp. 218-220.
46. India and Pakistan are part of the same subcontinent and ancient culture. However, Pakistan chose to follow a culture and structure based on its religion (Apurba Kundu in her 1995 research work *Civil Military Relations in British and Independent India 1918-1962, and Coup Prediction Theory*, argues that Islam predisposes towards

authoritarianism) whereas India is predominantly Hindu (not in religious sense as brought out in the previous chapter) with cultural continuity with its past.

47. Lt Gen S.K. Sinha (Retd), n. 10, p. 35.
48. Ibid.
49. Parts of the First Administrative Reforms Commission Report are available in the "Organisational Structure of the Government of India" as part of *Thirteenth Report, Second Administrative Reforms Commission* (April, 2009), p. 57, available at https://darpg.gov.in/sites/default/files/org_structure_gov13.pdf, accessed on February 23, 2021.
50. Wg Cdr (Dr) Venkataraman, n. 17, p. 181.
51. R Chandrashekhar, n. 14, p. 111.
52. Ibid.
53. Second Report of the Standing Committee on Defence (1996-97), Eleventh Lok Sabha (December, 1996), p. 12.
54. Ibid.
55. P.S. Raghavan, "The Evolution of India's National Security Architecture", *Journal of Defence Studies*, vol. 13, no. 3, July-September 2019, p. 34, at https://idsa.in/jds/13-3-2019-evolution-of-india-national-security accessed on August 06, 2020.
56. Ibid., p. 35.
57. Gurmeet Kanwal., "Introduction: The Need for Defence Reforms" in *Defence Reforms-A National Imperative*, ed., by Gurmeet Kanwal and Neha Kohli (New Delhi: Pentagon Press (IDSA), 2018), p. 4.
58. PS Raghvan, n. 55, p. 36.
59. GoM Report on National Security 2001, available at https://www.vifindia.org/sites/default/files/GoM%20Report%20on%20National%20Security.pdf, accessed on August 10, 2020.
60. Ibid., p. 122.
61. Ibid., p. 99.
62. Anit Mukherjee, "Defence Reforms: The Vajpayee Years" in *Defence Reforms-A National Imperative*, ed., by Gurmeet Kanwal and Neha Kohli (New Delhi: Pentagon Press (IDSA), 2018), p. 71.
63. GoM Report on National Security, n. 59, p. 104.
64. PS Raghvan, n. 55, p. 36.
65. Gurmeet Kanwal, n. 57, p. 8.
66. R Chandrasekhar, n. 14, p. 127.
67. Ibid., p. 129.
68. Jaswant Singh, *Defending India* (Bangalore: Macmillan India Ltd., 1999), p. 109.
69. Manu Pabby. "Work divided for Rawat-led dept of Military affairs" *The Economic Times*, (January 18, 2020) athttps://economictimes.indiatimes.com/news/defence/work-divided-for-rawat-led-dept-of-military-affairs/articleshow/73346897.cms. accessed on March 03, 2021.

5. Analysing India's National Security Architecture Dealing with External Security

No real change in history has ever been achieved by discussions.

– Subhash Chandra Bose

Introduction

Civil Military Relations (CMR) is the interplay between the military and the various organisations of the government which either control the military or interact with it. One of the primary aims for studying CMR is to enhance the effectiveness of the military and consequently the hard power of the nation for achieving its security objectives. In a democracy the responsibility of the security of the country is of the elected executive. The executive head of the government in India is the Prime Minister. Apart from the military, there is an entire security apparatus in the country responsible for external security. This security apparatus consists of many organisations starting from the political executive at the top. The chapter will attempt to analyse the present security structure of India dealing with external security.

The executive is formed from the elected representatives of the country and hence the actions of the political executive have the direct backing of the Parliament. Therefore, it is important to understand that final decisions in all matters will always be that of the political executive. The executive works under the Government of India Allocation of Business (AoB) Rules and Transaction of Business (ToB) Rules, 1961.

These Rules emerge out of Article 77(3) of the Constitution, which says that "the President shall make rules for the more convenient transaction of the business of the Government of India, and for the allocation among Ministers of the said business. The Rules mandate the minister-in-charge of a department (ministry) to dispose of all business allotted to a department under him or her".[1] Here it is vital to understand that the ministries and the departments mentioned in the AoB Rules are the permanent formal structures in the government for transacting government business and decision making, on the subjects entrusted to them by these Rules. A clear understanding of this fact is important while analysing the security structure of the country. However, when the subject affects more than one department, no decision can be taken "until all such departments have concurred, or, failing such concurrence, a decision thereon has been taken by or under the authority of the Cabinet".[2] The Prime Minister constitutes Standing Committees of the Cabinet and sets out the specific functions assigned to them. He can add or reduce the number of committees.

Key Committees of the Cabinet

The important committees of the Cabinet are as follows:

- **Appointments Committee:** This is an important cabinet committee. It makes appointments to posts of the CDS, the three service chiefs, C-in-C of all Army, Navy and Air Force Commands, all PSOs at Army, Navy and Air HQ, Chief of Integrated Defence Staff to the Chairman Chiefs of Staff Committee; C-in-C Andaman and Nicobar Command, C-in-C Strategic Force Command, Director General of Armed Forces Medical Services, Director General of Defence Intelligence Agency, Scientific Advisor to the Defence Minister, Director General of Ordnance Factories, Controller General of Defence Accounts, Director General of Defence Estates, Director of Institute for Defence Studies and Analyses, Solicitor-General, Governor of the Reserve Bank of India, Chairman and Members of the Railway Board,

Chief Vigilance Officers in Public Sector Undertakings and posts of Secretaries above the rank of Joint Secretary in the Central Government.

- **Accommodation Committee:** The Cabinet Committee on Accommodation decides the guidelines and rules of the allotment of government accommodation. It also determines the allotment of government accommodation to non-eligible persons and organisations.
- **Economic Affairs Committee:** This Committee continuously reviews economic trends, problems and prospects for evolving a consistent and integrated economic policy framework, coordinates all activities requiring policy decisions at the highest level and deals with fixation of prices of agricultural products and prices of essential commodities.
- **Parliamentary Affairs Committee:** The Cabinet Committee on Parliamentary Affairs watches and directs government business in Parliament. It reviews "legislations undertaken by State Legislatures from an all-India point of view; and considers proposals to summon or prorogue the Houses of Parliament".[3] It also has to scrutinise, and consider the attitude of the Government on non-official Bills and resolutions to be presented to Parliament.
- **Political Affairs Committee:** The Cabinet Committee on Political Affairs "deals with problems relating to Centre-State relations; economic and political issues that have to be judged with a wider perspective; and policy matters concerning foreign affairs that do not have external or internal security implications".[4]
- **Security Committee:** The Cabinet Committee on Security deals with issues of national security, foreign policy affecting national security, law and order and internal security. It also looks after economic and political issues related to national security. It deals with all cases involving defence capital expenditure of more than Rs 1,000 crore. The composition and function of the Cabinet Committee on Security (CCS) are as follows:

Cabinet Committee on Security

Composition

- Prime Minister.
- Minister of Defence.
- Minister of Home Affairs.
- Minister of External Affairs.
- Minister of Finance.

Functions: The functions of the CCS as enumerated in the ToB Rules, 1961 are as follows:

1. "to deal with all Defence related issues;
2. to deal with issues relating to law and order, and internal security;
3. to deal with policy matters concerning foreign affairs that have internal or external security implications including cases relating to agreements with other countries on security related issues;
4. to deal with economic and political issues impinging on national security;
5. to review the manpower requirements relating to national security including proposals concerning creation of posts carrying the pay scale or pay band plus Grade Pay equivalent to that of a Joint Secretary to the Government of India and higher, and setting up new structures to deal with security related issues;
6. to consider all cases-
    a. involving capital expenditure of more than rupees one thousand crore-
        i. in respect of
            A. the Department of Defence Production; and
            B. the Department of Defence Research and Development;
        ii. in respect of the Capital Works projects, Services Capital Acquisition plans, schemes, projects, procurement of security related equipment, non-scaled and new items in respect of Department of Defence; and
    b. involving security related expenditure of more than one thousand crore rupees in respect of Departments not included in item (a),

except in cases where higher powers for disposal of cases or class of cases have been delegated to the specified authorities;

c. involving capital expenditure of more than two hundred fifty crore rupees in respect of land acquisition by the Department of Defence where land acquisition is undertaken separately;

7. all matters relating to atomic energy; and
8. to consider cases of
   a. increases in the firmed-up cost estimates or revised cost estimates of schemes, projects, acquisition, or procurement in respect of items covered by entry (6), for reasons such as time overrun, changes in scope, or under-estimation, to the extent such increase is more than twenty percent of the original cost estimates already approved by the competent authority;
   b. any further increase of more than five percent in the revised cost estimates referred to in item (1):

   Provided that no case of revised cost estimate where such revised cost estimate is one thousand crore rupees or less or other cases falling within the powers delegated to other authorities by the Central Government, shall be required to be brought before the Cabinet Committee on Security except in cases, where the Minister-in-charge directs any case to be placed before the Committee".[5]

The AoB Rules, 1961 state that "the business of the Government of India shall be transacted in the Ministries, Departments, Secretariats and Offices specified in the First Schedule to these rules (all of which are hereinafter referred to as 'departments')".[6] As per the First Schedule, departments dealing with security are the Ministry of Defence (MoD) and the National Security Council Secretariat (NSCS). The NSCS has been added to the First Schedule of the AoB Rules, 1961, only in 2019 vide Amendment no. 351 dated August 06, 2019. As per the Second Schedule of the AoB Rules, the NSCS is the secretariat of the National Security Council (NSC), which is chaired by the Prime Minister. The responsibility of the NSCS is 'to assist the National Security Adviser

(NSA), the Principal Adviser on National Security matters to the Prime Minister; and the National Security Council'[7].

National Security Council

CCS is the apex decision making body on security related issues in India. The next most important body which deals with national security is the NSC. The NSC in its present form was set up through a Cabinet Secretariat Resolution dated April 16, 1999, based on the recommendations of a task force set up under the chairmanship of the then chairman of the Planning Commission late Shri KC Pant. The NSC consists of the following structures:

- NSC
- Strategic Policy Group (SPG)
- National Security Advisory Board (NSAB)

The NSC is chaired by the Prime Minister and comprises the ministers of Defence, External Affairs, Finance and Home Affairs. The NSA and Deputy NSAs are also members of the NSC. Other experts or members can also be invited for its meetings as and when required. The major difference between the CCS and the NSC is that the CCS is an executive decision-making body which deals with major decisions related to security, approval of major transformations in the defence forces, acquisition of major weapon systems, etc; whereas the NSC deals with the long-term policy planning. The NSC structure provides inputs and assists the apex political leadership of the country in the decision-making process.[8] The role of the NSC when it was formed in 1999, was to advise the govt on the following broad matters:

- "external security environment and threat scenario;
- security threats involving atomic energy, space and high technology;
- trends in the world economy and economy security threats in the areas of energy, foreign trade, food, finance and ecology;
- internal security, including counter-insurgency, counter-terrorism and counter-intelligence;

- patterns of alienation emerging in the country, especially those with a social, communal, or regional dimension;
- security threats posed by trans-border crimes such as smuggling and traffic in arms, drugs and narcotics; and
- co-ordination in intelligence collection and tasking of intelligence agencies so as to ensure that intelligence is focussed on areas of concern for the nation".[9]

The SPG when it was first created in 1999 was headed by the Cabinet Secretary. It has been reconstituted in 2018 and is now headed by the NSA, Mr Ajit Doval. It has the following members:

- Vice Chairman of NITI Ayog
- Cabinet Secretary
- Chief of Defence Staff (CDS)
- Chiefs of Staff of the Army, Navy and Air Force
- Governor of the Reserve Bank of India (RBI)
- External Affairs Secretary
- Home Secretary
- Defence Secretary
- Finance Secretary
- Secretary (Defence Production)
- Secretary Revenue
- Secretary of the Department of Atomic Energy
- Secretary of the Department of Space
- Secretary of the R&AW of the Cabinet Secretariat
- Director of the Intelligence Bureau
- Scientific Advisor to the Defence Minister
- Secretary, NSCS

The meetings of the SPG are convened by the NSA. Members from other ministries and departments may be invited to these meetings as and when required. A notification issued by the NSC Secretariat in September 2018 states that "The SPG shall be the principal mechanism for inter-ministerial coordination and integration of relevant inputs in the formulation of national security policies"[10]. The strength of the SPG is that it has senior functionaries of most of the departments and ministries which have direct or indirect relevance to national security. Therefore, it can be a very effective body for formulation of policies which requires coordination across ministries and departments. It can also provide a wholesome input on issues and recommendations that are placed before it. But its large size also makes it an inappropriate structure for decision making. One tends to concur with Mr Arvind Gupta the previous Deputy NSA and present director of Vivekananda International Foundation (VIF) when he states that "the SPG is too large a body for effective decision making".[11] SPG was the first body established by the government for inter-ministerial co-ordinations on issues of national security. It was supposed to undertake periodical reviews of the strategic defence requirements of the country and come up with policy options which would then be deliberated by the NSC; in this task it was supposed to be supported by the NSAB.

The NSAB is an important but informal component of the NSC. The NSAB consists of a Convenor and senior retired officials (civilians as well as military), academics and professionals from civil society who have expertise in security, foreign affairs, science and technology and economy. As per its original mandate, the NSAB considers subjects referred to it by the NSC or by government departments or agencies. Their task is to provide non-official, independent advice to the government on various national security related issues. The tenure of the members of the NSAB is two years[12]. The NSAB has "produced a Draft Nuclear Doctrine in 2001, a Strategic Defence Review in 2002 and a National Security Review in 2007".[13] NSAB till 2015 had 14 members which were subsequently reduced to four. The NSAB has been reconstituted in 2019 and presently has 11 members. It can also co-opt other domain experts for specific studies if required. Apart from giving advice to the government the "NSAB aims to develop into a bridge between the national security establishment and think tanks/research institutions working on national security and strategic affairs, so as to enhance communication and understanding of national security policies and perspectives".[14] The present chairman of the NSAB, PS Raghvan in an article written for IDSA has stated that the NSAB "could also act as a receptacle of public views on national security-related issues, which it could funnel back to the national security establishment"[15].

National Security Advisor and National Security Council Secretariat

The post of NSA was created in early1999 on the recommendations of a task force headed by late KC Pant with late Jaswant Singh and late Air Commodore Jasjit Singh as members. As per its mandate, this task force had studied the national security structure in other countries and based on it recommended the creation of a NSC structure in India. It also recommended the setting up of the National Security Council Secretariat similar to the one in the USA. The recommendations of the task force were accepted by the then AB Vajpayee government. However instead of appointing a separate NSA the govt decided to confer this as an additional responsibility on the then Principal Advisor to the PM, Brajesh Mishra. Thus, he functioned as both the Principal Advisor to the PM as well as the NSA. The existing Joint Intelligence Council (JIC) was renamed as the NSCS and it was given the additional responsibility of NSCS along with its previous responsibility of the functions of the JIC. The following role was envisaged for the NSCS:

- "All Ministries/Departments shall consult the Secretariat on matters having a bearing on national security.
- The NSCS will prepare or cause to be prepared papers for consideration of the SPG or the NSC.
- An officer of the level of Secretary to the Government of India, designated as Secretary, NSCS, will head the Secretariat.
- The NSCS will be located in the Cabinet Secretariat and will also service the SPG and the NSAB."[16]

Since the NSA wore a dual hat, therefore to assist him in his functioning and to take care of the day-to-day affairs of the NSCS a post of secretary to the NSCS was created. The NSCS was part of the Cabinet

Secretariat till 2002 after which it was shifted under the PMO. Thus, it got completely integrated with the NSA who was also part of the PMO. The Secretary NSCS was renamed as deputy NSA.

The Cabinet Secretariat Resolution of April 16, 1999 had stated that the NSC "shall have a National Security Adviser who shall function as the channel for servicing the National Security Council"[17]. The Group of Ministers (2001) which was established for giving recommendations on national security after the Kargil Review Committee (KRC) report, had accepted the KRC recommendation that the post of NSA should be separated from the post of Principal Secretary to the Prime Minister (PM). In 2004 the post of NSA was separated from that of the Principal Secretary to the PM. The NSA continued to be in the PMO and became the principal advisor to the PM on matters of external security, internal security, foreign policy, defence, atomic energy and space issues. The NSA is directly appointed by the PM and enjoys his confidence. The Nuclear Command authority of the country has a political council and an executive council. The PM heads the political council and the NSA heads the executive council. India and China have appointed Special Representatives to address their boundary problem from a political perspective under the direct supervision of their leaders. The NSA has since been India's Special Representative (SR) since the time this arrangement was formulated. The NSA as an institution exists in many countries, and since they have direct access to the highest leadership of the country, are the best means to gain access to the highest levels of the government during times of crises. "In March 2003, NSA Brajesh Mishra telephoned U.S. NSA Condoleezza Rice on the eve of our Parliamentary debate on the U.S. invasion of Iraq and asked her to inform the U.S. President of the expected criticism of the House. This advance warning softened the U.S. response somewhat, at a delicate stage of India's negotiations of the Next Steps to Strategic Partnership (which eventually led to the nuclear deal of 2008)"[18]. During the recent India China standoff at Ladakh, the initial de-escalation took place only after the political dialogue between the two countries was escalated to the level of the Special Representatives and India's NSA Mr Ajit Doval spoke to his counterpart SR in China.

The NSA which earlier was a Minister of State rank was elevated to Cabinet Minister status in June 2019.

NSCS was created as a secretariat for the NSC. Its mandate was to service the NSC, SPG and the NSAB. It also performed the functions of the JIC which was to collate intelligence from various agencies, extract relevant strategic information and provide the concerned decision makers with options to deal with various issues and challenges concerning national security. Secretary NSCS who was subsequently renamed as Deputy NSA used to perform the functions of the chairman of the JIC. Later on, the JIC division was resurrected in 2004 as a separate department in the NSCS and its chairman started reporting directly to the NSA. Along with the revival of the JIC, three more separate divisions were created in the NSCS. They were the project division to deal with nuclear doctrinal and other issues along with monitoring the nuclear doctrines of other countries; policy division, to prepare policy papers and to service the SPG and NSAB; and a defence division to deal with the modernisation of the defence forces and credibility of India's nuclear deterrence[19]. In 2015 a post of National Cyber Security Coordinator was created along with a cyber wing. National Cyber Security Coordinator is a special secretary rank officer and reports directly to the NSA.

The NSCS has evolved over the years and its role in the security architecture of the country has enlarged considerably. The NSCS represents India in the Shanghai Cooperation Organisation's (SCO) Regional Anti-Terrorist Structure (RATS). It functions as the secretariat for multilateral NSA-level dialogues, in the Bay of Bengal Initiative for Multi-Sectoral Technical and Economic Cooperation (BIMSTEC), which includes India, Nepal, Bhutan, Bangladesh, Myanmar, Thailand and Sri Lanka; Russia–India–China dialogue on Afghanistan; BRICS (Brazil–Russia–India–China–South Africa); and the India–Maldives–Sri Lanka Maritime Trilateral. It functions as the coordinator for bilateral NSA and Deputy NSA-level dialogue with over 20 countries.[20] The structure of the NSCS has expanded over the years and now it influences policy making in as diverse fields as "space security, environmental security, geospatial sciences, maritime security, blue economy, strategic minerals, rare earths, pandemics and technology security, involving coordination of actions by various departments and agencies and drafting of national policy papers".[21]

National security today encompasses external security, terrorism, internal security challenges, crime, environment security, energy security, information warfare, cybercrime, water security, data security, trade and commerce and various other social issues. To meet these challenges the NSCS is consequently being expanded and domain experts are being inducted from both within and outside the government. As per P.S. Raghvan, the current convenor of the NSAB, the structure of the NCSC is as follows:

> "Its work is now organised in four verticals, three headed by Deputy NSAs and the fourth, the military vertical, headed by a Military Adviser of the same rank. The strategic affairs vertical will deal with strategic and security interests in the neighbourhood and in key geographies. The technology and intelligence vertical will work on infusion of the latest technologies for intelligence, civil and military applications, and coordinate efforts to plug technology gaps. The internal affairs vertical will focus on next-generation threats, in addition to the ongoing issues in Jammu and Kashmir, the North-East, counter-terrorism and counter-insurgency. The Military Adviser will provide a military perspective to security policymaking; his vertical will also focus on military developments in the neighbourhood and defence requirements in India's strategic environment. These are broad indicative descriptions; there will be a number of cross-cutting issues, requiring coordination between various verticals. In addition, the plan is to induct professionals who can work on economic, sociological, ecological and legal aspects of national security policy".[22]

The military adviser works with all three verticals and also functions as an interface between the NSCS and the Service headquarters. The NSCS has evolved into an organisation with expertise across multiple domains. It can serve as an institution for amalgamating ideas and policies across ministries. It can prepare policy papers and advise ministries in the formation of their policies. The ministry which deals with the external security of India is the Ministry of Defence (MoD).

Ministry of Defence

The MoD before December 30, 2019, had four departments. On December 30, 2019, the government of India announced the creation of the post of CDS and the Department of Military Affairs. The AoB Rules, 1961, were modified vide Amendment Series no. 353 dated 30.12.2019. The five departments of MoD are now as follows:

- Department of Defence (DoD)
- Department of Military Affairs (DMA)
- Department of Defence Production (DDP)
- Department of Defence Research and Development (DDRD)
- Department of Ex Servicemen Welfare (DESW)

The responsibilities of these departments as per the AoB Rules, 1961 amended as of April 29, 2020, are as follows:

- **Department of Defence**:
    1. "Defence of India and every part thereof including defence policy and preparation for defence and all such acts as may be conducive in times of war to its prosecution and after its termination to effective demobilisation.
    2. The Reserves of the Army, Navy and Air Force.
    3. The National Cadet Corps.
    4. Remounts, Veterinary and Farms Organisation.
    5. Canteen Stores Department (India).
    6. Civilian Services paid from Defence Estimates.
    7. Hydrographic surveys and preparation of navigational charts.
    8. Formation of Cantonments, delimitation/excision of Cantonment areas, local self-government in such areas, the constitution and powers within such areas of Cantonment Boards and authorities and the regulation of house accommodation (including the control of rents) in such areas.

9. Acquisition, requisitioning, custody and relinquishment of land and property for defence purposes. Eviction of unauthorised occupants from defence land and property.
10. Defence Accounts Department.
11. Purchase of food stuffs for military requirements and their disposal excluding those entrusted to Department of Food and Public Distribution.
12. All matters relating to Coast Guard Organisation, including-
    - (a) surveillance of maritime zones against oil spills;
    - (b) combating oil spills in various maritime zones, except in the waters of ports and within 500 metres of off-shore exploration and production platforms, coastal refineries and associated facilities such as Single Buoy Mooring (SBM), Crude Oil Terminal (COT) and pipelines;
    - (c) Central Coordinating Agency for Combating of Oil Pollution in the coastal and marine environment of various maritime zones;
    - (d) implementation of National Contingency Plan for oil spill disaster; and
    - (e) undertaking oil spill prevention and control, inspection of ships and offshore platforms in the country, except within the limits of ports as empowered by the Merchant Shipping Act, 1958 (44 of 1958).
13. Matters relating to diving and related activities in the country.
14. Capital Acquisitions exclusive to the Defence Services.
15. All matters relating to Border Roads Development Board and Border Roads Organisation.
16. Institute for Defence Studies and Analysis, National Defence College and any other organisation within the Ministry of Defence whose remit is broader than military matters."[23]

- **Department of Military Affairs**:

1. "The Armed Forces of the Union, namely, Army, Navy and Air Force.

2. Integrated Headquarters of the Ministry of Defence comprising of Army Headquarters, Naval Headquarters, Air Headquarters and Defence Staff Headquarters.
3. The Territorial Army.
4. Works relating to Army, Navy and Air Force.
5. Procurement exclusive to the Services except capital acquisitions, as per prevalent rules and procedures.
6. Promoting jointness in procurement, training and staffing for the Services through joint planning and integration of their requirements.
7. Facilitation of restructuring of Military Commands for optimal utilisation of resources by bringing about jointness in operations, including through establishment of joint/theatre commands.
8. Promoting use of indigenous equipment by the Services."[24]

- **Department of Defence Production**: This department deals with Ordinance Factory Board and Ordinance factories. It is also responsible for all PSUs dealing with defence production in India viz, HAL, BEL, BDL, BEML, Mazagaon Dock Ltd., Garden Reach Shipbuilders and Engineers Ltd., Goa Shipyard Ltd., Mishra Dhatu Nigam Ltd. and Hindustan Shipyard Ltd. It also handles Defence Quality Assurance Organisations including Directorate General Quality Assurance and Directorate General Aeronautical Quality Assurance. It is responsible for the development of the aerospace industry and its coordination with users except for those areas which are the responsibility of Ministry of Civil Aviation and Department of Space.
- **Department of Defence Research and Development**: It is responsible for informing and advising the Defence Minister of all the developments and advancements in the field of science and technology which have a bearing on national security. It is also supposed to render advice to the three services and inter-service organisations on scientific aspects of weapons and military operations and logistics in all likely theatres of conflict.

- **Department of Ex Servicemen Welfare:** It looks after all issues of military veterans, their pensions and their contributory health scheme.
- **Defence Finance Division:** In addition to the above departments of the MoD there is a component of the Finance Ministry in the MoD known as Defence Finance. It is headed by the Financial Advisor Defence Services (FADS). The Defence Finance division is fully integrated with the MoD. The MoD has delegated financial powers, these powers are exercised in consultation with the Defence Finance division. For all cases which are beyond the delegated financial power of the MoD, the Defence Finance can directly access the Finance Ministry or the Finance Minister through the Secretary (Expenditure). As per the Controller General of Defence Accounts (CGDA) website "before according financial concurrence to any proposals involving fresh expenditure, it is the duty of the Finance Division to seek complete and comprehensive justification for the proposals. The division may even challenge the necessity for spending so much money or on such a scale to secure a given object".[25] All procurements of MoD are done in compliance with either the Defence Acquisition Procedure (DAP) which is used for capital procurements or the Defence Procurement Manual (DPM) which is used for revenue procurements.

Headquarter Integrated Defence Staff (IDS)

After the Kargil war, one of the major recommendations of the Group of Ministers (GoM) which deliberated on the Kargil Review Committee (KRC) report was the setting up of Headquarters Integrated Defence Staff (IDS). This was the first step after independence towards creating a structure for developing integration between the three services. IDS used to function under the Defence Secretary and DOD. After the creation of CDS and DMA, IDS now is under the CDS and organisationally under the DMA. The main role of Hq IDS is to integrate the planning process of the three services to achieve better synergy and capability development between them. IDS consist of four main branches which look after the following:

- Capability development;
- Operations and training;
- Defence Intelligence Agency (DIA)/intelligence and;
- Medical

Capability Development looks after the formulation of long-term policy, planning and force structuring of the three services, budget (general and defence) analysis, acquisition, procurement, and technology management. Once a specific service decides to procure a particular weapon system/equipment or platform; it includes it in its Long Term Perspective Plan (LTPP). The LTPPs of all three services are vetted by IDS and inter-se prioritization is carried out. After this, a Long Term Integrated Perspective Plan (LTIPP) is prepared and budgeting and procurement process as per DPP or DPM is initiated after acquiring the relevant approvals either at the stage of the Defence Minister (through Defence Acquisition Council) or at the level of the CCS as the case may be. Defence procurement is carried out under three broad plans, the LTIPP which is a 15-year perspective plan, the Services Capital Acquisition Plan (SCAP) which is a five-year vision document and the Annual Acquisition Plan (AAP) which as the name suggests is an annual plan. The AAP is what is budgeted and provides an actionable roadmap for acquisition.

The planning process for acquisition has changed with the appointment of the CDS and the creation of the DMA. A new Defence Acquisition Procedure (DAP) published in September 2020, has replaced the earlier Defence Procurement Procedure (DPP). As per the new DAP, the erstwhile LTIPP of the three services has been replaced with an Integrated Capability Development Plan (ICDP), which is prepared by IDS. Based on RM's Op directive a threat assessment is carried out and based on this threat assessment military objectives are defined. From these military objectives, the Military Mission Team at IDS works out a plan for desired capabilities for all three services. This is a consultative process and the three Service headquarters are consulted at every level. Based on the desired capabilities required for each service, capability gaps are analysed and worked out. This leads to the preparation of the ICDP. The ICDP is for a period of 10 years, unlike the LTIPP which was for 15 years. SCAP and AAP are now based on the ICDP; their durations remain the same as earlier.

The operations and training branch of IDS is responsible for conceptualisation and preparation of joint plans for threats that involve a response from all three services and training policy. It is responsible for the preparation of the Raksha Mantri's Operational Directive (RM's Op Directive), based on which the services prepare their own service specific operational directive. While preparing the RM's Op Directive, IDS also consults the External Affairs Ministry. Humanitarian Assistance and Disaster Relief (HADR) operations, planning and conduct of tri-services exercises, multinational exercises and international exercises involving more than one service is also in the charter of this branch. An important mandate of IDS is net assessment. The Net Assessment Directorate has the responsibility of "initiating and coordinating net assessments of the standing trends and future prospects of India's security capabilities and military potential in comparison with those of other countries, or groups of countries, so as to identify emerging or future vulnerabilities, challenges and opportunities for India"[26]. This branch is also responsible for coordinating the joint doctrine of the three services and formulating joint doctrines of military capability for joint operations. A joint doctrine for the services was promulgated for the first time in 2017. It is responsible for all joint training institutes like National Defence Academy (NDA), Defence Services Staff College (DSSC), Military Institute of Technical Training, and the School of Foreign Languages.

The head of the Defence Intelligence Agency (DIA) is the Deputy Chief (DC) IDS (Intelligence) and Director General DIA. He is responsible for providing intelligence inputs related to defence to the Defence Minister, CDS, the three service chiefs, Defence Secretary and NSCS. DIA obtains intelligence inputs from the intelligence arm of the three services and other intelligence agencies and prepares an integrated intelligence analysis and assessment. "It is also the interface between the military intelligence directorates and the Research and Analysis Wing (R&AW), Intelligence Bureau (IB) and NSCS".[27]

The head of the medical branch of IDS is the Deputy Chief IDS (Medical). The medical branch functions as an interface between the Office of the Director General Armed Forces Medical Services (DGAFMS) and HQ IDS on all matters about med manpower, induction, training, development of med tactical doctrines, med eqpt and stores as well as providing technical and professional inputs for all publications/guidelines/books and pamphlets on medical matters to be published under the aegis of the IDS.[28] IDS was a first and significant step towards ensuring better coordination and synergy between the three services. To address the issue of inter-ministerial coordination and input for defence planning, the government of India formed the Defence Planning Committee (DPC) on April 18, 2018.

Defence Planning Committee

DPC is headed by the NSA. It has CDS, three service chiefs, Defence Secretary, Secretary (Expenditure) from Finance Ministry and Secretary External Affairs as members. The Chief of IDS is the member secretary of the DPC. The DPC was notified by the MoD in April 2018. It was tasked to prepare draft reports on "national security strategy, international defence engagement strategy, roadmap to build (a) defence manufacturing ecosystem, strategy to boost defence exports, and priority capability development plans".[29] The MoD notification for the DPC stated that it is supposed to have four sub-committees to deal with "policy and strategy; plans and capability development; defence diplomacy; and defence manufacturing eco-system". The inputs of these sub-committees are to be put up to the Defence Minister for further consideration. The mandate of the DPC is also to "prepare military doctrines and, in line with this, establish the strategic objectives of Indian military power. Future operational directives of the defence minister will emerge from the doctrine and strategy worked out by the committee".[30] The dictate of the DPC is thus to provide higher directions to the MoD.

CDS and DMA

The post of the CDS and the institution of the DMA was created by the government on December 31, 2019. The CDS has been designated as the Principal Military Advisor to the Defence Minister and the Permanent Chairman of the Chiefs of Staff Committee. He is the head of all tri-service organisations and is also the Military Advisor to the Nuclear Command Authority. He heads the DMA as its Secretary in the MoD; being designated as Secretary, he is an executive functionary of the Government of India. This gives him the authority to originate policy decisions of the government; a first for a military officer since India's independence. This aspect of the CDS and DMA reform makes it the most important since independence wherein the military has been integrated into the government functioning. It has demonstrated the government's resolve to free the military from the stranglehold of the bureaucracy to a large extent. It is an important first step in giving the military the rightful place that it had in India's Strategic Culture. As per the reply given by the Raksha Rajya Mantri in the Rajya Sabha, the responsibilities of the CDS are as follows:

- "To bring about jointness in operation, logistics, transport, training, support services, communications, repairs and maintenance, etc of the three Services.
- To ensure optimal utilisation of infrastructure and rationalise it through jointness among the Services.
- To bring about reforms in the functioning of three Services with the aim to augment combat capabilities of the Armed Forces by reducing wasteful expenditure.
- To assign inter-services prioritisation to capital acquisition proposals based on the anticipated budget".[31]

The government's focus on optimum utilisation of resources comes out from the mandate given to the DMA, "facilitation of restructuring of Military Commands for optimal utilisation of resources by bringing about jointness in operation including through establishment of joint/ theatre commands".[32]

Decision making process of the MoD

The decision-making process of the MoD follows the bottoms-up approach. Responsibilities of various departments are distributed broadly among the various Joint Secretary level officers and below them to the Director or the Under Secretary level. Whenever a case or file is moved by any of the three services requiring government approval, it moves up the chain for obtaining requisite approval from the respective branch head of that service (army, navy or air force) before going to MoD. After obtaining the branch head approval the case goes to the section/desk level where it is prepared for moving up the chain in MoD. "The cases are generally processed at the Section/Desk level and the files are submitted to Under Secretary/ Deputy Secretary/Director/Joint Secretary/Additional Secretary/ Special Secretary/Secretary/Ministers, as per the requirement of each case".[33] Before the creation of CDS and DMA, the entire chain of appointments from the Deputy Secretary upwards was manned by generalist officers from the central services. Needless to say, no strategic value addition was done to the proposals. To its credit, the MoD did function as an audit agency ensuring the services followed the laid down rules and procedures. However, because of its inherent structure, it was handicapped in providing any strategic directions to the military. Inspite of having a hostile neighbourhood and facing many wars since independence it is indeed surprising that India followed this structure for 72 years before changing it. With the CDS and the DMA now being part of the structure, the consultative process between the Service Headquarters and DMA (earlier DoD) remains the same, however, the process has been speeded up as the proposals of the Services are now being perused by officials of the DMA who are again mostly military officers and hence have domain knowledge on the subject. The DMA has replaced the DoD as far as the handling of the three services is concerned but has the consultative or the decision-making process changed? It hasn't.

India's National Security – Concept

Before analyzing the security structure of the country, it would be imperative to first understand the concept of national security. National security encompasses the complete security of the nation. It is linked to national interests. Factors that influence national interests are both tangible and intangible. Intangible factors of national interests are linked to the national ethos. In the third chapter, the study of the strategic culture of India brings out that the Indian nation has followed a certain approach towards war, which has been predominantly guided by value systems even in war-fighting. The lessons learnt, bring out that Indians never adopted an approach for aggressive use of force. The Indian society itself was based on value systems. The national ethos are the intangibles that affect national security. However, the chapter predominantly deals with the tangible factors.

The effect of tangible factors comprises external as well as internal security. Although on the face of it there appears to be a clear distinction between external and internal security there are areas and domains where they merge; like the case of state-sponsored covert terrorism. Is there an ideal way to deal with the external security of the country? Walter Lippman an American political analyst states that "A nation has security when it does not have to sacrifice its legitimate interests to avoid war, and is able, if challenged, to maintain them by war."[34] This situates the national security of a country specifically in its geographical location and hence would be definite to a country. National security will not be a one glove fits all and hence cannot be a theoretical construct, it will be rooted in its geography and to a certain extent in its history.

Another factor influencing India's external security is its strategic partners. How much should India rely on its strategic partners? Satish Kumar while evaluating India's external security rightly states that "India must bear in mind that it does not occupy a prime of place in the national security strategy of any of its strategic partners, like the US,

Russia, Britain, France, Germany, Japan, and Australia".[35] He further amplifies that each of these countries would like to have defence and economic cooperation with India to boost their economies and to maintain a global geostrategic balance, but India will have to stand on its own in times of military conflict with its adversaries. Each nation is predominantly guided by its national interests. This was evident in India's ongoing military stand-off with China, wherein Russia did not condemn China even once for its aggression towards India whereas it was quick to condemn QUAD as a grouping against China. Similarly, the USA while conducting Freedom of Navigation Operations (FONOPS) in India's Exclusive Economic Zone (EEZ), issued a strongly worded statement for the same. The USA has conducted such FONOPS in India's EEZ even in the past, but what was different in 2021 is the strongly worded press release supporting it and challenging India's excessive maritime claims.[36]

China has been hostile to Indian interests since the late 1950s. Satish Kumar in his analysis has brought out that China has influenced all the South Asian countries in a manner inimical to India. Diplomacy has failed to resolve the boundary dispute with China. India at present does not have an answer to the China challenge. The situation is similar to 1950 when China invaded Tibet and India did not have an option to respond. Pakistan since 1947 has proven that it will always remain hostile to India. India's External Affairs Minister S. Jaishankar has rightly brought out that "there are very few major states that still have unsettled borders to the extent that we do. Of equal relevance is the very unique challenge that we face of years of intense terrorism inflicted on us by a neighbour".[37] The Indian Ocean region is becoming one of the most contested areas for influence by major powers of the world. Jaishankar in his talk emphasised the importance of hard power for the security of India. This brings us to Walter Lippman and his stress on the importance of power for national security. It is also the most important lesson that emerges from India's Strategic Culture as brought out in the third chapter; there is no alternative for India to acquiring comprehensive national power for its security. Should the thought process of dealing with external security be influenced by the strategic culture of the nation? It should.

The external security realm of a nation is an arena wherein many structures and organisations operate. In the case of India, they are MoD, MEA, MoF, MHA (Border Security Force (BSF) and Indo-Tibetan Border Police (ITBP) are under MHA) NSC and its structures, Intelligence agencies, Commerce Ministry to name a few. Of these, MoD, MEA, MoF, intelligence agencies, NSC and its structures are direct actors, while others indirectly influence external security. As brought out earlier external security of a nation is not a theoretical construct. It has to be geo-situated in its geography, history and the evolution of its neighbouring states. It will be affected by national requirements in terms of food security, energy security, trade security, cyber security and national approach to global affairs which would be dictated by the national philosophy of the country. To explain this further, the USA followed a national philosophy of promoting democracy and market economy as it suited it, while the erstwhile USSR tried to propagate communism. A country like China is following a path of hegemony. External security in the present milieu is not only about protecting borders but about the capability of India to be able to protect its interests in all domains as specified above. Thus, the external security apparatus of a country should continuously evolve and be a reflection of its future trajectory. The interplay and cohesiveness of the various tangible factors affecting national security will determine the robustness and capability of the national security architecture.

Analysis of the Security Structure of India

The composition of the CCS and the NSC are the same. The major difference between the two is that the CCS is a decision-making body while the NSC is an advisory body. The CCS deliberates on issues and recommendations that are placed before it by various ministries and departments and takes executive decisions on it for further implementation. It is thus the apex decision making body of the government of India on matters of national security. There is no professional military input available in the CCS meetings unless the CDS or the Service Chiefs are invited for specific briefings. The appointment of CDS has created a single point of contact for the government for all military matters. If the CDS evolves in a manner wherein it is able to integrate the functioning of the three Services and becomes the guiding authority for capability development of hard power then will it not be prudent that he becomes a special invitee to the CCS?

The NSC along with its supplementary organisations like the SPG, NSAB and NSCS are supposed to deliberate and discuss long term issues in all their aspects and dimensions by considering all the available options to develop a well thought out and coordinated approach. The NSC is thus supposed to evolve a coordinated approach path towards national security which can serve as policy guidelines for various ministries and departments. All matters concerning national security that require interdepartmental deliberations or that are required to be put up to the CCS for deliberations and decisions are to be routed through the NSCS and the NSC structure. However, things are not as smooth as they are supposed to be, is indicated by the fact that in 2019 the Cabinet Secretariat had to pull up the MoD and the Ministry of External Affairs for failing to consult the NSA and the NSCS on matters of national security.[38]

The SPG comprises senior government functionaries who have their departmental responsibilities to deal with. Therefore, the SPG at best can only function as a platform to resolve inter-ministerial issues. It may not be able to focus de novo on aspects of national security. The NSAB is an advisory body that offers advice on issues placed before it. This leaves only the NSA and the NSCS to function as not only the think tank of the government but the only institution dealing with coordinating inter-ministerial national security aspects.

The foundation of the NSC structure is the NSCS with its four verticals. Each of the verticals analyse issues under their purview without the constraints of a domain which the ministries have. This results in a comprehensive evaluation of national security issues and the generation of policy guidelines affecting several ministries. The NSCS involves itself in constant consultations with different arms of the government and hence can evolve policies and guidelines which have a coordinated approach to security.

The entire NSC architecture comprising of the NSC, SPG, NSAB, NSA and NSCS does not form part of the executive arm of the government. This has been highlighted by Arvind Gupta in his book *How India Manages its National Security*, where he states that the NSC is an advisory body that lacks the power to enforce its advice.[39] Before 2019 the NSA and NSCS had no executive responsibility as per the AoB/ToB Rules of the government; now the responsibility of the NSCS is to function as the secretariat of the NSC and to assist the NSA.[40] Being an advisory body the NSC structure is not accountable to the Parliament of India.

NSC and the Ministries

The executive arm of the government of India functions through its various ministries and departments. The functions of these departments are specified in the AoB Rules, 1961. Each ministry is headed by a cabinet minister. In the Indian form of governance, executive decisions have to be taken in the ministries and ratified by the committee of the Cabinet as required. The ministers of the important ministries like defence, external affairs, economic affairs and home affairs are part of the CCS. The NSC structure with the NSCS and the NSA has become an overarching body on the ministries. Mr Sekhar Gupta in his analysis of the NSC and NSA argues that it may lead to undermining the authorities of the Defence, Finance and External Affairs Ministers.[41] This may not be the case as these ministers and ministries are represented in the NSC and the SPG where disagreements and coordination issues can be resolved.

The NSCS as per the AoB Rules is to function as the secretariat of the NSC and to assist the NSA; it does not have formal authority over the ministries and its advisory capability originates from the NSC. The ministries are supposed to be the expert and repositories of knowledge for their domain. The proposals which emanate from them are after careful deliberations and approval by the respective minister. It thus represents the total of the knowledge and ideas of that ministry and the respective minister who are domain experts. The notes and proposals are then subject to scrutiny by the NSCS and the NSA. The verticals of the NSCS deal with issues across domains and hence the question of domain expertise between the ministries and the NSCS may arise leading to disagreements. If the NSCS policy advisories are made binding on the ministries then it weakens the ministerial system of governance of India. More ever it assumes that the NSCS will always be right in its analysis and assessment. If the NSCS utilises inputs from the ministries and only coordinates then it is no more than a mere coordinating agency. This makes this informal system of interaction between the NSCS and the ministries susceptible to incoherence and leadership issues with the relevant minister representing the ministry and NSA representing the NSCS. At its best, it will provide seamless coordination between the ministries and the NSCS and at its worst, it may lead to disruption of coordination. To highlight the inherent weakness of this system it would be well to remember Prime Minister PV Narshimha Rao's statement on NSC in the Indian Parliament in 1995, as quoted by late Jaswant Singh in his book *Defending India*.

> "the national security council set-up is found in countries where the Presidential form of Government has been adopted, the most notable example being that of the United States. We find that it is difficult to have such a system transplanted in India because here the business of the Central Government has to be ultimately transacted in the Cabinet or Cabinet committee with Ministers Incharge being responsible for their subjects to Parliament."[42]

Much has changed since 1995, the NSC set-up in India is now well established, it has become the only platform for an inter-ministerial holistic analysis of India's security. However, because it only generates policy advisories to the ministries it is not an institutionally integrated structure in the governmental system. It is personality-driven to some extent and is dependent on the dynamism of the NSA, deputy NSAs and the military advisor.

Ministerial functioning

Executive decisions of the government are taken by the ministries. The issue of lack of coordination between the various ministries and government departments has been brought out by many analysts of national security. Arvind Gupta in his analyses in *How India Manages its National Security* brings out that "the various departments and agencies work in silos and efforts to coordinate their functioning proves difficult and sometimes impossible".[43] He further argues that this leads to decisions being taken piecemeal and not being enmeshed, leading to a disintegrated approach to national security. Power as a resource is the total capability available to the nation to influence others for national benefit. Ministries of Defence, External Affairs and Finance directly affect the hard power of India. The functional outcomes of these ministries are intricately linked to each other and are tangible measures of national power. Military and diplomacy are two sides of the same coin. The aim of both is to protect national interests. India in the past has relied more on diplomacy to provide a solution to its problems. India's first Prime Minister Jawaharlal Nehru effectively utilised diplomacy to follow a path of non-alignment as a tool for national security. However, relying only on diplomacy without having corresponding hard power had its failings as India learnt in 1962.

Indian diplomacy has performed admirably since independence, it negotiated the path of non-alignment, utilised the erstwhile USSR as a balance against the USA in 1971 and has looked after Indian interests well. However, while diplomacy has generally done well on the international relations front, it has failed to provide a solution for India's external security problems. Diplomacy has failed with Pakistan, that it has failed with China is amply clear from the continuing Ladakh imbroglio with China. It has also failed in preventing China from influencing

India's neighbourhood in a manner inimical to India's interests. India has also not utilised its military power to find a solution to its security concerns. Brig Rumel Dhaiya (Retd) in his article on National Security Strategy argues that there is a lack of appreciation at the highest levels of the government about the use of force as an instrument of international politics and this leads to a lack of direction for the military. He further states that in India "security policy has become subservient to foreign policy".[44] All the wars that India has fought since independence were wars that were thrust upon it by either Pakistan or China. Indian diplomacy since independence has generally functioned in isolation without the backing of hard power capability. The Indian state has rarely utilised power as a tool for achieving foreign policy objectives. A nation's capability and credibility in international relations would depend on its hard power, both military and economic and hence its intent would be measured against its capability to influence. Diplomacy and military are two sides of the same coin for achieving national aims and therefore a synergised and integrated approach between them is essential. As brought out in the second chapter, ancient India 1800 years ago during the period of the Gupta Empire had integrated military and diplomacy. Is there an imminent requirement for India to do the same today for an effective approach to national security?

The military capability of a nation is directly affected by its economic capability. In India's ministerial form of governance, the Ministry of Finance (MoF) is responsible for the financial planning and MoD is responsible for the military capability of the nation. In its annual budgeting exercise, the MoF earmarks a certain amount of the nation's financial resources known as Defence Budget for the military. This is an annual independent mathematical exercise of the MoF, and it does not reflect or is not dependent on the requirements of the military. MoD prepares its ICDP for a period of 10 years which is a wish list for capability development. It utilises the annual defence budget as per the AAP prepared by it (by a process as discussed earlier). The MoF and the MoD operate in their silos as per their perception of national requirements to fulfil their individual responsibilities. This operating in silos results in the MoF having no stake in the security capability of the nation and the MoD preparing its capability development plans detached from the other economic requirements of the nation. By having an integrated approach can these ministries propel India on a path to build-up a military industrial complex?

India's strategic culture and ancient past bring out that security along with the welfare of the people is the most fundamental responsibility of the state. The three most important ministries tangibly affecting national security on the external front viz. MoF, MoD and MEA operate in different silos without having an integrated approach to national security. However, inspite of functionally overlapping in each other's domain, they also have their distinct functions. For a cohesive approach towards building up comprehensive national power is there a requirement to integrate these ministries to an extent where they functionally synergise with each other? Is there a requirement to evolve from MoD to Ministry of External Security? a ministry responsible for comprehensive national power?

Application of hard power – the Military

The next step would be to analyse the utilisation of hard power to meet national objectives. When a country decides to use hard power, it is a national decision. In such a situation there are certain fundamental questions that need an answer. They are whom to fight? why to fight? when to fight? where to fight? with what to fight? and how to fight? The word 'fight' denotes the kinetic application of national power. Of these questions 'why' and 'whom' is a national decision in which the military has no role to play, however, the MEA and MoF would be involved. The questions 'when', 'where' and with 'what' would involve the political leadership, MEA, MoF and the military. 'How' is the domain of the military and should be best left to it. The question 'why' is a political question and does not concern the military. But the question 'whom' and 'where' will determine the capability build-up of the military, it will determine the solution to the 'with what' question. The geographical expanse of India is immense. Its location places on it the responsibility to be the dominant power in the Indian Ocean to ensure its security. The expanse of its borders varies from high mountainous terrains to deserts and to areas with large expanse of canals and rivers. Air power has long back expanded to Aerospace power. This places an onus on India to develop capabilities across varied geographical terrains, in the seas and the aerospace dimension. Therefore, the resources that India needs for the 'whom', 'where' and 'with what' question is humongous. It is a question for which the answer cannot be only military, neither does it belong in the realm of diplomacy. There can only be a diplo-military approach to these questions until India reaches an economic capability, where it can earmark adequate resources for its military power across dimensions. Does the present Indian security setup have the institutional structures which can provide comprehensive options to the political executive for these questions to enable decision-making? This brings us to the current procedure of capability build-up followed by the military.

The army, navy and air force of India require modernisation and capability enhancements. All are short of the capabilities that they would ideally need to meet their responsibilities. The ICDP path that has been charted in the present DAP 2020 caters for extensive consultation between the three Service Headquarters and IDS, while the ICDP is being prepared. The non-availability of adequate resources leads to each Service prioritising and compromising on what it needs and ICDP is only a conciliation path between them. This exercise happens based on the Raksha Mantri's Op directive. This entire process does not provide comprehensive guidance to the 'whom', 'where' and 'with what' questions. Indeed, the present system is an improvement over the individual service approach of the past. But does the present system provide effective guidance to the military and does it enable the military to approach capability development in an integrated holistic manner? When capability development happens disjointedly and is a compromise by each Service, can Integrated Commands be the ideal solution? Will an effective answer to the 'whom', 'where' and 'with what' questions at the politico-military level enable an integrated capability development?

Conclusion

The security architecture of India which deals with external security starts at the top with the CCS. It is the executive body of the government responsible for all policy matters related to defence, policy matters of external affairs affecting national security, economic and political issues affecting security and all such matters which impinge on national security. It is the highest decision-making body on all matters of national security. In India the executive is answerable to the parliament. Therefore, all decision-making structures of the government are accountable to the Parliament.

After the CCS, is the NSC structure comprising of the NSC, SPG, NSA, NSCS and NSAB. The NSC structure is supposed to function as the think tank of the government. The composition of the CCS and the NSC is the same, the difference being that the CCS is responsible for taking executive decisions on matters placed before it, whereas the NSC is the highest body of the NSC architecture and is responsible for deliberating on issues brought up to it by the various components of the NSC structure. The SPG comprises the Cabinet Secretary, CDS and defence and bureaucratic heads of ministries affecting national security either directly or indirectly. It is the highest body for inter-ministerial coordination. The members of the SPG have the tremendous responsibility of their departments and therefore may not be able to provide undivided attention to national security. The NSA and the NSCS under him are the primary structure that focuses on aspects of national security. The NSA is the primary national security adviser to the Prime Minister. The NSA and the NSCS are not responsible to the Parliament primarily because they are an advisory body and because they are an advisory body, they do not have an executive role as defined by AoB / ToB rules except for functioning as the secretariat of the NSC and to assist the NSA.

The primary ministry which deals with the hard power of the country is the MoD. Before December 2019, the MoD was dominated by the bureaucracy. All the affairs of the military earlier were handled by the DoD headed by the Defence Secretary. Post the establishment of the

CDS and the DMA, all military affairs have now shifted to the DMA with the CDS being its secretary. This has integrated the military with MoD and a military officer for the first time has been given executive powers of the government; though as per the AoB rules, defence of India is still the executive responsibility of the Defence Secretary. IDS working under the CDS is the primary agency now to bring coordination between the three services. It is also responsible for integrated capability building of the military.

MoD, MEA and MoF are the three important ministries responsible which tangibly affects India's hard power for external security. All these three ministries work in silos and even though there is consultation between them on important issues, they do not have an integrated approach to national security. Traditionally India's strategic calculations for its external security have been dominated by its foreign policy. India has rarely used power as an instrument of international relations or as means to resolve its external security issues. Diplomacy alone has not been able to provide India with a solution for its security conundrum. So, is there a requirement to evolve a diplo-military approach towards it? The present modus operandi between the MoD and MoF has not yielded the desired results. The MoF has no stake in the military capability of the country as much as the military prepares its capability build-up plans without being aware of the economic commitments of the country. Therefore, is there a requirement for an integrated approach between the MoD, MEA and MoF for build-up of comprehensive national power? Can the MoD spur the growth of the industrial capability of the country?

With the creation of the CDS and the DMA and the promulgation of the new DAP, the military has adopted a much-needed integrated approach to capability build-up which is currently based on the RM's op directive. This integrated approach however is a compromise and prioritisation by each service of its capability requirements due to budgetary constraints. Although better than the previous approach it still is not the most optimum. The present security structure does not provide a comprehensive multi-ministerial answer to the fundamental questions for utilising military power viz, 'who' to fight, 'where' to fight, 'when' to fight and 'with what' to fight. The answer to these questions has to be a comprehensive whole of nation approach to provide the right direction for not only capability build-up but to also provide options to the national leadership for utilising power for not only security but also for securing national interests.

The next chapter will attempt to situate the military in India's democratic set-up. It will try and provide an answer to the questions raised in this chapter. While attempting to do so, it will also examine the defence reforms of countries like the USA and China. The difference of India's strategic culture with these countries and its strengths and weaknesses will also be taken into account while analysing the defence reforms. The final aim is to propose a change in the present MoD to enable a comprehensive approach to external aspects of national security.

Notes

1. Pradeep Kaushal, "Why Cabinet Committees are formed, what are the functions of each". *The Indian Express*, (June 07, 2019) at https://indianexpress.com/article/explained/why-cabinet-committees-are-formed-what-are-the-functions-of-each-5768896/ accessed on July 24, 2020.
2. Ibid.
3. Cabinet Secretariat of India, "Business Rules/Transaction of Business Rules", (April 03, 2020) https://cabsec.gov.in/businessrules/transactionofbusinessrules/ accessed on July 26, 2020.
4. Ibid.
5. Ibid.
6. Cabinet Secretariat of India, "Business Rules/Allocation of Business Rules", (April 29, 2020), https://cabsec.gov.in/businessrules/allocationofbusinessrules/completeaobrules/ accessed on July 29, 2020.
7. Ibid., p. 177.
8. Narender Kumar, "Defence Planning: A Review" in *Defence Reforms-A National Imperative,* ed., by Gurmeet Kanwal and Neha Kohli (New Delhi: Pentagon Press (IDSA), 2018), p. 22.
9. Cabinet Secretariat Resolution No. 281/29/6/98/TS, dated 16 April 1999, The Gazette of India, 19 April 1999, available at https://archive.org/details/in.gazette.e.1999.383, accessed on August 13, 2020.
10. IANS. "Strategic Policy Group reconstituted, Ajit Doval is Chairman". *The Hindu*, (October 10, 2018) at https://www.thehindu.com/news/national/strategic-policy-

group-reconstituted-ajit-doval-is- chairman/article25175468.ece accessed on August 04, 2020.

11. Arvind Gupta, *How India Manages its National Security* (Gurgaon, India: Penguin Random House India, 2018), p. 340.
12. Ibid., p. 341.
13. PTI. "National Security Advisory Board reconstituted with ex-envoy to Russia Raghavan as head". *The Economic Times*, (July 13, 2018) at https://economictimes.indiatimes.com/news/defence/national-security-advisory-board-reconstituted-with-ex-envoy-to-russia-raghavan-as-head/articleshow/54765284.cms accessed on August 10, 2020.
14. P.S. Raghavan, "The Evolution of India's National Security Architecture", *Journal of Defence Studies*, vol. 13, no. 3, July-September 2019, p. 45, at https://idsa.in/jds/13-3-2019-evolution-of-india-national-security accessed on August 06, 2020.
15. Ibid.
16. Cabinet Secretariat Resolution, n. 9.
17. Ibid.
18. PS Raghvan, "Re-Energising India's National Security Structures". *Strategic News International,* (April 22, 2019) at https://sniwire.com/2019/04/22/re-energising-indias-national-security-structures-2/ accessed on August 11, 2020.
19. Refer S.D. Pradhan, 'National Security System—Evolution', in Satish Kumar (ed.), *India's National Security: Annual Review 2010*, (New Delhi: Pentagon Press, 2010), pp. 444–45 for further details of the reorganisation.
20. P.S. Raghavan, "The Evolution of India's National Security Architecture", *Journal of Defence Studies*, vol. 13, no. 3, July-September 2019, p. 41, at https://idsa.in/jds/13-3-2019-evolution-of-india-national-security accessed on August 06, 2020.
21. Ibid.
22. Ibid., p. 43.
23. Cabinet Secretariat of India, n. 6.
24. Ibid.
25. CGDA, "Role & Functions of the Finance Division" at https://cgda.nic.in/index.php?page=deffinaccessed on August 27, 2020.
26. Satish Dua, "HQ Integrated Defence Staff in the National Security Structure", *Journal of Defence Studies*, vol. 13, no. 3, July-September 2019, p. 62, at https://idsa.in/jds/13-3-2019-evolution-of-india-national-security accessed on August 28, 2020.
27. Ibid.
28. Integrated Defence Staff, "Medical" at https://www.ids.nic.in/medical-issues.php accessed on August 29, 2020.
29. Sishir Gupta, "India to create super-committee for defence planning", *Hindustan Times*, (April 19, 2018) at https://www.hindustantimes.com/india-news/india-to-create-super-committee-for-defence-planning/story-PQSPeTpZ8Xm2QKjINXzxnK.html, accessed on August 29, 2020.

30. Manoj Joshi, "Higher defence management with Indian characteristics", *Observer Research Foundation*, (April 21, 2018) at https://www.orfonline.org/research/higher-defence-management-indian-characteristics/, accessed on August 29, 2020.
31. Press Information Bureau, Government of India, Ministry of Defence, February 03, 2020, at https://pib.gov.in /newsite/PrintRelease.aspx?relid=198899, accessed on March 07, 2021.
32. Ibid.
33. MoD, Department of Defence, "Procedure followed in the decision-making process including channels of supervision and accountability" at: https://www.mod.gov.in/dod/proactive-disclosuresaccessed on August 29, 2020.
34. Lieutenant General Philip Campose (Retd), *India's National Security Strategy: Imperative of Integrating Defence Policy*, (CLAWS Journal, Winter 2016), p. 18.
35. Satish Kumar, 'Unmitigated Threats Diffident Responses', in Satish Kumar (ed.), *India's National Security: Annual Review 2016-17*, (New York: Routledge, 2018), p. 426.
36. Shreemoy Talukdar, "US FONOP in India's EEZ: Storm in a teacup, but issue highlights residual baggage of Cold War era", *First Post*, (April 12, 2021) at https://www.firstpost.com/india/us-fonop-in-indias-eez-storm-in-a-teacup-but-issue-highlights-residual-baggage-of-cold-war-era-9519091.html, accessed on April 17, 2021.
37. HT Correspondent, "Greater integration between foreign and military policies key to cope with challenges: Jaishankar", *Hindustan Times*, (December 13, 2020) at https://www.hindustantimes.com/india-news/greater-integration-between-foreign-and-military-policies-key-to-cope-with-challenges-jaishankar/story-ua1YejUQQ6d9hPNDVrDKgO.html, accessed on April 18, 2021.
38. Manu Pubby, "Cabinet Secretariat raps MoD, MEA for not involving NSA" *The Economic Times*, (August 21, 2019) at https://economictimes.indiatimes.com/news/politics-and-nation/cabinet-secretariat-raps-mod-mea-for-not-involving-nsa/articleshow/70776972.cmsaccessed on August 23, 2020.
39. Arvind Gupta, *How India Manages its National Security* (Gurgaon, India: Penguin Random House, 2019), p. 61.
40. Cabinet Secretariat of India, "Business Rules/Allocation of Business Rules", (April 29, 2020), https://cabsec.gov.in/businessrules/allocationofbusinessrules/completeaobrules/ accessed on July 29, 2020.
41. Shekhar Gupta. "The new Doval Durbar reduces India's layered security system to a top-down Caliphate" *The Print*, (October 13, 2018) at https://theprint.in/national-interest/india-gets-a-national-security-adviczar-it-is-ajit-doval/133795/ accessed on April 18, 2021.
42. Jaswant Singh, *Defending India* (Bangalore: Macmillan India Ltd., 1999), p. 272.
43. Arvind Gupta, n. 38, p. 60.
44. Rumel Dhaiya, 'Reforming the Military Institutions and National Security Strategy', in Krishnappa Venkatshamy, Princy George (ed.), *Grand Strategy for India 2020 and Beyond*, (New Delhi: IDSA, Pentagon Press, 2012), p. 77.

6. Transforming Ministry of Defence to Ministry of External Security

Do not be led by others, awaken your own mind, amass your own experience, and decide for yourself your own path.

– Atharva Veda

In India there are various institutions and departments that deal with external security. Of all these institutions, the military represents hard power and is the pivot of external security. The Indian Constitution envisages the military as an instrument of the State. Analysis of the present security structure that deals with external security has brought out the need for integration between the various arms of the government which influence the execution of external security responses. The study of military history and strategic culture of India also provide lessons which are relevant even today in shaping India's security responses. This is primarily because India being a continuous civilisation has undergone a certain conditioning throughout its history, leading to the shaping of its strategic thought and attitude to war. Instead of doing piecemeal alterations in the security structure there is a need to carry out a major overhaul to bring this structure in synchronisation with the present and futuristic security needs of the nation. While attempting this overhaul it would be prudent to amalgamate the present deficiencies with the lessons of the past so that the new structure is able to cater for both.

The present chapter aims to amalgamate the present deficiencies of India's external security system with lessons from the past and then tries to provide a solution in the form of a structure which meets both the requirements. Before attempting a solution for the shortcomings in the present structure, the military reforms of the USA and China have also been looked at to understand any relevant lessons for India. While doing so, the attempt has been to analyse whether India should follow them or chart its own path depending on its requirements, as its strategic culture is distinctly unique.

In a democratic system the effectiveness of the military is dependent upon the civil military setup and the Higher Defence Organisation (HDO). The primary aim of understanding civil military relations is to increase the effectiveness of military power and consequently national power to an extent where it can fulfil all security requirements. Therefore, it would be pertinent to begin with understanding the civil-military relation as envisaged in the Indian Constitution.

Role of the Military as per the Constitution

To develop a correct understanding of the civil-military relation in India and its external security set-up, it would be relevant to understand the role of the military as envisioned in the Indian Constitution. As per the Constitution is the military responsible for protecting the territorial integrity of India? Is it responsible for protecting the people of India? or is it responsible for protecting the constitution of India? As per Article 53 (2) of the Constitution of India "the supreme command of the Defence Forces of the Union shall be vested in the President".[1] As per the same Article 53(1) the executive power of the Union is vested in the president. Hence, as per the Constitution, the President is the supreme and executive commander of the defence forces. As per Article 74 of the Constitution, the President exercises his executive powers on the advice of a Council of Ministers headed by the Prime Minister. Therefore, the Indian Constitution provides that the functional control of the military though exercised by the President is actually guided by the Council of Ministers headed by the Prime Minister. Thus, effectively the functional control is with the Prime Minister and his Council of Ministers. The responsibility of the military is therefore to the government of the day. As per the Constitution of India the military is an instrument of the government represented by the Prime Minister and his Council of Ministers and its responsibility is to carry out orders as issued by the government. As per the Constitution the military does not have any other responsibility and therefore is not empowered to act independently of the government on any issue including threat to the territorial integrity of India, threat to the people or threat to the Constitution. This is the foundation of the Civil Military Relations of India. With this as background, before moving on to analysing India's security structure dealing with external security it would be germane to understand the security reforms of the USA and China and its relevance to India.

Higher Defence Organisation of the USA

The USA has a presidential form of government. As per the constitution of the USA, the President is the Commander-in-Chief of the armed forces and "he is authorised to direct the movements of the military forces placed by law at his command, and to employ them in the manner he may deem most effectual to harass and conquer and subdue the enemy".[2] The military in the USA have dual control; they are also controlled by the Congress. The Congress has the power to declare war, to raise and support the military and to make rules for the regulation of the military.[3] The authority to declare war is with the Congress and to execute that war is with the President. In contrast, as per the Constitution of India the entire executive powers with respect to the military are vested in the President to be exercised on the advice of the Council of Ministers headed by the Prime Minister. Thus, the Cabinet in India has complete authority over all functions including employment and maintenance of the military in India.

Jointness in the US military began in 1903 when a joint board was established comprising military heads of the Army and the Navy; it was not effective and had no impact during the first World War. The US Joint Chiefs of Staff (JCS) was established in 1942 to meet the requirements of jointness in the Second World War; it had no legislative sanction or formal Presidential definition. The JCS was formally established by the National Security Act of 1947.[4] The JCS consisted of the Service Chiefs of the Army, Navy and the Air Force. They were made responsible for preparing joint plans for strategic direction, logistics, training and education. They were also to establish unified commands in strategic areas where such commands are in the interest of national security. The JCS was to act as the principal military advisor to the President and the Secretary of Defence. The Act of 1947 also led to the establishment of the National Security Council (NSC) to advise the President on foreign and defence policy and Central Intelligence Agency (CIA) for collection, analysis and distribution of intelligence.

On August 10, 1949, the US President signed the 'National Security Act Amendments of 1949'. It led to the National Military Establishment being redesignated as Department of Defence headed by the Secretary of Defence under the President. It also created the post of Chairman JCS who was to preside over the JCS but had no command authority over them or the Services. The entire JCS was designated as the principal military advisor to the President, Secretary of Defence and the National Security Council with its own staff of 210 officers.[5] Each of the Services were controlled by a Military Department with a Secretary as its head, functioning under the Secretary of Defence. The Service Chiefs apart from being part of the JCS were also responsible for the functioning of their individual Service under the Secretaries.

Reorganisations were again carried out in 1953 and the commands of the operational unified and specified commands were placed under the military departments. In 1958 another review was carried out and the chain of operational command of the unified commands became from the President to the Secretary of Defence to the JCS and then to the commanders of the unified commands. The military departments were removed from the chain of command. The JCS became the immediate military staff of the Secretary of Defence and became responsible for strategic plans and strategic directions of the armed forces.[6] The Service Chiefs were responsible to organise, train, equip, support and administer their combat forces but had no operational control over them. In 1978 the Commandant of Marine Corps also became part of the JCS.

The next major changes happened by the Goldwater-Nichols Defence Reorganisation Act of 1986. The Chairman JCS became the principal military adviser rather than the corporate JCS. It ended the consensus decision making of the JCS. Post of Vice Chairman was created to assist the Chairman and to act in his absence or disability. All functions of the JCS were assigned to the Chairman. The other members of the JCS could provide their advice if they differed from the Chairman or when sought by the President.[7] The operational control of the combined commands ran from the President to the Secretary of Defence to the commanders of the combined commands; however the Secretary was authorised to use the Chairman JCS as his channel of communication to the combined commanders. The US DoD presently functions with this structure.

Analysis of USA HDO

The US DoD structure originated with its experiences form the Second World War. During this war it operated with Britain in combined command structures and had to create JCS structure to coordinate the war with Britain. As a result, when it reorganised its military in 1947 and 1949, it opted for combined commands and JCS structure for operations. The responsibility for organising, equipping and training each component of the combined command, was not of the commander of the combined command but that of the individual Service headquarter. It thus followed a dual structure, one for operations and other for training and sustenance of individual service components. Inspite of following a structure of combined or joint commands, desired integration between the services did not happen before 1986, which is 37 years after the combined commands were created.

The major factors which led to the Goldwater-Nichols Reform were many. During the botched-up Operation Desert One, in 1980, the US tried to extricate American hostages from Tehran; however, it was a major failure as the Services were unable to operate together effectively.

During investigations into the failure of the operation, the NSA testified before the Senate Committee that individual service interests dictated military actions and hampered joint mission requirements. Similarly, the Grenada operations of 1983 brought to the fore the lack of joint communication equipment leading to communications breakdown during operations. The analysis of the Beirut bombings of 1983 indicated that the individual component commanders in the combined commands often prioritised orders from their service's headquarters in Washington over those of the commander of the combined commands.[8] The Goldwater-Nichols Act tried to overcome these problems. Kathleen J. McInnis in her Congressional Paper on the analysis of Goldwater-Nichols Act cites a study conducted by the National Defence University of the USA of operations conducted after September 11, 2001. She brings out that in 2006 operations in Iraq, the President went against the advice of his military and defence leadership as they failed to provide him with comprehensive military options. She further states that civil-military cooperation is required for making effective strategy and that a whole of government effort is required for policy formulation rather than focussing too much on the military in national-level decision making.[9]

The USA experience with its DoD brings out that merely establishing joint commands for operations is not sufficient to ensure jointness. More important is joint creation of capability to ensure interoperability between force structures. Joint creation of capability will ensure commonality in equipment and procedures wherever required and possible. It will not only enable integration of operations but also the economy of effort. Jointness or integration in planning of strategic military aims and acquisition of capability for achieving it, is the basic requirement for integrated operations. The US, being a global power conducts military operations across the world and therefore it carried out structural reforms to meet its requirements, which were different than any other nation's necessity and hence it charted its own path. That is the lesson learnt from the USA experience; each country must chart its own path based on its requirements, its strengths and its weaknesses.

Higher Defence Organisation of China

In 2015 President Xi Jinping of China led his country down the path of major reforms in the organisational structure of the People's Liberation Army (PLA). These reforms intended to transform all the major elements in the area of defence and national security. The goal was to create a modern Chinese military to implement the Chinese dream of renewal of the great Chinese nation. The aim was also to emphasise the leading role of the Communist Party of China (CPC) in all major aspects of the country.[10]

In China the PLA is subordinate to the CPC and it does not have an independent role. This stems from the lesson that China had learnt in the beginning of the 20th century. In 1911 dictator General Yuan Shikai seized power after the fall of the Qing dynasty. His death was followed by a number of military coups and counter coups with the military substantially interfering in politics. The Kuomintang (China Nationalist Party) ruled China from 1919 to 1949 when in the civil war it was defeated by the CPC. Subsequently the PLA played an important role during the cultural revolution in China. The main control over the PLA is by the Military Council of the CPC Central Committee. The Military Council has existed since the 1930s and its government counterpart is the Central Military Commission (CMC) of the PRC established in 1949 when the CPC took control of China. The Military Council and the CMC are two parallel organisations of the CPC. The reforms of 2015 affect the CMC and not the Military Council of the Central Committee of the CPC. Philip C. Saunders and Joel Wuthnow in their analysis of the military reforms state that the first basic principle in the military reforms was "to consolidate and perfect the basic principles and system of the Party's absolute leadership over the military".[11]

The PLA structure prior to the reforms comprised of the following:

- three services (army, navy and air force) and Second Artillery Force,
- four general departments viz. General Political Department (GPD), General Staff Department (GSD), General Logistics Department (GLD) and General Armaments Department (GAD) and
- seven military regions based on geography.

The navy, air force and Second Artillery were under the control of their headquarters, while the army was controlled by the General Staff Department. During peacetime the service headquarters had operational control over their forces and not the theatre commander of the military regions. All the general departments, the service headquarters and the military regions were directly controlled by the Central Military Commission (CMC).

The 2015-16 reforms changed the CMC structure. The GPD, GLD and GAD were renamed as departments looking after Political Work, Logistics Support and Equipment Development. The GSD was broken up into smaller departments now directly under the CMC. Second Artillery Force was renamed as PLA Rocket Force. The PLA Army headquarters was created under the CMC to look after the army. The seven military regions were changed to five theatre commands viz. Northern, Central, Eastern, Southern and Western theatre commands. A Joint Staff Department was created to deal with command-and-control functions for all the theatre commands and the headquarters of the army, navy and air force. The military structure of China after the reforms is as follows (image courtesy Philips C. Saunders and Joel Wuthnow, 2016):[12]

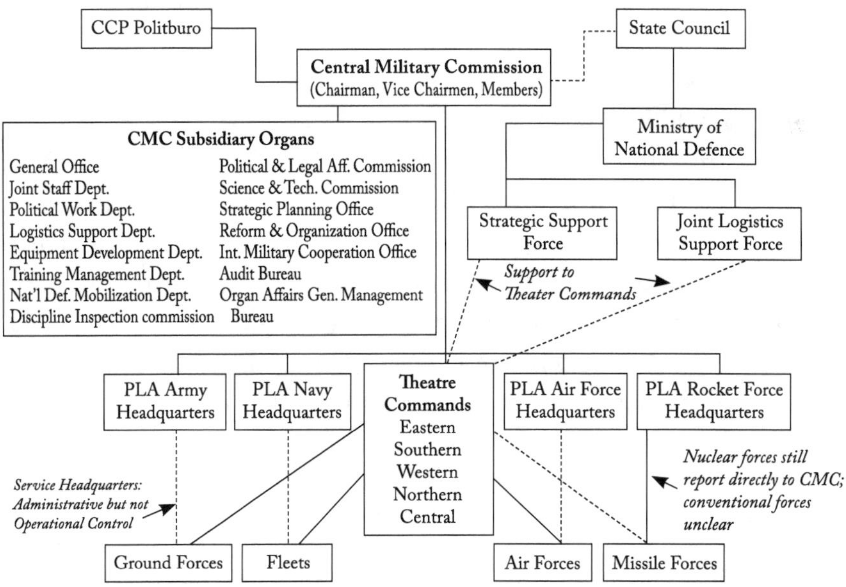

In the new structure, individual services are administratively managed by the Service headquarters while operationally they function under the theatre commands. CMC provides overarching control over the entire structure with the theatre commands and the Service headquarters functioning directly under its control in two parallel branches. A joint operations command centre has been created as part of the Joint Staff Department (CMC level) and also in each of the theatre commands. These are supposed to provide the Command and Control (C2) structure for operations and will function both during war and peace. At the theatre level they provide the link between the theatre commander and the component commander and combat units.[13] In the theatres, the individual service component commander will be under his Service headquarters for administrative control and under the theatre commander for operational control. The status of the Rocket Force component of the theatre command however is still unclear; with reports suggesting only a certain degree of control by it. It will not be completely under the control of the theatre commander.[14] The PLA had a dual command system in which the commander as well as the Political Commissar exercised authority at various levels of command, right from the theatre command down to the combat units' level; this has not been affected by the reforms.

Analysis of China's HDO

The CCP in China was founded in July 1921. The CCP created an armed force (Red Army) in 1927, after its members were persecuted by the Nationalist government in China. In 1948 the CCP renamed the Red Army as People's Liberation Army (PLA).[15] It defeated the Nationalist Army of China in a civil war in 1949 and took over control of China. The PLA therefore is an army raised by a political party (CCP) and the party has throughout ensured that the PLA continues to be a military belonging to the party and that it has a strong hold over it. One of the important aims of the military reforms of 2015-16 was to strengthen this control over the PLA by the CCP also known as the Communist Party of China (CPC).

After taking over as party chairman and President, Xi Jinping found that the PLA had inadequate supervision by the CPC. The CPC structure within the PLA was ineffective in exercising control over it. Joel Wuthnow and Philip C. Saunders argue in their analysis that there was reducing attractiveness of Marxism within the PLA, there was fear that the PLA might become a national army rather than a party army.[16] The general departments had gained too much power and this had led to corruption in the officer corps and undermining of the authority of the CMC. The functions of auditing and discipline were being done at the level of the general departments and this had rendered it susceptible to influence; hence there was a need to shift it to the level of the CMC.

China had a semblance of joint structure before the reforms, in the form of the Military Regions (MR). During operations the MR were supposed to control the forces within its geographical boundaries under the control of CMC, but during peacetime the Service headquarters controlled the combat units. There were problems of coordination and cooperation between the Service Headquarters and the MRs. China realised that the system that it followed had problems with command and control. It also realised the importance of joint operations from the conduct of US operations in the Middle East. Thus, China followed a path of military reform based on the structure that it had and its political needs of CPC control over the PLA. It has created new joint planning and command and control structures while following the path of dual control of its forces viz administrative control by the Service headquarters and operational by the theatre commands. This command and control structure is still not completely clear and how it will pan out is in the realm of the future.

What should India learn from the USA and China's military reforms

India is an ancient and continuous civilisation with 4000–5000 year old history and culture. It is continuous because in spite of invasions and colonisation there has been no break in its culture and consequently its strategic culture. As seen in the third chapter this continuation has led to its conditioning which can be termed as its strategic culture. The military structure of India may be what it inherited from the British, but the ethos of soldiering is as old as its culture and has been described in the third chapter. While trying to learn from the USA and China experiences, it needs to be remembered that both have evolved their structure from their own ethos and experiences.

As per a Congressional research paper prepared by the Congressional Research Service of the US Congress, "the designers of the Constitution were deeply sceptical of a standing army; as such a military instrument could also overthrow the government it professed to serve".[17] It cites Oliver Cromwell's disbanding of the British Parliament in 1653 to give an example of the military becoming a threat. Charles A. Stevenson in his work *Warriors and Politicians* states that the founders of the American republic were aware of the role that the military had played in making and unmaking of governments in Athens and Rome. He cites Samuel Adams to say that "a Standing Army, however necessary it may be at some times, is always dangerous to the Liberties of the People".[18] He further states that the revolt of the Americans in 1776 was "not only against British taxation but also against military domination".[19] Thus it is found that the American nation emerged with a deep mistrust of the military. This mistrust of the military has been the foundation of all military structures and reforms ever since and is reflected in all studies done on the civil-military relationship in the US.

China like India is one of the earliest continuous civilisations in the world with an ancient military history. Ancient China had a peasant-based army in which the emperor used to call upon the peasants to fight for him for protecting their state. Fighting for the king was an obligation for the farmers.[20] In contrast ancient India evolved a system wherein the responsibility of one varna (caste) was only warfighting and protection of the state. The common man in ancient India generally remained unaffected by the travails of war. Militaries evolved differently in China and India. When the CCP created the Red Army in 1927 it went on to become an army with mass mobilisation. In China militaries involved mass mobilisation of people, whereas in India militaries never became a mass mobilisation of the common man.

Contrast the US mistrust of the military with India's strategic culture. As brought out in the study of India's strategic culture done in the third chapter, the Indian military has an ancient legacy of non-interference in the affairs of the state. This is because soldiering in India evolved based on the concept of dharma, which in India defined the responsibilities of individuals as well as societal structures. In India, the responsibility of the king was defined by Raj-dharma and soldiering evolved based on the principle of Kshatriya-dharma. As a result, the military did not become a threat to the established mode of governance in the Indian subcontinent till the Turkish invasions. Instances of military coup happened during the Muslim Sultanate rule but there are no chronicled instances of military coup in empires and kingdoms ruled by kings following ancient Indian concepts like dharma. Post-independence, India and Pakistan inherited the same military and governance structures from the British; while Pakistan has undergone many military coups, the Indian military has never been a threat to the government (covered in the third chapter). This is a continuation of a military ethos and strategic culture that is 4000-5000 years old. This is one of the foundational differences between the US and Indian strategic cultures and needs to be taken cognisance of.

The ethos of soldiering that has evolved in India is very different from what has evolved in the USA or China. The Indian military ethos has its own strengths and weaknesses, and Indian policy makers need to recognise these. India's security architecture needs to be based on India's strategic culture; it needs to capitalise on its strengths and take care of its weaknesses. India would utilise a unique Indian strength, a legacy of its strategic culture since ancient times, if it integrates its military in the national security decision making structure, without fearing its interference in state affairs. Therefore, while it is prudent to learn from other's successes and failures, it is important that India finds its own solutions for its security problems. India's security architecture needs to be based on Indianness.

Questions before India's security architecture

In the previous chapter, while analysing India's security architecture, certain questions were raised. It would be prudent to revisit them before attempting to find a solution. The backbone for India's security structure is the NSC architecture. It has become the most important structure for inter-ministerial coordination and national security policy formulation. In the NSC structure the vital component is the NSCS which works de novo on national security.

NSCS advises the ministries on policy formulations. Implementation of policies is the responsibility of the ministries and they are the arm of the government responsible to the Parliament and to the people of India. They are the face of the government; success or failure on the part of a ministry is the success or failure of the Minister in-charge and consequently that of the Prime Minister. NSCS functions as a coordinator for either resolving an issue between ministries or to coordinate a policy affecting various ministries. It does not have any de facto authority over the ministries and its authority stems from the personality of the NSA. Issues on which the NSCS deliberates are decided either by the deputy NSAs or even by the members of the NSCS organisation. If the minister of a particular ministry is politically strong the ministry may overlook the NSCS. There may be a question of domain expertise between the NSCS and the ministries. Therefore, the NSCS never gets down to issues which challenge the expertise of the ministries. It follows an approach of conciliation and coordination to resolve issues and evolve consensus between various stakeholders. Policy guidelines generated by the NSCS are advisories; whether a ministry follows the inputs of the NSCS or not, the responsibility or accountability of the outcomes of its decisions will be of the ministry and the minister. The primary governance structures of India are the ministries. They are not only administrative structures, but they also represent the total capability of the Indian state in their respective domains and hence are representative of the best competence that the nation has in that domain. Therefore, a comprehensive approach to national security would need to be based on the ministerial system.

An international event affecting India's security would generally evoke a response from the ministries of Defence, Foreign Affairs and Finance. Response may be in the form of posturing of national power or political signalling, demonstrating the resolve of the nation to react to a situation. A nation's capability and credibility in international relations depends on its hard power both military and economic, and more importantly its will to utilise that hard power. Therefore, India's intent in the international arena would be measured against its capability to pursue and enforce that intent. An analysis of the ministerial way of working in the previous chapter has brought out that the present system of functioning in silos by the MoD, MEA and MoF has resulted in a disjointed approach to national security and does not provide a synergistic capability to respond. There is a requirement to synergise and integrate the functioning of these ministries to develop comprehensive national power and a coherent approach to national security.

The previous chapter also deliberated on the kinetic application of national power. It brought out the need for an institutional structure based on the ministerial architecture of governance, which can provide comprehensive answers to the questions 'why to fight', 'whom to fight', 'when to fight', 'where to fight' and 'with what to fight'. These questions are not for only the military to answer. These are national questions and need comprehensive answers. These questions will dictate the path that the capability development of national power would follow. It would need a cohesive approach both from the civil and the military, as it deals with the economic, military and diplomatic capability of the nation. These three are the foundational platforms on which several other offensive and defensive security capabilities are being built viz. information warfare, cyber warfare, electronic warfare, energy security, etc.

The threat from the nexus of China and Pakistan will always loom large on the Indian horizon. India's response would require a whole of government approach. Like the USA and China, India has security requirements which are very specific to it and therefore it needs to find a solution which corresponds to its necessities. The answer to most of the questions that have been deliberated above point in the same direction of an integrated civil-military institution combining the relevant expertise from different ministerial domains into a cohesive ministerial structure of the Ministry of External Security. India's evolution through the ages and its strategic culture from the ancient times is unique to India. Adopting institutional solutions from other nations even with alterations may not be the ideal answer for India's security. It would need to be based on its own strengths and weaknesses.

Challenges before the Military

The Indian security structure needs realignments and readjustments in its structure. There is also a requirement for greater integration among the various arms of the Indian military. The deficiencies in the military have been brought into the foreground by the government through assigning futuristic responsibilities to the newly created Chief of Defence Staff (CDS) and the Department of Military Affairs (DMA). The DMA, while being responsible for the routine affairs of the military, is also responsible for 'promoting jointness in procurement, training and staffing for the Services'. It is responsible for bringing jointness in operations by restructuring military commands including through establishment of joint commands.[21] The futuristic responsibilities of the CDS are to bring "jointness in operation, logistics, transport, training, support services, communications, repairs and maintenance etc of the Services and to ensure optimal utilisation of infrastructure".[22] The responsibilities of the CDS and DMA between them cover all aspects of the military from staffing to equipment and training. They indicate the requirement of bringing jointness or integration in all aspects of the military's operation. That is the task that has been cut out for the CDS and the DMA. It is mandatory for the Indian military to be able to achieve this to ensure that national resources are effectively utilised so that the military capability remains the pivot of national power.

The military needs to bring in jointness and integration in its operations, equipment, logistics, staffing and other aspects to ensure seamless interoperability of common platforms and services between the three arms of the military. The importance of this for integrated military operations can be understood from the USA experience wherein it established theatre or joint commands immediately after 1947, however during Operation Eagle Claw (to extricate hostages from Iran in 1980) which was 33 years after theatre commands were established, it found that interoperability was one of the main reasons for failure of the operation.

The military's capability should be able to provide effective options to the national leadership for utilisation of power. This would only happen if this capability development is not done in isolation only by the military, but as a national approach through civil military cohesion. The military's capability is not only its own, it is a representation of national power and hence all stakeholders need to be responsible to ensure this capability. This brings us back to the requirement of an integrated institution utilising civil and military competence for development of national power. As would be seen subsequently, such an institution would be able to bring about jointness among the Services and synergise their operation.

Lessons from India's Strategic Culture

It would be pertinent at this juncture to revisit the lessons from ancient India's military history and strategic culture. The second and third chapter of the book covers India's military history from ancient times in brief and India's strategic culture. The two most fundamental responsibilities of the State or the kingdom has been security, and welfare of the people, since the evolution of states in India. From the Vedic Period, India evolved a separate group or varna called the 'Kshatriya' for war fighting and his dharma was the Kshatriya-dharma. This ensured that the common man remained aloof from the travails of war (refer second chapter). As brought out earlier this was very different from the concept of war as it evolved in China, where it was basically people's war with masses participating. The Kshatriya varna was treated with utmost respect in society and consequently soldiering in India has always remained a very exalted occupation. Concepts of dharma and ethics of war which India developed millennia ago shaped India's approach to war fighting. Because of these factors India's strategic culture evolved very distinctly than any other civilisation of the world.

Indian history shows that whenever Indian kingdoms resorted to assertive or aggressive postures it resulted in almost pan-India kingdoms which defended India against external invasions. This mostly remains true throughout India's history since ancient times. *The first lesson that ancient India teaches is that aggressive pursuit of national interests and assertiveness are vital for security*. Examples of the empires of Mauryas, Guptas, Satvahanas, Lalitaditya, Cholas, Yashovaraman, Harshvardhan, Rashtrakutas, Gurjar-Pratiharas, Palas, Chalukyas, Mughals and many others bear testimony to it.

One prominent weakness displayed in the evolution of the strategic culture was India's penchant for dharmayuddha (fighting with ethics, refer third chapter). Weakness, because it could not match treachery and guile utilised by invaders in the tenth and twelfth century. There were other factors for defeat of Indian kings, but proclivity for dharmayuddha blunted the offensive edge of the Indian militaries and they mostly resorted to pitching strength against strength and war for defence. This does not mean that Indian kings were pacifist in their approach, but the approach to war was heavily influenced by the concept of dharmayuddha and it was followed in the wars of the subcontinent till the Turkish invasions happened. This proclivity for ethics in war did not manifest as weakness whenever India had strong militaries. This brings forth the second important lesson which is *the requirement of formidable military power (national power in today's parlance) to ensure security in consonance with Indian strategic culture's penchant for ethics in war and in pursuit of national interests.*

Indian subcontinent has been a witness to many great empires and military leaders. What is of significance is that some empires lasted for centuries while some existed only during the lifetime of their leaders. Examples of the former are the empires of Mauryas, Satvahanas, Guptas, Cholas, Vijaynagar, Mughals and many others and examples of the latter are Lalitaditya, Yashodharman, Kharavela, Yashovarman, Ranjit Singh and many others. The reason for some empires lasting many centuries is that they created effective military and administrative institutions which empowered these empires to create a great legacy. The effectiveness of great leaders lasts only for their lifetime whereas efficient institutions created by great leaders serve as an empowerment tool for society. *The great empires of India created prodigious military institutions which were supported by equally competent administrative structures.* This is the next important lesson from the strategic culture of India.

Indian empires even at the zenith of their power never indulged in territorial expansion beyond the Indian subcontinent. Inside the subcontinent the desire for a pan-India empire extending to all Jambudvipa (Indian subcontinent was known as Jambudvipa in Ancient Indian literature) always existed and hence wars were fought amongst Indian kings for supremacy. Military and strategic inadequacies of Indian kings in the medieval period resulted in their military defeat in the tenth and twelfth centuries, which resulted in destruction and carnage of Indian culture and society by invaders. India's history has ample lessons which demonstrate that military weakness adversely affected not only the security of the state but also led to the destruction of its culture and inflicted savagery and plunder on its people. India has faced continuous military threats right from ancient times till the colonisation by the British and even after independence in 1947. India's geography and history makes it incumbent on it to have a formidable national power pivoted on its military to ensure security.

Amalgamating the past and the present

Analysis of the present security structure dealing with external security as carried out in the previous chapter has brought out that the various important ministries which directly affect external security like MoD, MEA and MoF act in silos dictated by their responsibilities as assigned to them by the AoB Rules. It has also been brought out that the ministries are the main executing agencies of the government. In the present structure the NSCS led by the NSA is the only body which looks into inter-ministerial issues and does coordination and consensus building between the ministries for a definite outcome like evolving a policy or building consensus on a particular issue. However, the NSCS is not an execution agency of the government.

The three major ministries through their ministers provide their inputs and options to the Cabinet which is then responsible for taking decisions. But if a situation requires a response which is inter-ministerial like a particular security situation which warrants a response from MoD as well as MEA and maybe also the MoF, then there is no institution in the security framework which can generate these integrated or amalgamated options for the Cabinet to choose from. The first level at which these can be generated or deliberated is at the level of the CCS, which is a major shortcoming. Ideally the CCS should be able to choose from options which are presented to it and not generate them. In the past the response to external situations have been mostly single ministry controlled, like either a diplomatic response or a military response to an act of aggression or an economic response to a certain stimulus. But the Chinese aggression in Ladakh has demonstrated that India's response in the future will have to be a whole of nation approach, a comprehensive application of national power across multiple domains. In such a situation the present institutional security structure is woefully inadequate. It is incapable of generating options for the national leadership by utilising all domains of national power for an integrated response. As brought out earlier, at present the first level where such an integrated response can be generated is the CCS. Therefore, there is a requirement of an integrated institution comprising elements of MoD, MEA, MoF and intelligence agencies as part of a ministry, for capability build-up as well as for utilisation of comprehensive national power.

Will such an integrated institution be able to amalgamate the past and the present? Will it be able to take care of India's strategic shortcomings as displayed by its strategic culture brought out in the previous paragraphs? Will it be able to provide a solution to the questions posed to India's present security architecture dealing with external security? It would be prudent to begin with the lessons from analysing India's Strategic Culture, amalgamate them with the present objectives and examine as to what extent the present set-up is deficient in meeting them and the effectiveness of an integrated institution to meet those objectives.

National Objectives

Aggressive pursuit of national interests

Present

No national institution or ministry in the present structure empowers or enables the government with options for this approach. The only ministry which advises the government on dealings with other nations is the MEA and it is not empowered to follow an assertive approach. The MoD generally is consulted only when the territorial integrity is threatened.

Proposed

An integrated institution of MoD, MEA, MoF and Int agencies would be able to provide the options for an assertive approach to national interests should the government choose to exercise it.

The External Affairs Minister, S Jaishankar in a talk given at Manohar Parrikar IDSA, has highlighted the requirement of aligning the military and external affairs policy of the country and even going beyond aligning only policies for effective foreign policy.[23]

Requirement of formidable military power

Present

To MoD is responsible for development of military power. The only document which guides it in doing this is the RM's Op Directive which is for a period of five years and in most parts is prepared by it based on intelligence inputs. It also obtains inputs from the MEA while preparing the RM's Op directive but there is no continuous or seamless integration of diplomatic and military inputs and policies.

Proposed

An integrated institution will be able to correctly chart the path for capability build-up of national power. It will be able to predict and allocate resources as well as provide the right inputs and guidance for capability build up. It will be able to satisfactorily provide the answers for kinetic application of national power viz. the questions whom to fight, where to fight and when to fight. It will thus provide guidance to the capability build up question viz. with what to fight.

RM's Op directive is prepared by Integrated Defence Staff (IDS) in consultation with the Service headquarters. Based on available intelligence inputs a threat assessment is carried out by IDS in coordination with the three Services. Based on the threat analysis, measures to counter the threat are evaluated and forms part of the directive. It has inputs from other departments of MoD as well as from the Defence Planning Committee (DPC). Before finalisation it is sent for comments to MEA as well. It is revised every five years. Thus, it is found that RM's Op directive is an assessment of threats as perceived by IDS and the three Services and this perception of threats is based on intelligence inputs available at that period. The RM's Op directive is not integrated with the MEA's assessments of the international situation in India's neighbourhood. It is not a vision of the nation's approach to employment of military power. It is mostly based on the assessment by the MoD and therefore while it may represent the Indian military's response to military threats, it is an incomplete document when it comes to comprehensive capability build-up and utilisation of national power. This approach to security was able to meet national requirements in the past when the military was the only respondent to security threats but is a redundant approach to national security today. The Integrated Capability Development Plan (ICDP) of the MoD is based on this document and hence it will be inadequate in its scope for comprehensive capability development. This deficit can be met by an integrated institution of national power.

In the present security structure, it is solely the military's responsibility to build-up and sustain, power. It has to persuade the national leadership of its requirements and resources. There is a resource deficit between what the military wants and what it gets. However, because capability build-up is only the domain of the military, what prevents it from going overboard and building capability that may not be immediately required? India does not have unlimited economic resources to allocate to the military. In such a situation in the present set-up there is incoherence between what is demanded by the military and what it gets. This often leads to non-availability of resources even for critical requirements. The result is that India had to resort to emergency purchases for the military

Institution for build-up and sustenance of national Power

Present

The military is solely responsible for development of capability as well as its sustenance. In the present security structure, it is responsible for assessing threat, evaluating deficiencies in capabilities, convincing other government structures of its requirements and procuring it. Before the CDS and DMA the military was only an attached office of the MoD and was not a part of the government structure.

Proposed

An integrated institution will be able to comprehensively analyse not only threats to security but would be able to generate options for utilisation of power for the executive to fulfil national aims. It will ensure a whole of government approach towards this and capability build-up will happen in consonance with national requirements and national resource. It will provide a national institutional structure for development and sustenance of power.

when faced with imminent threats in the past.[24] The present security structure does not bring a whole of government approach to creation and sustenance of power. Security and welfare are the two most fundamental responsibilities of the state, since the evolution of state in ancient India. What has to take priority and when has to be a national decision with the military being a part of this decision making process as it is the military that has to ultimately bear the cross. Victory and defeat do not belong to only the military, the defence minister and the Prime Minister; it is attributable to every component of the government machinery which influences national power. Therefore, creation and sustenance of national power cannot be only the military's responsibility; it has to be a national responsibility. A cohesive institution comprising both civil and military, from ministries like MEA, MoD, MoF and intelligence agencies will bring a comprehensive approach and provide an option for one of the most important lessons from India's Strategic Culture.

In the present security scenario, soft power capabilities are as important as hard power. Offensive and defensive cyber capabilities and information warfare capabilities are domains where the lines for war and peace have blurred. These domains are continually engaged in a no war no peace scenario. With the fusion of Artificial Intelligence (AI) capabilities, the cyber domain has become a deadly space. The NSCS has made a timely intervention in this field with the National Cyber Security Coordinator and the Cyber Wing. Since the domain of NSCS includes both internal as well as external security it is the right organisation to develop executive capabilities in the soft power domain. Its mandate in these fields should not be restricted to policy advisories but to execution as well.

The above analysis brings out that the external security structure (dealt with in the fourth chapter) that India adopted post-independence did not cater for its strategic culture and is inadequate for its present security requirements inspite of few attempts to amend it. The structure was a mere continuation of the vestiges of the British empire. Therefore, there is a need for a major revamp of this structure instead of a disjointed approach to reform it.

Before, attempting a solution for India's external security structure based on its past and the present, it would be pertinent to remember a few aspects of the greatness that its strategic culture had achieved. The art of war was well understood and practised in India. There were detailed military and administrative structures for maintaining the massive military might of the Mauryan Empire comprising 6,00,000 infantry, 30,000 cavalry, 9000 elephants and 2000 chariots. Inspite of having a powerful military the Mauryan Empire did not attempt military conquest outside the Indian subcontinent. The same proclivity for not venturing outside the subcontinent was repeated in the next powerful empire that India witnessed, the Gupta Empire. History amply proves that Indian military power never ventured territorial conquest beyond the Indian subcontinent. If contrasted with European colonisation it serves to provide a reassuring intent of Indian power through millennia.

However, these empires ensured that the Indian subcontinent remained the domain of their influence.

The Gupta Empire integrated military and diplomacy into the office of 'Mahasandhivigrahika' (minister of war and peace). He worked closely with the military and the king. He advised the king on the relationship that the kingdom maintained with others and provided critical advice on the use of military power. It was a novel concept wherein he advised the king on which kingdoms could be annexed and which could remain feudatory states. This innovative concept has been utilised while proposing an external security structure for India.

India's strategic culture was rooted in ethical concepts. Society was based on dharma (explained in detail in the third chapter). It was the socio-political and philosophical basis of societal functioning and influenced all aspects including war. It led to the development of ethics in war fighting as early as the period of the Epics (approximately 1000 BC). It is a factor which influences Indian society even today. The concept of dharma relates duty and responsibility to morality in a manner which is distinctly unique. Shri Krishna emphasised the importance of military victory to ensure dharma and this importance of military power needs to be factored in India's statecraft. While it is not only prudent but also necessary to learn and adopt the latest in technology, but institutions need to be based on own requirements and societal structures. Having brought out the importance of an Integrated Institution as a structure which can effectively utilise the lessons from India's strategic culture as well as provide a solution for its present weaknesses, it would be astute to understand the outcomes that are desired from such an institution.

Outcomes from an Integrated Institution of National Power

India's External Affairs Minister (EAM) Dr S Jaishankar delivered a talk on the topic 'Contours of India's Foreign Policy: Diplomacy, Security and Trade'at the Manohar Parrikar Institute of Defence and Strategic Studies (MPIDSA) on December 13, 2020. In his talk the EAM emphasised on the need for India to give primacy to hard security, because of the security challenges that it faces. He stated that as India's interests expanded in the world it was imperative for it to focus on hard power. But what was more important, especially because it came from the EAM himself, was that foreign policy could not be conducted by the MEA alone. He said that "the complexity of national security issues requires serious specialisation and that also means it requires equally serious integration".[25] Acceptance of the need to integrate diplomacy and military could not have come from a higher government functionary. Before examining the contours of an integrated institution, it would be pertinent to understand the outcomes that would be required from such an institution.

Integrated analysis of external security imperatives

Various intelligence agencies are involved in gathering intelligence related to external security of the country. They provide inputs to NSCS, DIA, MEA and various other organisations. These organisations also have their own means of accessing intelligence. These inputs are analysed by these ministries and departments and inferences suitable to them are drawn out. There are no holistic or integrated analyses of these inputs. The Integrated Institution would be able to analyse a situation, an input or an issue comprehensively from various perspectives like diplomatic, military, economic and intelligence. This comprehensive analysis will lead to generation of options which will be integrated and represent a cohesive national approach to an issue. This analysis and response can then be provided to the political leadership of MoD, MEA, MoF and the CCS and NSC.

Countries in India's neighbourhood which directly affect the security of India would be the responsibility of this institution. It would be the main recipient of inputs about these countries from all domains like, military, diplomatic, economic and intelligence. These inputs would be analysed in all its dimensions at this institution and the output in the form of comprehensive information, analyses and options would be provided to the leadership of the ministries of MoD, MEA, MoF, CCS and the NSC. Since the information and analyses would be done by an integrated set-up therefore the action by the various ministries based on these inputs and analyses would present a coordinated approach or response by the government of India. This institution would be able to generate various options for the political executive which can then base its decisions on the direction that it wants the country to follow. The inputs can be in the form of weekly or fortnightly briefings. It would be a whole of nation approach. Presently the same is done in different departments and ministries leading not only to duplication but also to a disjointed approach. It would elevate the functioning of the national security apparatus to a realm where it would be a completely coordinated approach utilising both the civil and the military in a cohesive manner.

Creation of options for national response to forecasted security contingencies

Diplomatic analysis is an important aspect for understanding a country and forecasting the relationship that needs to be developed with it. However, only diplomatic analysis would be inadequate for a comprehensive understanding of a country. Analysis of intelligence, diplomatic, economic and military inputs would provide a better assessment of the path that a nation should take and therefore would be the key to developing its own response to it, be it in the economic, diplomatic or military domain. It will enable India to better develop its capabilities in the desired domain to respond to a particular country. It will enable the optimum utilisation of either economic power, diplomatic capability or military power. It would be a synergistic national approach. Intelligence agencies would be able to have a more coordinated and focussed approach. It would overcome the present disjointed approach that the various ministries follow by working in silos.

Synergised capability build-up of military power

The Integrated Institution would also be responsible for military strategy. It would be responsible for creating offensive capabilities to not only deter but also to punish belligerence. Since it would have the most comprehensive inputs and analyses about India's neighbourhood therefore, it would be responsible for identifying weaknesses and developing capabilities to exploit that weakness. One of the lessons of the strategic culture of India is the requirement to have an assertive approach for protection of national interests. The country's capability build-up needs to cater for the availability of requisite offensive capability across domains and interest areas. Analysis by the integrated institution would thus be the key to guide the national capability build-up. The security analyses would be done by all components including military, diplomacy, economic and intelligence. It would provide inputs to the political leadership about capability build-up which is immediately required and which can be gradually acquired. Since the institution is integrated therefore it would have economic and diplomatic inputs and analyses apart from military before arriving at the solutions for capability creation. Thus, capability creation would be the outcome of an integrated approach by economy, military and diplomacy right from the stage of analysis to generating solutions. This approach would synchronise national power with the resources that can be allocated for it. National security at times would require much more resources than can be allocated to it by the present method of defence budgets and at times development would take priority over capability creation. The integrated institution would completely synergise this process. MoF and MEA would be an equal stakeholder in the creation of national power as much as MoD. This would ensure the most optimum utilisation of national resources. Creation of national power would be a national responsibility rather than being the responsibility of only the military.

Analyses of security situations in an integrated manner would result in a coordinated diplo-military approach. A diplomatic outcome or end for a military action would be pre-coordinated. Similarly, a diplomatic approach to a situation would have the tacit backing of military power. The response to an emerging security or diplomatic situation can be in both domains with diplomacy usually being the primary responder. It would overcome the failure that Indian diplomacy has endured while engaging in protecting India's security interests.

The Integrated Institution would evolve military strategy based on its comprehensive analyses. This analysis would be a comprehensive diplo-military, intelligence and economic evaluation. It would estimate its own weaknesses and strengths against the adversary's weakness and strengths. Based on this analysis it would identify military objectives for various contingencies and situations. It would also need to work out the modalities of integrated application of military power for achieving the military objectives. From these modalities it would derive operational objectives for each Service. The Army, Navy and the Air Force have all got their inherent capabilities and strengths. Each of them would be required to achieve certain objectives independently and certain objectives jointly. These operational objectives and the modalities for achieving them would need to be specified by the Integrated Institution, for each Service. Effectively the Integrated Institution would be the **Centralised Joint Strategy Planning Institution** for the military. Operational responsibility for achieving the objectives set by the Integrated Institution will be that of the Chiefs of Staff Committee (COSC). Because military and operational objectives are being set-up by this Integrated Institution, therefore it would be the responsibility of this institution to ensure that each Service has the requisite military capability to achieve the operational objectives that are being set for it. Needless to say, capital procurement for the military would be the responsibility of this institution. The mandate of the Integrated Institution would be complete analyses, creation and strategising of national power. Based on the capability of national power that it creates it would be able to provide options to the national leadership for utilisation of national power. The Integrated Institution would be the principal executive institution for external security.

Fountainhead of indigenisation

The Integrated Institution would chart the path for the military capability build-up of India. It would be able to comprehensively project short term, medium term and long term procurement requirements specific to the Indian military. Presently India has no option but to import equipment that is available in the world market. To illustrate this, India, even after 73 years of fighting its first battle with Pakistan and 70 years after acknowledging China as a threat (China annexed Tibet in 1950 and forcibly became a threat to India), does not have the right military hardware for a battle in the mountains, whereas its entire border with China and its disputed areas with Pakistan are all in high mountainous terrain. Military equipment specific to Indian requirements would be specified by the Integrated Institution. Building military equipment specific to Indian needs would require huge investments in research and development. In the absence of requisite technical knowhow in the Indian defence manufacturing sector it would need collaboration with major world arms manufacturers. This would only happen if there are firm and long term commitments. The Integrated Institution would be able to offer such firm and long term commitments to the industry to enable them to invest heavily in R&D and collaborations. It would spur the growth of many ancillary industries. Therefore, it would become the fountainhead for creating a military-industrial manufacturing base in India.

Structure of the Integrated Institution

Unlike the NSCS the Integrated Institution would be an executive structure of the government. It would need to be part of a ministry. Depending on the outcomes that are required from the Integrated Institution it would be best suited if the Integrated Institution is a part of the MoD. Since the Integrated Institution would be responsible for a comprehensive approach to most aspects of external security, the MoD could be renamed as the Ministry of External Security (MES).

The Integrated Defence Staff of the MoD is presently responsible for strategic planning for the military in consultation with the Service Headquarters. It could be completely subsumed in the Integrated

Institution. Procurement directorates of the three Service Headquarters would become part of the Integrated Institution. Strategic planning cells of the three Service Headquarters would also need to move to the Integrated Institution. The COSC and the three Service Headquarters would be responsible for implementing operational strategy and achieving operational objectives as provided to them by the Integrated Institution. COSC would parallelly interact with the Integrated Institution.

All structures/country specific desks of the MEA which deal with India's neighbouring countries would integrate with the Integrated Institution. This would include all countries which directly or indirectly affect the external security of India. Similarly military officers would be posted to MEA to be part of country specific desks which deal with countries with which India has substantial defence engagements like the USA, Russia, Australia, European Union countries, Middle East countries, etc. There is a requirement to merge military and diplomatic expertise and hence the new MES and MEA would need to function in a more integrated manner. Components of MEA which deals with countries immediately affecting India's external security and would substantially influence national power build-up should integrate with the present MoD to form MES while military officers could be integrated with the MEA to assist diplomacy for those countries with which India has substantial military engagements.

The MES would function under the Defence Minister who would become the Minister for External Security. In the MES structure the newly created DMA would become the responsibility of the Chief of Integrated Staff to the COSC (CISC) or the Vice Chief of Defence Staff (VCDS). The CISC/VCDS could be Secretary of DMA. The CDS could play a larger role as being responsible for external security under the Minister in the MES. The Integrated Institution would be the responsibility of the CDS. The CDS would thus be the principal advisor to the Defence Minister and the CCS for external security. The MES and MEA would have the same inputs and would function in unison. NSA would be the principal advisor to the Prime Minister for all aspects of national security while the CDS would be responsible for external security. Will the Integrated Institution, MES and CDS dilute the role of the NSA? No. Presently the NSA is overburdened with all aspects of security. The proposed structure would take off some of his burden and provide him with coordinated options for external security, something which is not possible in the existing system.

Domains of cyber security and information warfare blend the realms of internal and external security. These domains therefore should be the responsibility of the NSCS. The NSCS already has a National Cyber Security Coordinator. It needs to create another wing for information warfare. The Integrated Institution however should have an External Cyber Cell and an External Information Warfare Cell, primarily for offensive operations. The Defence Secretary would be responsible for administration of the MES. He would also be the liaison between the MES and the industry for capability development. He would be responsible for the development of military industrial manufacturing base in India. He would also be responsible for coordination of MES with other ministries.

The above mentioned steps would necessitate a major change in the Allocation of Business (AoB) and Transaction of Business (ToB) rules. After independence the Service Chiefs were invitees to the CCS meetings which was subsequently diluted and they ceased to be a part of it. In the proposed structure the CDS should be an invitee to CCS meetings. The status of CDS would need to be elevated to that of the Cabinet Secretary. Security and welfare have been the primary responsibility of the state and security needs to be given its due importance, in the government scheme of things. The Integrated Institution would have elements of MoF and MEA. It would be pertinent at this stage to briefly look at the structure of these ministries and the proposed changes.

Structure of Ministry of Finance

MoF has six major departments, each headed by a secretary. These are as follows:

- Department of Economic Affairs

- Department of Expenditure
- Department of Financial Services
- Department of Revenue
- Department of Investment and Public Asset Management
- Department of Public Enterprises (shifted from Ministry of Heavy Industries and Public Enterprises in July 2021).

As per the MoF website, Department of Investment and Public Asset Management deals with all matters of the government related to investments and disinvestments. The Department of Revenue deals with all matters related to direct and indirect taxes of the government of India. The area of responsibility of the Department of Financial Services includes the functioning of financial institutions, banks, insurance companies and the National Pension System.[26]

The Department of Expenditure is responsible for managing the finances of the Central government and matters related to the finances of the various States of India. It has the responsibility for implementing the recommendations of the Finance Commission of India. "The principal activities of the Department include overseeing the expenditure management in the central Ministries/ Departments through the interface with the Financial Advisers".[27] The finance division of the MoD (covered in detail in Chapter 5) is headed by a secretary level officer. He acts as the integrated financial advisor for the Defence Minister for utilising the delegated financial powers of the defence ministry. In its present role the finance division acts to provide financial advice to the MoD and ensures adherence to financial procedures by it.

The Department of Economic Affairs formulates and monitors policies which affect both the domestic and international management of India's economy. It is responsible for the preparation and presentation of the Union Budget. Through various divisions like the bilateral cooperation division, infrastructure policy and finance division, investment division and international economic relations division, it coordinates India's economic interaction with other countries. It analyses and guides India's international economic policy. Economic evaluation of countries is carried out by this department and it also spearheads India's economic response.

The Central Government in its terms of reference for the 15th Finance Commission mandated it to recommend funding for defence and internal security. This was an important and unique step by the Government of India to find resources for security apart from the routine budget allotment for defence which happens every year as part of the routine budget exercise. The Finance Commission in its report, "re-calibrated the relative shares of Union and States in gross revenue receipts" to set aside resources for defence.[28] The Commission has recommended the creation of a "dedicated non-lapsable fund, Modernisation Fund for Defence and Internal Security (MFDIS)" in the Public Account of India with a corpus of Rs 2,38,354 crore over the period of 2021-26.[29] The Commission has recommended that 1.5 lakh crore would be transferred from the Consolidated Fund of India and the rest would be generated by monetising defence lands and disinvestment of defence public sector companies.[30]

Proposal

The present system of defence budgeting is inadequate to meet the requirements for capability build-up. The annual defence budget should only earmark finances for routine revenue expenditure and not for capital expenditure. Finances for capital expenditure should be earmarked into a non-lapsable modernisation fund as has been recommended by the 15th Finance Commission. This corpus should be utilised as and when required on the directions of the Integrated Institution. The Integrated Institution will ensure that capability build-up happens as a national responsibility thus ensuring the most optimum utilisation of this consolidated fund.

There would be a requirement to expand the role of the Financial Advisor Defence Services (FADS)/Secretary Defence Finance. The Secretary of the MoD finance division instead of being only a financial advisor would need to be integrated in the capability build-up process of the Integrated Institution. He would be responsible for not only providing economic advice but also provisioning of finances for capital expenditure in consultation with the Expenditure Division of the MoF. In case of emergent requirement of funds for security, he would be responsible to liaise with the MoF for provisioning the same. This would require modifications in the present budgeting and accounting procedures of the MoF. As a component of the Integrated Institution, Secretary Defence Finance would be an integral part of the decision making process for capability build-up. He should not function only as a financial auditor for proposals of capital acquisition but should be part of the proposal creation process. He and the finance structure under him would be a stakeholder in the development of national power. The ambit and responsibility of the defence finance division would need to be enlarged to enable it to shoulder this responsibility.

The Secretary Defence Finance will also be the link between the Economic Affairs Division of the MoF and the Integrated Institution. He would be responsible for getting economic inputs from the MoF about countries which affect India's external security and provide security inputs to the MoF about these countries. Alternatively, he could have the capability for economic analysis of these countries as part of the Integrated Institution. It would involve relocating some resources from the Department of Economic Affairs', Bilateral Cooperation Division (China desk) and International Economic Relations Division. It would fulfil the requirement of integrating economic analysis with external security as part of the Integrated Institution. The next step would be to analyse the structure of the Ministry of External Affairs.

Structure of the Ministry of External Affairs

The MEA operates through structures called divisions. These divisions are either functional in nature like the administrative division or based on geography (countries or regions). Each division based on geography has many countries under it. MEA functions through five secretaries under the External Affairs Minister (EAM). The secretaries are the Foreign Secretary, Secretary East, Secretary West, Secretary Economic Relations and Secretary CPV (consular, passport and visa) and OIA

(Overseas Indian Affairs). The Foreign Secretary is responsible for overall coordination and supervision. In addition, he looks after the affairs of China, Japan, USA, Nepal, Bhutan, Indian Ocean Region, Pakistan, Afghanistan, Iran, UK, France, Germany, Russia and other divisions of MEA like Centre for Contemporary China Studies (CCCS), administration, finance, etc. Secretary East is responsible for countries to the east of India and Secretary West for countries to the west of India except the ones under the Foreign Secretary. Subordinate to the secretaries the MEA has seven additional secretaries looking after various divisions.

The MEA divisions based on geography are AMS (Americas) Division dealing with the USA and Canada, BM division dealing with Bangladesh and Myanmar, Central Europe division dealing with central European countries, Central and West Africa division, East Asia division dealing with China, Mongolia, North Korea, South Korea and Japan, Eurasia division dealing with Russia, Ukraine, Georgia and other Central Asian countries, Europe West division, East and Southern Africa division, Gulf division, Indian Ocean Region division, Indo-Pacific division, LAC (Latin America and Caribbean) division, Northern division comprising Nepal and Bhutan, Oceania division dealing with Australia, New Zealand and Pacific Island countries, PAI (Pakistan, Afghanistan and Iran) division, Southern division dealing with South East Asian countries and WANA (West Asia and North Africa) division. The MEA also has a Policy Planning and Research division.

Proposal

The divisions of MEA which deal with countries directly influencing India's external security should be merged with the proposed Integrated Institution under the Ministry of External Security. The divisions which should be merged are PAI (Pakistan, Afghanistan and Iran) division, Northern (Nepal and Bhutan) division, Indian Ocean Region division, BM (Bangladesh and Myanmar) division and the section of East Asia division dealing with China. Simultaneously military officers should be deputed to function in the other geographical divisions of MEA during peacetimes. Pure diplomatic analysis of countries should be replaced by diplo-military analysis and option generation for formulation of diplomatic policies. Similarly military analysis of countries affecting India's external security should be replaced with diplo-military analysis for capability build-up.

Proposed Changes in the Ministry of Defence

The structure of the MoD was covered in detail in the previous chapter. With the proposed change of the MoD to MES, the structure of the MoD would need to change. The government has announced the dissolution of the Ordnance Factory Board and the creation of seven new PSUs in its place to manage the 41 Ordnance factories of India.[31] While describing the outcomes of the Integrated Institution it has been proposed that the Defence Secretary would be the liaison between the Integrated Institution and the industry to meet the procurement requirements of the military. In synchronisation with this role of the Defence Secretary it is proposed that the Department of Defence Production be merged with the Department of Defence and function under the Defence Secretary. The Integrated Defence Staff (IDS) would be completely merged with the Integrated Institution. With the proposed mandate of the Integrated Institution, it would also be possible to merge the Department of Ex-Servicemen Welfare with the Department of Military Affairs (DMA). It is proposed that the Secretary of the DMA should be changed from the CDS to VCDS. Operations of the military would be the responsibility of the Chiefs of Staff Committee (COSC) with the Army, Navy and the Air Force functioning under them. Joint military structures would also function under the COSC. Operational employment of the military would be the domain of the COSC. As mentioned earlier the procurement directorates and the strategic planning structures of the three services would shift from their individual headquarters to the Integrated Institution. The CDS would be responsible for all these structures under the Defence Minister. He would be the highest government functionary below the ministerial level dealing with external security of the country. Routine matters of the three services would be dealt by the DMA functioning under the VCDS. The protocol status of the CDS should be made equivalent to the Cabinet Secretary and he would be a non-member invitee of the Cabinet Committee on Security (CCS). The CDS could be renamed as Chief of External Security.

Organisational Structure of the Ministry of External Security

The organisational structure of the Ministry of External Security would be as follows:

The COSC would be responsible for execution of military operations. It would implement the operational directives as conceived by the Integrated Institution. The Integrated Institution would also provide inputs to the MEA and the MoF. Having seen the outcome expected from the Integrated Institution it would be pertinent at this stage to understand its structure.

Integrated Institution

The proposed structure of the Integrated Institution of External Security would be as follows:

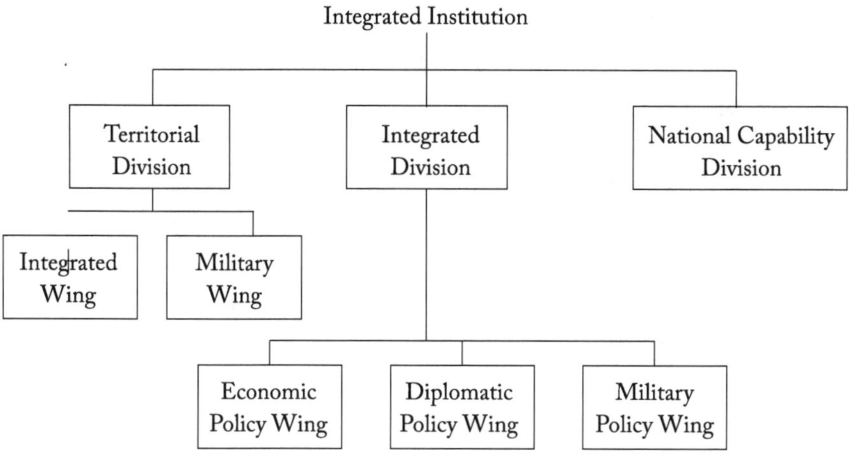

The Integrated Institution will have three divisions viz. Territorial Divisions, Integrated Policy Division and National Capability Division. The Territorial Divisions would be similar to the territorial division of the MEA. It would be either country specific or region specific. Some of the proposed territorial divisions would be China division; Pakistan division; Afghanistan, Iran and Tajikistan (AIT) division, Northern (Nepal and Bhutan) division, Bangladesh and Myanmar (BM) division and Sri Lanka and Maldives (SM) division.

Each of the territorial divisions would have two wings, an Integrated Wing and a Military Wing. The Integrated Wing would have officers from all the three Services, diplomats dealing with that country or region, economic officers dealing with that region and intelligence officers. The intelligence section would ensure that intelligence inputs from all sources for that region are available for analysis. The Integrated Wing would ensure that it has comprehensive input from all domains about its specific country or region. It would have the most complete knowledge about its region of interest. It would be responsible to carry out a complete analysis of its region of responsibility and prepare a 'comprehensive report'.

The comprehensive report of the Integrated Wing would be provided to the Military Wing of the Territorial Division. Based on this report it would carry out a comprehensive military analysis of its region. Based on this analysis it would generate options for utilisation of national power for specific goals as generated from the comprehensive report. Based on the options that it would generate for utilisation of power; it would also analyse and project capability requirements for the options that it has generated. These options would be for the present national capability as well as future projected capability. It would generate a 'military options and capability' paper.

The 'comprehensive report' and the 'military options and capability paper' would be provided to the Integrated Policy Division and the National Capability Division. The Integrated Policy Division would collate the report from the various territorial divisions and forecast security contingencies for various regions. It would amalgamate the reports and the forecasted security contingencies to generate national response options in various domains for it. It would deliberate on policy options for diplomatic engagement, economic engagement, options for employment of military power for various contingencies and capability development plan for the military. To help it in doing so it would have an economic policy wing, diplomatic policy wing and military policy wing. This division would be responsible for setting up military, diplomatic and economic objectives for utilisation of national power. While doing so, it would setup military operational objectives for the COSC, in consultation with it.

This division would generate a comprehensive document with economic options, diplomatic options, military options for each region/country being dealt with by the Integrated Institution and a comprehensive military capability requirement for the short term as well as for the long term. It would fuse the military requirement plan with the current military capability and in consultation with the economic policy wing and diplomatic policy wing, create a military capability development plan. The military capability development plan would also have an economic plan for achieving the capability build-up. It would also **create options for national security objectives based on present and forecasted comprehensive national power for the national leadership.** The options report and the military capability development plan of this division would be provided to the ministers of Finance, External Security, External Affairs, NSA, NSCS and the political leadership.

The National Capability Division would be responsible for the current national power capability and to ensure that it is capable of meeting national requirements. It would be in direct communication with the field forces and would interact with the three Services. It would be responsible for providing information of current capability to the Integrated Policy division. The military capability development plan when approved by the national leadership would be provided to the National Capability Division. It would be responsible for executing the capability development plan. It would fuse military requirements with national industrial capability and create an enabling environment for growth of military industrial complex. It would liaise with the Defence Secretary for fulfilment of projects and procurements. The Defence Secretary would liaise with the industry for procurements. The National Capability Division would be responsible to ensure timely completion of projects in coordination with the Defence Secretary. This division would have an external cyber cell and external information warfare cell for offensive purposes. Keeping abreast of the latest technological advancements in warfare would be the responsibility of this division. It would interact with the Department of Research and Development of the MES.

The Integrated Institution would parallelly interact with the COSC while formulating the military options as well as while preparing the capability development plans. The three Service headquarters under the COSC would be responsible for all military operations. The Integrated Institution because of its structure and mandate, would have comprehensive and updated information about its area of interest. This would enable it to immediately generate options for responding to any emerging military/diplomatic/economic situation that has the potential to affect India's security.

The tenure for personnel in the Integrated Institution should be a minimum of 10 years with adequate overlap during rotation. It would be prudent that military and civilian officers before getting posted to the Integrated Institution should undergo a 3-6 months course for getting familiarised with their area of interest and with strategic perspectives of the country at one of the designated think tanks. Operational control of the three Services would be with the COSC.

Control of the Military

The COSC would be subordinate to the CDS (CES) and would be responsible for operational control of the military. The Integrated Institution (Centralised Joint Strategy Planning Institution) would be responsible for joint strategic planning and setting up operational military objectives for the COSC. The CDS would cease to be the Chairman COSC. The senior Service Chief would be the Chairman COSC. In case of formation of theatre and joint commands, the theatre commands would report to the COSC, since it would be responsible for operations. The COSC would be accountable to the CDS for achieving its objectives, but the CDS would not interfere in operations. However, setting up military and diplomatic objectives would be the responsibility of the CDS in consultation with the CCS.

The allotment of military resources to the theatre commands depending on the objectives to be achieved will be done by the COSC. The COSC will hold adequate reserves under its command (COSC Reserve Forces) to be allotted to a theatre command as required. This would be done during peace as well as during war. The Commands would not have fixed assets of their own. The assets of the theatre commands/ single service commands would be dynamically controlled by the COSC. Strategic assets would be centrally controlled by the COSC.

Blending the Integrated Institution and MES in the present structure

The proposal recommends transforming the present MoD to MES by integrating certain elements of MEA and MoF with MoD and by strengthening institutions like the Secretary defence finance. It also aims to integrate capability build up, strategising and setting up operational objectives for the three arms of the military. This integration of the military was the aim that the government had set before the CDS and the DMA. The present discourse on theatre commands has veered in the direction of making the CDS an operational commander of the military. The proposal provides an alternate structure wherein the CDS or the CES is a functionary at the governmental level with operations being handled by the COSC. It brings a whole of government approach to external security by integrating military with diplomacy and economy to an extent where such an integration is not only desirable but mandatory to deal with future challenges.

The proposal though transformational, in effect recommends creation of only one new structure, the Integrated Institution. The Integrated Institution utilises existing structures of IDS and the Secretary defence finance. It recommends shifting of 5-6 territorial divisions of the MEA (it has 59 divisions) to the MES. It envisages the shifting of the procurement directorates and strategic planning directorates of the three Services from their individual headquarters to the Integrated Institution. It makes these functions the responsibility of the MES rather than individual service headquarters. It therefore integrates capability creation and military operational strategising not only between the three services but also with diplomacy and economy. Major restructuring would be required between the three Service headquarters. However, the process would not significantly affect the operational capability of the military as it does not affect the field forces. It breaks the present system of functioning in silos by the ministries wherein the MES would provide inputs and options to three different ministers viz. Minister for External Security, External Affairs Minister and the Finance Minister, all of whom are part of the CCS. It integrates the CCS and government functioning like never before. It simplifies decision making at the political level by presenting it with comprehensive options enabling it to steer the country in the desired direction. It thus reduces the effort of decision making at the ministerial level in a democratic structure where the political leadership also belongs to a political party, who have to face elections almost every year and have to devote considerable time and effort towards it.

Is the NSCS capable of doing the same functions as required from the MES? No. The outcomes desired from the MES and the Integrated

Institution can only be performed by an executive structure like a ministry. In a democratic setup like India, any institution responsible for the outcomes as required from the Integrated Institution has to be accountable to the Parliament and thus to the people. On the other hand, it is important to have an institution like the NSCS which holistically examines security and provides an alternate viewpoint and advice to the Prime Minister, but it should not be the only institution to do so as is happening in the present structure, and therefore the importance and imperative requirement of a ministry like the MES. The mandate of the NSCS is overview of national security in its entirety. The NSCS cannot be accountable to Parliament. It should be free from the responsibilities of implementation and should only be advisory for it to function effectively, else it would become a ministry.

Will the MES undermine the authority of the PMO? No. The Prime Minster and the PMO will always remain the highest decision making body in India as per its Constitution. The MES will in fact strengthen the capability of the PMO by providing it with options and execution capability which do not exist in the present security structure. Similarly, the MES and its minister would not undermine the authority of the NSA as explained earlier in the chapter. If external security is comprehensively taken care of, it would have a much desired impact on internal security as well. The MES therefore would indirectly enhance internal security.

Significance of the Ministry of External Security

The Ministry of External Security and the proposed integrated setup would considerably ease and speed up the ability of the government to respond to any external security situation with a comprehensive national approach. Options for national external security objectives would be proposed by the MES to the national leadership (CCS). The choice made by the national leadership would decide the national objectives. The MES from these national objectives would chart out diplomatic, economic and military objectives. It would not only ensure territorial protection of India but a comprehensive approach to protect its national interests across domains. It will be an organisation to effectively synergise military and civil competence to function as an enabler for policy making at the highest level. It would ensure cohesion of the civil and military to chart a synergistic approach for India's external security.

Such a system has not been attempted elsewhere but each nation needs to plan its path as per its own requirements. Ancient India is the best example wherein the culture and philosophy of India was distinctly unique. The USA undertook theaterisation of its military at a time when it was a unique concept not attempted anywhere else; it adopted it because that was what it needed. India needs to do the same; chart its own path for achieving the goal of comprehensive national power and comprehensive approach to security.

Conclusion

As per the mandate of the Indian Constitution, the military is an instrument of the state. The state is represented by the political executive and hence the military is the instrument of the government of the day. This is the foundation of civil military relations of India. For national security requirements, the USA and China charted their own paths depending upon their past experiences, their existing structures and their strategic culture. India needs to do the same. It has millennia old strategic culture which teaches many lessons that are still relevant since they are about India's conditioning that it has undergone for the past more than 4000 years. There are inadequacies in its existing external security and governance structures which are mostly a remnant of colonial times. India therefore needs to comprehensively review its external security structure and also account for its weaknesses and strengths as brought out by its strategic culture.

The present and the emerging security challenges of the future would require a whole of government or a comprehensive national approach to external security. The present ministerial system of India results in a disjointed approach to national security by the various ministries. While the government has created a CDS and DMA to ensure integration and jointness between various arms of the military, the same needs to be done between various arms of the government too, for a comprehensive national approach to security. This is important not only for an all-inclusive approach to security but also for a broad based national approach to build-up of military power in synchronisation with national requirements and availability of national resources.

The present ministerial system functions with consultations that happen at the apex bureaucratic level and the political level, but is disjointed, works in silos and does not provide the political executive with integrated options which emerge from real time analysis. An Integrated Institution is required which can evaluate and analyse events holistically in all their dimensions and evolve options for the political executive to choose from. It should be able to enmesh security, diplomacy and economy. It should be able to continuously evaluate and then calibrate India's response to events either in multiple domains or in the specific domain which warrants a response. This institution cannot have a bureaucratic approach of analysing and generating options on file. Responses if not immediate lose their significance and effectiveness.

The present MoD would need to be transformed to the Ministry of External Security with a part of MoF and MEA integrated with it in an Integrated Institution. It would require changes in the AoB/ToB Rules and in the mandate of the CDS. It would also require reorganising the MoD. Structures like the IDS, FADS in the MoD and territorial divisions in the MEA already exist; they would need to be integrated with a change in mandate to support the new structure. MES would bring a comprehensive whole of nation approach to external security. The Integrated Institution would also ensure that military strategy and military objectives are not only integrated between the three services but also get integrated with national objectives. It would be able to earmark military objectives at the operational level for execution by the COSC. It would be able to provide comprehensive options in all domains to the national leadership for protecting national interests.

The proposed structure would readjust civil military relations to evolve it into a cohesive framework. It would realign the Higher Defence Organisation so as to integrate it with the national security decision making structure. It would lead to creation of a security architecture which would empower decision making by the political leadership with comprehensive options for national security and national interests.

Notes

1. Government of India, Ministry of Law and Justice, Legislative Department, *The Constitution of India*, (December 09, 2020), p. 37.
2. Congressional Research Service – In Focus, *Defense Primer: President's Constitutional Authority with Regards to the Armed Forces* (December 16, 2020), at https://fas.org/sgp/crs/natsec/IF10534.pdf, accessed on May 19, 2021.
3. Congressional Research Service – In Focus, *Defense Primer: Congress's Constitutional Authority with Regards to the Armed Forces* (December 16, 2020), at https://fas.org/sgp/crs/natsec/IF10535.pdf, accessed on May 19, 2021.
4. USA Department of Defence, Joint Chiefs of Staff, *Origin of Joint Concepts,* at https://www.jcs.mil/About/Origin-of-Joint-Concepts/ accessed on May 19, 2021.
5. Joint History Office; Office of the Chairman of the Joint Chiefs of Staff, *Organisational Development of the Joint Chiefs of Staff 1942-2013* (April 2013), p. 22.
6. Ibid, pp. 29-43.
7. Ibid, pp. 62-63.
8. Kathleen J. McInnis, Congressional Research Service, *Goldwater-Nichols at 30: Defence Reforms and Issues for Congress* (June 02, 2016), pp. 3-5, at https://fas.org/sgp/crs/natsec/R44474.pdf, accessed on May 20, 2021.
9. Ibid, p. 23.
10. Andrei A. Kokoshin, *2015 Military Reform in the People's Republic of China* (Massachusetts: Harvard Kennedy School, 2016), p. 1. Translated by Kirill Leonov.
11. Philip C. Saunders and Joel Wuthnow, "China's Goldwater Nichols? Assessing PLA Organisational Reforms" *INSS Strategic Forum, National Defence University* (April 2016), at https://inss.ndu.edu/Media/News/Article/ 713451/chinas-goldwater-nichols-assessing-pla-organizational-reforms/ accessed on May 23, 2021.
12. Ibid.
13. Ibid.
14. Joel Wuthnow and Philip C. Saunders, "Chinese Military Reform in the Age of Xi Jinping" *INSS, National Defence University* (March 2017), at https://ndupress.ndu.edu/Portals/68/Documents/stratperspective/china/ChinaPerspectives -10.pdf accessed on May 25, 2021.
15. Xiaobing Li, *A History of the Modern Chinese Army* (Kentucky: The University Press of Kentucky, 2007), p. 46.
16. Joel Wuthnow and Philip C. Saunders, n. 14, p. 33.
17. Congressional Research Service – In Focus, *Congress, Civilian Control of the Military, and Nonpartisanship* (June 11, 2020), at https://crsreports.congress.gov/product/pdf/IF/IF11566, accessed on May 27, 2021.

18. Charles A, Stevenson, *Warriors and Politicians, US Civil-Military Relations Under Stress* (New York: Routledge, 2006), p. 2.
19. Ibid.
20. Xiaobing Li, n. 15, p. 15.
21. Cabinet Secretariat of India, "Business Rules/Allocation of Business Rules", (April 29, 2020), https://cabsec.gov.in/businessrules/allocationofbusinessrules/completeaobrules/ accessed on July 29, 2020.
22. Press Information Bureau, Government of India, Ministry of Defence, February 03, 2020, at https://pib.gov.in /newsite/PrintRelease.aspx?relid=198899, accessed on March 07, 2021.
23. HT Correspondent. "Greater integration between foreign and military policies key to cope with challenges: Jaishankar". *Hindustan Times*, (December 13, 2020) at https://www.hindustantimes.com/india-news/greater-integration-between-foreign-and-military-policies-key-to-cope-with-challenges-jaishankar/story-ua1YejUQQ6d9hPNDVrDKgO.html, accessed on June 18, 2021.
24. Bureau correspondent. "India purchases $3 billion worth emergency weapons, ammunition: Report". *Defense World.net*, (January 19, 2017) at https://www.defenseworld.net/news/18268/India_Purchases__3_Billion_Worth_ Emergency_Weapons__Ammunition__Report#.YM3nVmgzZPY, accessed on June 18, 2021.
25. HT Correspondent, n. 23.
26. Website of the Ministry of Finance, Government of India, at https://finmin.nic.in/, accessed on June 28, 2021.
27. Website of the Department of Expenditure, Ministry of Finance, Government of India, "About the Department", at https://doe.gov.in/about-department, accessed on June 28, 2021.
28. Press Information Bureau, Delhi, "The Report of the Fifteenth Finance Commission" (February 01, 2021), at https://pib.gov.in/PressReleasePage.aspx?PRID=1693868, accessed on June 28, 2021.
29. Ibid.
30. XV Finance Commission, Volume-I Main Report, October 2020, p.351, available at http://finance.cg.gov.in/15%20Finance%20Commission/Report/XVFC-VOL-I%20Main-Report-E.pdf, accessed on June 28, 2021.
31. Krishn Kaushik, "Govt approves restructuring of OFB into 7 new corporate entities", *Indian Express* (June 17, 2021), at https://indianexpress.com/article/india/govt-approves-restructuring-of-ofb-into-7-new-corporate-entities-7362296/, accessed on June 30, 2021.

Index